THE
WEALTHY
GARDENER

THE
WEALTHY
GARDENER

Life Lessons on Prosperity
Between Father and Son

John Soforic

PORTFOLIO / PENGUIN

PORTFOLIO / PENGUIN
An imprint of Penguin Random House LLC
penguinrandomhouse.com

Most Portfolio books are available at a discount when purchased in quantity for sales promotions or corporate use. Special editions, which include personalized covers, excerpts, and corporate imprints, can be created when purchased in large quantities. For more information, please call (212) 572-2232 or email specialmarkets@penguinrandomhouse.com. Your local bookstore can also assist with discounted bulk purchases using the Penguin Random House corporate Business-to-Business program. For assistance in locating a participating retailer, email B2B@penguinrandomhouse.com.

Originally self-published in the United States by the author in Mt. Pleasant, Pennsylvania, in 2018.

ISBN 9780593189740 (hardcover)
ISBN 9780593189757 (ebook)

Printed in the United States of America
1 3 5 7 9 10 8 6 4 2

Book design by Nicole LaRoche

FATHER & SON
(before we grew up)

To Mike,
Little did I know at the start,
That I couldn't finish without you.
You are why this book exists,
And why my soul is in it.
—Dad

CONTENTS

ABOUT THIS BOOK

The Wealthy Gardener is a hybrid. It is half fiction, half non-fiction. Chapters are divided into life lessons, each opening with a fictional story followed by real-life anecdotes. Why this format? As a father, I wanted to engage my son in many lessons on wealth, but I didn't want to preach at him. A better way to do it, then, was to create a parable. Like reading a bi-ography for pleasure and insight, learning through stories can be more enjoyable and profound. While this approach comes at the risk of oversimplifying principles, it is a risk chosen for the greater good of clarity. The hybrid format remains the best way to entertain, engage, and explain the lessons of prosperity.

THE
WEALTHY
GARDENER

PART I

Master Gardening

We come from the earth, we return to the earth,
and in between we garden.

ANONYMOUS

Chapter 1

USE THE DAYS

LESSON 1-1 · SEEK PROSPERITY

Prosperity: Financial comfort; life without money worries.

The seeds of every harvest are the hours of days.

THE WEALTHY GARDENER

He sat alone on the solitary bench overlooking the pond at the corner of his property. There was a hardcover book on his lap, his hand grasping a pen. The Wealthy Gardener scribbled a verse as an introduction to his finished manuscript:

> *The moral is clear as I look back*
> *At these lessons, now that I'm of age.*
> *That the book of one's life is determined*
> *By the courage contained in each page.*

These lines would serve as an opening to a subject more complex than most people imagined. The truth is, he believed, there was never just one ingredient that led to his financial freedom. It was always a way of life.

And this way of life was noble.

The Wealthy Gardener recalled how, in the early days, his friends had judged him to be a workaholic without work-life balance. They had advised him to slow down, take it easy, enjoy more leisure, and live for the day. Why not be content with your life? Can't you be satisfied with normal conditions?

"Many things in life are more important than money," they had told him. "Why work so hard?"

"Many things are indeed more important than money," agreed the Wealthy Gardener, "but overcoming the 'money problem' allows us to focus on those important things. Without money and time, we wield little power over life."

His friends meant well, of course, but they just didn't get him. He wasn't trying to be better than them, nor did he care to be a high-income earner with an affluent lifestyle. Many others had achieved that level of success. He was seeking a rarer outcome. He always knew exactly what he wanted—and he was after the financial holy grail.

As his material success burgeoned over the years, his good fortune became more visible. The same people who had judged him began calling him lucky. They again advised him to be content with his success and relax. "You can't take it with you," they would remind him. "What's the point of money if you can't enjoy it?"

They never suspected his deepest motivation—it wasn't about piling up cash in the bank for the sake of hoarding money. It was about gaining the upper hand, not over others, but over his life's financial condition. It was about living with no economic concerns and, ultimately, experiencing his fullest life through financial freedom.

"When we're faced with a problem that money can solve and we have the money to solve it," he had always said, "then we face a trivial problem. But lacking this money, even the smallest of life's problems can turn into the worst of life's problems."

Later, in the twilight years of his life, when his wealth had multiplied into extraordinary sums, he allowed himself the luxury of traveling to see and experience the world. No matter where he went, he saw how all people faced the same underlying economic challenges.

It seemed that almost everyone thought about money, wanted it, but did not clearly choose to accumulate it. In this way, he had been unlike others. His success was a testimony to disparate outcomes from different goals. Wealth grows from the seeds of desire.

And in the end, his friends returned. Old men mellow with age, and those lifelong rivals became the most regular patrons of his winery.

They dubbed him "the Wealthy Gardener" due to his passion for backyard gardening. The silly nickname stuck, and he did not object to it. Instead, within a year he renamed his vineyards the Wealthy Gardens.

He enjoyed the name because it reminded him of a metaphor comparing life to a plot of land. Gardeners are not afraid of working hard to shape the landscape, but they are also aware of a mysterious Unseen Force that operates behind the scenes to make the plants grow.

At any rate, time was running out, thought the Wealthy Gardener, and his days were numbered. Now it was finally time to return home.

He tucked his book under his arm and trekked a mile through his fields. As he walked, he couldn't help but ponder the greatest question of all: Was the price of success worth the rewards? He had lived his life, had achieved uncommon prosperity, but did it matter, now that he was about to die?

Yes, it was worth the price, he believed, for the rewards of prosperity were found in the work, the freedom, and the personal growth so necessary to attain his wealth. Most unexpected, he had come to see the prosperous life as a spiritual journey.

He hoped he had conveyed these truths in the pages of his book.

Arriving home, he went to his garden. It was November, and the ground was not yet frozen. He wrapped the book in a plastic bag, feebly lowered himself to the ground, and buried it in the dirt. Either Jimmy would find the book, or the lessons of the Wealthy Gardener's life would be lost to eternity. He offered a prayer to Fate to decide.

IN THE REAL WORLD, I attended a Catholic grade school and high school. By the time I graduated, I had been indoctrinated in the evils of excessive wealth and prosperity: A rich man cannot get into heaven any more than a camel can fit through the eye of a needle. Money is the root of all evil. And what good is it to gain the world yet lose your very soul?

But during my twenties, as I moved into the financial challenges of adulthood, I learned about money from a different perspective. I witnessed how a lack of money leads to fear, restlessness, and chronic despair. I discovered that work-life balance is not so wonderful when you spend your spare time in an uneasy state of financial anxiety.

We never know the value of money until we know the fear of its absence. Money, like oxygen, is not too important until there is not enough of it. But when levels run low, every waking hour is consumed by it—either spent working for money or worrying about it.

At the age when I learned the worth of money, I was married with a small child. Others depended solely on me to provide for them. With these responsibilities, my options were limited. I was trapped in a middle-class struggle for decades. I slowly determined that to win my freedom, I would need to succeed financially.

I would earn a life of prosperity, or a part of me would die.

I have gained this life of financial freedom.

Prosperity is the power to take a walk in the woods on a weekday, pay for college tuitions, and live with choices, options, and power. It is waking up without money worries. It is living without the pressure of time. It is the ability to spend one's daily hours in meaningful pursuits. And it required me to grow spiritually in the struggle.

Be wary of those who tell you to be content with your condition in life. Only you can know the condition that will satisfy your soul. And only you can feel the pull of your ambition.

THE LIFE LESSON: SEEK PROSPERITY

I was told that ambition for riches comes from the devil,
But found that the prosperous life was a spiritual adventure.

LESSON 1-2 · TIME

Time: The stuff our lives are made of.

Don't judge each day by the harvest you reap, but by the
seeds that you plant.

ROBERT LOUIS STEVENSON

TWO YEARS EARLIER

Our conditions reflect our doings, mused the Wealthy Gardener, in the
parade of passing days. For this reason, he routinely escaped on solitary
retreats to reassess his life and examine his weekly schedule.

On this day, he was set to embark on a twelve-month vacation. This
lengthy break would uproot him from his normal daily routines, and he
offered no explanation to his employees, who managed the thriving
farm, vineyard, and winery. Before departing, however, he called upon
his trusted operations manager, Santos, to review business matters during his absence. In addition to Santos's usual work duties, the Wealthy
Gardener presented him with an unexpected responsibility.

"I bought the farm next door," said the Wealthy Gardener, "and I
want you to improve its condition while I'm away. Turn it into something special. While I can promise no certainty of pay for your efforts,
you are free to use your imagination, use my employees at my expense,
and test your capacities to their fullest on this project. I want you to give
it your very best effort."

Santos warily considered the offer. At the age of sixty, he was a para-
gon of work ethic with little imagination. "So you're asking me to work
for an entire year, and to give up my free time, to fix up a run-down farm
with *no promise of additional pay?*"

"That is indeed what I'm asking of you."

With that, the Wealthy Gardener left for his retreat.

He returned exactly one year later and found that his own grounds were untidy and profits were down. Worse, the farm next door appeared to have been untouched and now seemed to be in a state of disrepair.

After a few prodding questions, Santos explained that the employees had balked at overtime hours despite being offered full pay. And because he had not found eager workers to help him, nor volunteered his own free time, the neighboring farm had been ignored and forgotten.

"You have been with me for decades," the Wealthy Gardener said, sighing. "In return for your loyal service, my hope was to gift you the property upon my return. The neighboring farm was to be yours." His eyes narrowed. "But now, as it is, since there is no opportunity there to sustain your life, I have no choice: I can only keep you employed in your current position."

Santos was aghast at the revelation. He finally admitted the unfortunate truth: "I didn't pursue this overwhelming project," he said meekly, "because I was busy on this farm, and you said there was no promise of additional pay."

For a thoughtful moment, the Wealthy Gardener gazed at his operations manager. "Don't you get it? There is *never* a certainty of future rewards," he said calmly, "but we go for it anyway, or we keep what we've got."

Santos nodded silently and turned away. The time was gone, and he simply hadn't known the stakes. His future was lost within the uneventful parade of ordinary days that had marched past in a silent procession.

"TODAY IS A KING IN DISGUISE," Emerson wrote. "Let us not be deceived, let us unmask the king as he passes."

Let us unmask the king as he passes . . .

If there is indeed a judgment in the next world, a focal question will be about the use of our time: What did we do? What occupied our days, weeks, and years? And won't we feel foolish to admit we were too busy and distracted to have clear goals that would have assured a greater impact in our time?

"Don't say you don't have enough time," advises H. Jackson Brown Jr. "You have exactly the same number of hours per day that were given to Helen Keller, Pasteur, Michelangelo, Mother Teresa, Leonardo da Vinci, Thomas Jefferson, and Albert Einstein."

We have used the same twenty-four-hour clock throughout history. The conditions of our lives—the circumstances that surround us—are very much an accounting of how we spend that time. Conditions reflect our purposes, effectiveness, and use of time.

At nineteen, while in college, I saw how my time leads to my conditions. My freshman college grades were atrocious. As I sat in a chair in the hallway outside the dean's office, I felt more vulnerable than ever before in my short life-span. I was defenseless. The facts were irrefutable. I was a lamb at the slaughterhouse. The door to the dean's office opened and I was ushered inside to receive my sentence.

The dean was an elderly gentleman who explained the purpose of our meeting as I sweated bullets in a chair opposite his large desk.

"There is no dishonor in seeking a less challenging curriculum," he said, and my mind whirled to process the situation. First, it seemed I wasn't being kicked out of college—not yet, at least. And second, this man thought I was mentally incapable. His judgment was fair.

It never occurred to him that I was googly-eyed over a girlfriend, had a host of fun buddies, and played cards every night. He was unable to fathom that a young adult would squander the opportunity of a college education in favor of a social agenda that left no time for academic study.

The dean figured I was powerless due to lack of ability, when in fact, I was powerless due to lack of daily purpose. When I wasted my hours, I wasted my potential. After the meeting, I wrote a list of my goals, planned my schedule, followed my plan, and earned straight A's.

When a change of condition is wanted, always seek to alter the weekly schedule. This lesson of using every passing day of life to the fullest is emphasized by the parable of the pearly gates.

Four people died and went to heaven. They formed a nervous line outside the pearly gates. In front of the gates stood Saint Peter, holding four books, each summarizing one of the four's lives.

The first man in the line stepped forward and stood in front of Saint Peter, who was scanning the summary page of this fellow's life.

This first person had possessed average intelligence and abilities. In his time, he had married and raised a family; applied himself and risen to the position of foreman at the local factory; volunteered faithfully at his church; participated as a Little League coach; and been on the school board.

"You've used your time well," said Saint Peter, looking up. "I need more like you down there. So I send you back to resume your life as a pillar of the community. You will have your dignity and the respect of others."

Poof. There was a cloud of smoke and the man vanished from sight.

The next person, a woman this time, stepped forward. Saint Peter studied her thin book of life, grunting several times. Finally, his gaze fell upon her.

"You had fair abilities and intelligence. You used none of them. You merely existed in your time. You avoided work and strain at all cost. Your love of idleness led to a life of frivolity. And so, since you have proven yourself worthy of little more than eating and sitting, I return you to earth as a cow. There you can graze in idleness until the day of your slaughter."

Poof. There was a cloud of smoke, and the woman was gone. The two people remaining in line thought they heard a *mooooooo.*

After witnessing this harsh judgment, the next person in line hesitantly stepped forward. He was a middle-aged man who fidgeted as Saint Peter thumbed through his book with heavy sighs.

"You were gifted with the genius to be a writer unlike the world has ever read, and you had the occasion to engage this ability," said Saint Peter. "You were compelled by an inner urge to write, but you drowned it in drink. Instead, you became a laborer. You spent beyond your means. And your wanton lifestyle trapped you into wage slavery. You failed your destiny, and the world will never know the books that only you could have written. Since you have proven yourself capable of work without thought, I return you now as an ox to plow fields in the hot sun, where your genius will be unneeded."

Poof. The man vanished in a cloud of smoke.

The final woman stepped forward with a sense of calmness unlike the others. Saint Peter looked up from her book and studied her with unveiled interest.

"You used your mind, you found your interests, you used your time with care, and you weathered the storms of life." A smile formed on Saint Peter's face. "You engaged with deep concern for others, and you learned the many rewards of selflessness. You raised a family, impacted the common good, lived by your values, and followed your inner voice.

"What am I to do with you?" Saint Peter shrugged. "I send you back as an earthen angel, where your influence will grow. Let your light shine."

WHAT'S THE MORAL of the story?

If you don't want to be thought of as a cow, engage your time and don't be lazy. If you don't want to work like an ox for eternity, use your gifts, work intelligently, and control your spending. At the very least, live with dignity and choose to contribute to a worthy cause, whatever you decide that is, by listening to your inner voice.

"The value of life lies not in the length of days," said Michel de Montaigne, "but in the use we make of them. A man may live long, but get very little."

Our potential is useless without our engagement of time. Every condition we desire, including prosperity and wealth, requires a price to be paid—our outcomes reflect our hours. We miss the height of our fullest potential by not engaging the quiet parade of days.

"Time management is the sun," Brian Tracy has explained so eloquently, "and everything that you do is the planets in orbit." Benjamin Franklin wrote: "Dost thou love life? Then do not squander time, for that's the stuff life is made of." Time is also the stuff our conditions are made of.

THE LIFE LESSON: TIME

I saw that my conditions trail the use of my time,
And I can change what I do or keep what I've got.

Impact activity: The work (action) that earns a goal.

Gardens are not made by singing "Oh, how beautiful,"
and sitting in the shade.

RUDYARD KIPLING

Two days later, the Wealthy Gardener met with Santos upon his insistent request. It came as no surprise that the man wanted a second chance to use his time to repair the neighboring farm. He now offered to resign as the operations manager to fully devote himself to the mission.

"I'll do whatever it takes," Santos vowed. "I'll work from sunup until sundown. I'll sleep less. If you give me this chance, I won't let you down."

The Wealthy Gardener listened patiently until the manager exhausted his pitch. And then, for a long moment, they sat in silence. Finally, the Wealthy Gardener cleared his throat and spoke: "How will you meet your living expenses during this renovation?"

"My family will work with me," Santos replied eagerly. "And my friends and cousins are willing to lend me the money to pay for my expenses. I ask for no help from your employees—just the same opportunity that I foolishly squandered last year."

The Wealthy Gardener sighed. "I admit to mixed emotions."

"If you give me this chance," Santos persisted, "I'll do my best this time."

"I know you will," the Wealthy Gardener said gently. "I have no doubt about your work ethic. But sometimes a person's best effort is not enough. Did you give your best effort to my farm, vineyards, and winery during my absence?"

"I never stopped for a minute," Santos said earnestly. "In my waking hours, I stayed busy. And I didn't let the others slack off, either."

"And yet the profits are down substantially this year."

The manager turned pale. "I could have worked no harder."

The Wealthy Gardener frowned. "The world is a judge and results are the verdict. I intended to gift you the farm on two conditions. First, I had to be sure that you could maintain profitability of my operations without me. Second, I needed to know that you were willing to offer your free hours. By both measures, you have failed."

Santos opened his mouth, but no words came forth. In the awkward silence that followed, the Wealthy Gardener considered his situation.

"But with clarity of goals and focus on results," he said with a sigh, "we can always improve our impact, and this should give us hope. If our best is not good enough this year, we can change our activities and improve our effectiveness in the upcoming season."

"You're giving me a second chance?" Santos asked.

"I'll consult with my advisers, and I'll get back to you."

The meeting ended, and the Wealthy Gardener sat alone for an hour in his small office. He wanted his loyal friend to have this opportunity, but now he had reservations. The bottom line was that Santos had failed despite his greatest effort. What if the Wealthy Gardener's generosity would doom his manager to financial calamity? Is it wise to give people more than they can handle?

AN IMPACT ACTIVITY is an action that earns a goal or condition. "If we're unhappy with the harvest we're reaping, we should sow different seed," said Phil Pringle. If we're busy every waking hour and getting nowhere fast, we need to change what we're doing so we use the hours better. We need impact activities that produce better results.

"Doing the right *thing* is more important than doing the thing *right*," Peter Drucker said. Doing the right thing means doing things that impact objective results. I learned this lesson after a crisis.

During the stock market crash of 2000–2002, I saw my life savings dwindle and, with it, my hopes of prosperity. I found that the misery of losing money was related to the years of labor required to earn it. When the money evaporates, we feel the pain of our futile efforts.

Prior to this loss, I had wanted a life of prosperity. After this painful crisis, however, I had a deeper conviction that I would accept nothing less than wealth. I would not tolerate stress, vulnerability, and money worries for life. My determination was mixed with deep emotion.

What followed was nearly unbelievable. I ascribe these results to the power of doing the right things and doing them consistently. I committed myself to making room for more impact activities. I revamped my weekly schedule, avoiding hollow hours to better use the days.

At that time I made my living as a chiropractor. In this career, I earned an ordinary income equal to the median income of a certified city plumber. But after the stock market crash of 2000–2002, my income skyrocketed, more than doubling during the unusual three-year period that followed. I then saved more money each month than the average chiropractor earned each month. And I did not advertise or market my services one bit differently.

What happened during this time?

I changed my activities as follows: I eliminated alcohol and entertainment; spent time in solitude and meditation; maintained an upbeat attitude; exercised daily; adhered to a perfect dietary regimen; wrote specific money goals; drew images of my goals; made a vision board of clippings; vividly imagined patients calling me; used affirmations nonstop; listened to personal development audiobooks while driving; planned my days; expanded my business hours; spent time with family; and revitalized my mind and body during nonwork hours.

If you scrutinize this list of activities with a careful eye and fail to comprehend what led to the doubling of my income, be patient. I will explain it entirely in later chapters and lessons. The point to digest at this early stage of the book is that there was a huge difference in the objective results, but little physical cause of these financial changes.

The world only saw that my clinic was insanely busy. My accountant saw that excess money was plentiful. My small staff repeatedly asked, "What is happening? Why is it suddenly so busy?"

The garden of my life was flourishing, I realized, due to many small and consistent actions. I sensed that my new focus and determination had caused a mysterious harmony with a cooperative energy.

What I know for sure is that my success during those years did not come from doing more or working harder; I wasn't seeking motion for its own sake. I was not a mindless gardener trying to get many things done. I did not have a long to-do list. If anything, I narrowed my focus to gainful activities. I sought simplicity. I concentrated on less.

If you follow this example, you will clarify a well-defined goal, search diligently to find your own impact activities, and then give your hours to the actions that lead to the greatest results.

I doubled my income by engaging in impact activities. Some of those activities were mental practices that I didn't reveal to even my closest friends. But in solitude, I concentrated daily on picturing my wishes fulfilled. And I generated emotion as I imagined the life of my dreams.

I was empowered during those years.

Little did I know, that period of satisfying productivity and spiritual enlightenment would soon embroil me in a new crisis—one that would stop my momentum, test me beyond my strength, and make the stock market crash seem like a tiny hiccup in comparison.

THE LIFE LESSON: IMPACT ACTIVITY

I saw that only a few actions earned tangible rewards,
And so I rearranged my schedule for the best activities.

LESSON 1-4 · IMPACT HOUR

Impact hour: Workload (time) that earns a goal.

All the flowers of tomorrow are in the seeds of today.

PROVERB

The days are long but the years are short, reflected the Wealthy Gardener. The recent week would have breezed by with little significance if not for his commitment to daily impact hours.

Despite his whirlwind of responsibilities, the Wealthy Gardener made time to use many hours for his own constructive purposes. His top priority today was to spend an hour meeting with his two advisors. With the counsel of their combined wisdom, he had never made a rash decision. To him, these advisors were as indispensable as living people, and they always steered him from future calamities.

Each evening, if a passerby were to look in his window, it would appear that the Wealthy Gardener was doing nothing at all. But to him, thinking was work; it was doing something. He believed that clear thinking was a learned skill, and since his thinking directed the days of his work, he considered it the single most impactful use of his free time.

He would begin each thinking session by dwelling on the day's urgent problems and considering possible solutions. To ensure wise decisions, he would rationally review the known facts. He'd even list the pros and cons of the potential courses of action. Finally, he'd close his eyes and seek a gut feeling about each available solution to his dilemma.

Sometimes he'd sense nothing, which was a signal to dig for more facts. Some courses of action just naturally felt right, while other options somehow felt wrong. He couldn't explain it, but he called these hunches his inner red light or green light.

His advisors may have only been in his mind, but to him, they were essential aids to his thinking. The first advisor was his faculty of reason. The second advisor was his voice of intuition. Together, these two guides proved to be a trustworthy team. On their own, however, either one of them could be a treacherous deceiver who could lead him into trouble. An hour with this pair shaped the hours of many days.

A week after his last conversation with Santos, the Wealthy Gardener met once more with his operations manager. They sat in the winery office to discuss their course of action.

"I am willing to give you another chance," said the Wealthy Gardener, "but I cannot agree to the conditions you requested. Rather, you will remain employed with me for another year to prove that you can maintain the profits of a business. You'll renovate the neighboring farm during your free time. And you must do all renovation without the aid of my employees."

He leaned back and waited in silence. Santos nodded with a grim expression. "Of course I appreciate your generosity," he said finally. "But must I work both jobs this next year? It would be my dream to do as I pleased with such an opportunity."

"First, it is the opinion of my advisors that you must prove yourself worthy," said the Wealthy Gardener. "The world is a place that weighs results—not efforts. You claim to have given your best effort in my absence last year, but profits are down. In this next year, you will figure out how to produce results with the same number of hours. Second, if you cannot give your free time to the pursuit of your dreams, then the seeds of achievement are not in you."

There was a long pause during which Santos shifted uneasily in his chair, seeming to consider a strategic response. Both knew, however, that only one of them had the power in this negotiation.

"But if I were able to quit my current job," Santos objected carefully, "I could start the improvements and finish the task much faster."

"You've heard my offer," replied the Wealthy Gardener. "You can use your free time to pursue your dreams, or you can remain exactly where you are. You must choose now—which will it be?"

Santos sighed in self-resignation. "I'll do it."

"So be it, but now there is one more condition," said the Wealthy Gardener, leaning forward. "I want you to hire a boy as an apprentice. Pay him minimum wage and give him obligations to help ease your burdens."

Santos squinted. "Who is it, and why do I need him?"

"His name's Jimmy," said the Wealthy Gardener. "He's an amazing kid, but he needs a break. I ask this favor due to my generosity, and I want no further questions about him."

Santos eyed him suspiciously. "It's a deal, due to your generosity."

AN IMPACT HOUR is sixty minutes of doing the right things that lead to a critical outcome. An impact hour is the opposite of a hollow hour, and it moves us forward toward our goals. It is an hour of effort that adds to the great volume of work that is required for achievement.

We all use the same time clock, but it is obvious that some people have more impact than others. An inspiring example is that of an attorney in Mississippi who created impact hours in his days despite an overcrowded life. His story discredits the excuse that we have no time to pursue our dreams. We make time, or we keep what we've got.

At thirty years of age, this man was busy. In fact, he worked sixty hours each week at his law firm, was married, and had two small children. His schedule was booked; he was in the midst of the most demanding season of his life.

But one day in a courthouse, this lawyer overheard the testimony of a young rape victim. He was deeply moved, and he couldn't stop thinking about it. He paused during this ordinary day, reflecting on what he'd witnessed, and was curiously inspired to write a novel along the lines of the testimony he had heard.

Let us slow down the story and consider this curious juncture of his life. This lawyer was inspired, in a fleeting moment, to write a novel. Why didn't he dismiss the idea as crazy? We are wise to notice that he paused, and only by so doing could he consult an inner wisdom that guided him into the unknown. It may very well be that this simple moment of pausing, when he gave his attention to this cockeyed idea, was the most valuable five seconds in the passing days of his life.

If the man had not paused long enough for consideration, the idea would have been ignored, and the world would not know the name *John Grisham*. But he chose to follow the silent pull of an inner voice. Much will be written in this book about the power of a wise pause when we are tempted to shrink from ideas and inspirations.

Still, where would he find the time for the work?

Our dreams may begin as inspiration, but dreams are earned by daily hours. Impact hours are the cement blocks that form the foundation of worthy achievement. Most dreams die in this plodding and action phase called work; they starve from lack of daily impact hours.

Since no time existed in his crowded days, Grisham needed to create impact hours outside of work and in addition to family time.

"I would wake up at five o'clock," he recalls in a *Writer's Digest* interview, "and I'd be at my office at five thirty. That was the only quiet time of the day. I'd make some strong coffee and sit down and start writing. My law firm was busy. I was in the state legislature, and my wife and I were having babies and life. And so from five thirty until eight thirty or nine, that was the only quiet time of the day. I remember I had to go to court sometimes at nine. And I can remember just sitting in court being dead tired, 'cause I'd already written for three hours. And it was draining. When you do it a lot it really takes a lot out of you."

In this story, we read the testimony of a person who used small increments of time, working for one hour, then another, giving birth to his dreams as the days and years marched along. We can see that these hours were engaged in worthy activity with deep focus and effort. And last, we can see that the person giving his free time had no certainty of success.

Grisham recalls: "I used to walk in a bookstore and see all those tens of thousands of beautiful books and I would say, 'Who wants to hear from me?' you know, and 'What have I got to say? How can I add to that?' And, you know, I just—I finished it. After three years. And was lucky enough to get it published."

John Grisham's initial goal was to simply "finish the book." And then—and this cannot be overlooked—he showed up and did the laborious work for years. He engaged hours with impactful activity and intense effort in the parade of days.

We are always too busy to add to our schedules, but we either change what we're doing, or we keep what we got.

In the end, John Grisham finished the manuscript for *A Time to Kill*. The published book proved to be a commercial flop. But he continued to write, giving daily hours to his dream while others lived normal lives. His steady use of days resulted in another manuscript.

When this second manuscript, *The Firm*, was published, it became a sensational bestseller. This success triggered new sales of his first book, which then also became a bestseller. Movies were made from these first two books, more books were written, and it all looks so glamorous now.

But we too often fail to observe the human being—alone and obscure, working in the face of uncertainty, propelled only by an inner ambition, with the demands of a family and a full life—who just made the time to do the gritty work. Grisham created impact hours in his days with no certainty of pay. All dreams are paid for with our time. We build a foundation of success by using the days, one hour at a time.

THE LIFE LESSON: IMPACT HOUR

I saw that most dreams died from lack of daily hours,
And so I rearranged my schedule for more hours of work.

Chapter 2

THE WORK
OF EARNING

LESSON 2-1 · FINANCIAL DIGNITY

Dignity: The quality of being worthy of honor or respect.

A garden gives the body the dignity of working in its own support. It is a way of rejoining the human race.

WENDELL BERRY

Any slacker can perform enjoyable work, mused the Wealthy Gardener as he tended his backyard garden, but it takes character to pay the daily price of steady work to reap an abundant fall harvest.

On this stifling summer day, he took a break and strolled to the picket fence dividing his property from the neighboring lot. On the other side of the fence was a garden in a state of widespread confusion.

In the lawn next to the garden, his neighbor Jared reclined on an Adirondack chair with his attention on his cell phone. The Wealthy Gardener looked upon him with concern. Jared was a thirty-two-year-old bachelor who'd recently lost both his job and his marriage. He'd moved back in with his parents to ease his financial pressures.

"I hope that phone has an app for pulling weeds!" shouted the Wealthy Gardener. Startled, Jared looked up, laughed aloud, and walked to the fence.

"How's it going, old man?" Jared joked as they shook hands. "You're looking dirtier and sweatier than usual today."

"It's called hard work," quipped the Wealthy Gardener. "Dirty gardeners are happy gardeners! So what are you up to this afternoon?"

"I'm still looking for a new job," Jared answered whimsically. "I'm only staying with my parents for a little while."

"I heard about your situation," the Wealthy Gardener said. "I'm sure you have a plan to make it all work out. How's the job search coming along?"

"Honestly, it's hard to replace my last job," said Jared. "I've sent my résumé to companies all over the country, but firms aren't hiring. What I don't want to do is start at the bottom again after all the years I've already spent doing the lowest grunt work."

"In your line of work, what does the grunt work entail?"

Jared exhaled audibly. "Basically, it's anything the managers don't want to do. It's the drudgery—the work that has to get done but nobody wants to do it."

The Wealthy Gardener smiled. "It's kind of like pulling the weeds in a garden."

Jared nodded, and then there was an awkward silence between them.

"You know, Jared," said the Wealthy Gardener, "this may be none of my business, but your mom has always kept a vibrant garden in her backyard. But now the landscape looks like a haphazard mess. Is she feeling okay, or should I be worried about her health?"

"Actually, her health is fine." Jared chuckled. "The sad truth is that the garden is my responsibility while I'm here. I guess I'm not a very good gardener, and it shows. I just don't understand the joys of gardening."

The Wealthy Gardener considered his next words. "The joy of gardening is found in the dignity of work. It's spending ourselves in a cause. And it's doing what we don't like, as well as what we do like, to best engage our lives."

Jared laughed. "Are you suggesting I'd be happier as a dirty gardener?"

The Wealthy Gardener winked at him. "I'm suggesting there is no work without dignity, and that we're all happier and more fulfilled with direction and purpose."

DIGNITY IS THE QUALITY of being worthy of honor or respect. As we mature into independent adults, we discover the dignity of work to provide for our living expenses. We won't love every aspect of our job, but any work beats the humiliation of being broke and dependent.

When faced with financial pressures after college, I was ashamed of my situation. I'd started my own business but felt powerless to make it work. I was defeated every day. In my eyes, I was inferior to others. Deep within, the money struggle affected my self-worth.

At the bottom of my frustration was the fact that advertising wasn't working for my new practice, so I endured idleness within the walls of a business. If I could only make that phone ring, I thought, everything would be okay. I only wanted the dignity of work.

As my bank account shrank, I grew desperate. The worst moment of despair came one day as I sat alone on a park bench gazing out over a tranquil pond. In a somber mood, I agonized about closing my new business. But in a moment of clarity, I realized that even if I failed in that line of work, I'd somehow survive. Failure in business wouldn't separate my body and soul. I would survive, and life would go on.

Several of my peers didn't realize this truth. From a graduating class of one hundred, two of my friends committed suicide during the first critical year after starting their businesses, and another took his life in the second year of running his own. I can imagine that they felt the desperation of financial ruin combined with the agony of their idle helplessness.

"Poverty is uncomfortable," James Garfield said, "but nine times out of ten the best thing that can happen to a young man is to be tossed overboard and compelled to sink or swim."

My father was tossed overboard with a splash at sixteen. His dad had died unexpectedly, leaving him to support his mother and three sisters. After the funeral services, my dad and his mother spread their bills on the kitchen table. It took only a few minutes to realize that they were in trouble. In that moment, my father, seeing the plight of destitution, broke down and cried over their financial misfortunes.

He had no choice but to find a job—any job—to earn money. He found work at a local publishing company. He was a janitor there three days a week and learned to set type without pay during the remaining two days. He went to work to earn and learn.

The desire or expectation to love the grind of daily work is a defeating belief that causes untold suffering. Success takes backbone to do many things we do not like to do. Work is a friend, not a lover; it is a sober, steady relationship.

My dad used his days to cultivate a friendship with work. He married and started a family of his own. He once told me the story of asking for a raise and receiving just a nickel more per hour. Ignoring the insult, he stayed the course at his job.

"Do what you can, with what you've got, where you are," advised Theodore Roosevelt. Whatever we do may seem insignificant, but it is most important that we do it. In our duty, we find our dignity.

In his free time, my dad began to renovate duplexes. Four duplexes provided excess income and a financial advantage that he used for more savings and investments. He co-purchased a lake house and renovated it, and also spent time with his family. In the end, his friendship with work was rewarded as he later became the president and CEO of that publishing business.

"Work is the best friend I've ever known," wrote George Clason. "It has brought me all the good things I've had." It is not the dirty gardeners who deserve our pity, but rather the clean ones, sitting on their porches, waiting for the perfect job while their gardens grow into disarray.

THE LIFE LESSON: FINANCIAL DIGNITY

I learned that lack of money erodes self-respect,
And a noble dignity arises by earning a living.

Security: The state of being free from danger or threat.

When the roots are deep, there is no reason to fear
the wind.

ANONYMOUS

The Wealthy Gardener observed the transformation of the neighboring landscape after a week of Jared's work. It was the result of man's exertion along with evidence of a silent harmony in the garden.

"The condition of that messy backyard," said the Wealthy Gardener, "has certainly improved with your shadow in it. So how did it feel to get dirt under your fingernails?"

Jared laughed as he wiped his forehead with a glove. "If I'm being honest," he said, "I didn't hate the work, but I didn't love it, either."

They were on opposite sides of the picket fence, and both were disheveled, sweaty, and dirty. The elderly gardener smiled about the love of work.

"Work is a loyal friend, not a passionate lover," remarked the Wealthy Gardener. "And in the end, haven't you found your work to be better than your idleness?"

"I must admit," Jared said reluctantly, "I felt good about the progress after a few days. And the work wasn't really that difficult, when I think about it."

"So tell me, Jared," said the Wealthy Gardener, "did you learn anything beyond the power of your own labors? Did you feel a connection with the energy of the garden during your work?"

"A connection with the energy of the garden?"

"You did a fine job, and your effort is clear to see," said the Wealthy

Gardener. "But while effort is critical, it's not everything in a garden. We too often fail to notice the honeybee as it pollinates, the emerging flower that attracts the bee, the seed falling on fertile soil, or the rain that activates the fallen seed. We fail to witness the coordination of Nature that constantly unfolds all around us. We fail to experience the wonders of the garden."

"I guess I missed it." Jared laughed, bemused. "Why does it really matter?"

"Because in nature we see the cooperative energy all around us, or at least we see the effects of it. We don't see the wind, but we see the rustling leaves. We see the effects of an Intangible Force in every garden— the same power that exists in our lives, that governs all of it."

Jared paused, seeming uncomfortable. Finally, he sighed and said, "Well, it seems we're getting a little too deep for me. All I know is that when I work my ass off, things eventually turn out just fine in the end."

It was an ironic statement, since Jared's life was in shambles. The Wealthy Gardener was careful not to mention that Jared was broke, divorced, unemployed, and aimless.

"I can tell you that in my own life, I've always found—"

"Why do you think I need your advice?" Jared interrupted.

The Wealthy Gardener was taken aback. "Now, listen to me, son, there's no need to be defensive. We all have hard times, and it's nothing to be ashamed of."

Jared glared at him. "How could you help me?"

"The one thing I know," said the Wealthy Gardener, "is how to prosper financially."

Jared grunted. "So you can make me financially secure?"

"No, only you can do that. But I can tell you what's worked for me, even though I can't always explain it. And for me, financial security has always been the effect of an Intangible Force—a power within."

Jared raised an eyebrow. "I think you've been in the sun too long."

. . .

SECURITY IS A STATE of being free from danger or threat. At the age of twenty-five, while I was struggling financially during the first year of running my business, a patient entered my failing chiropractic clinic. He was a sixty-year-old gentleman who came to me looking for relief from his back pain, but he would help me more than I'd help him.

He'd once been a minister, I learned, but in his late fifties had felt a curious inclination to change his life's course. He returned to school, earned a psychology degree, and eventually opened and operated his own private counseling practice.

In time we became friends. I shared my money struggles with him, and he offered to be my mental "success coach."

I considered the proposition and accepted an offer that forever changed the trajectory of my life.

I was open-minded to the coaching idea due to my background in sports. I recalled high school basketball games when I had scored over thirty points, but those rare performances occurred only when I was in a state of invincibility and otherworldly poise. Because I was familiar with mental conditioning for sports performance, I was open to "mental coaching sessions" for business success.

Or maybe I was just desperate.

A weekly coaching session with him went something like this: We would first discuss what was going on that week, focusing on my attitude and the relevant statistics that measured the success of my clinic. We'd then discuss my goals for the following week. After this conversation, the counselor would leave the room. I'd lie back on a recliner, slide headphones over my ears, and close my eyes. I would breathe deeply to quiet my consciousness.

Faint music came through the headphones, followed by my counselor's pleasant voice. He guided me through a visualization of business objectives for the upcoming week: new patients, total patients, money collected, and so on. I was directed to imagine and experience these critical outcomes. I was instructed not just to see, but actually to sense the patients calling the clinic.

At the end of each appointment, I was given a cassette recording of the session and told to listen to it with the emotion of faith every night and every morning for the rest of the week. This daily mental discipline was my homework between our weekly meetings.

Within the first week, my clinic's phone started to ring with new patients. It was probably a coincidence, I reasoned, but this suspicion was impossible to resolve. I could not be sure that the ringing phone *was* a coincidence; conversely, I could not be sure that it was *not* a coincidence.

All I knew for certain was that in my physical world, the phone was ringing. I witnessed this change, and I continued the daily mental practices.

By focusing on my desired outcomes, I began to gain control over my thoughts. When worries arose, I returned to a vision of my desires. The phone kept ringing. My hope that this *might* work started to grow, and soon this fragile hope developed into faith that it *was* working. As I became convinced of this cause and effect, my faith hardened into a conviction. Each week, the phone just kept ringing. It rang and rang and rang. In time, business at the clinic exploded!

Within six months of starting my mental imagery practices—and doing nothing else differently to improve my business—I could barely keep up with the volume of patients. The new problem was a weekly appointment book with no open spaces to accommodate the numerous patients calling the clinic.

My wife asked what was happening. I couldn't explain it, I said, but it felt like I was able to somehow draw people to me. Even in the safety of a marriage, I felt vulnerable about admitting that I believed in such a wonder. I was a reluctant participant who had witnessed the unfathomable. I could explain what I was doing each day, but I could not rationally explain the phenomenon.

During this time, I strove to generate a kind of faith that reminded me of the invincibility I knew before my rarest high school athletic performances. It wasn't hoping or wanting. It wasn't wishing or begging in prayer. Rather, it was knowing, beyond sanity, that my clinic phone would ring. And it rang off the hook.

I learned that financial security is a conviction, a certainty of results, a Power Within that commands an effect. I was financially secure the day I learned to focus my thoughts on what I wanted most, and then *experience these outcomes* in my imagination with an absurd faith.

THE LIFE LESSON: FINANCIAL SECURITY

I learned that financial security was a power within,
And I achieved true wealth while I was dead broke.

LESSON 2-3 · FINANCIAL EXCESS

Excess: Surplus, abundance, more than enough.

The farmer and manufacturer can no more live without profit, than the labourer without wages.

DAVID RICARDO

An income equal to living expenses is a precarious situation, mused the Wealthy Gardener, gazing out the window at the sparrows. Without more than enough income, we exist like caged birds, trapped without choices in a state of daily insecurity.

Within minutes, the business meeting began. Two guests sat in the chairs opposite the Wealthy Gardener's small desk. In one chair was Santos, the operations manager who was renovating the neighboring farm in his spare hours. In the other was Jimmy, Santos's new apprentice.

"So profit-*ability*," the Wealthy Gardener started slowly, eyeing his guests across the desk, "is the heartbeat of a business. How will you assure the profitability of your farm during the next year?"

"It's always been about the yield of the fall crop," Santos offered eagerly. "The fall harvest determines the margin of the annual profits."

"I agree that the harvest is a crucial factor," said the Wealthy Gardener, then turned his attention to Jimmy. "What do you say on this matter?"

"Profit is about income and expenses," Jimmy said. "A big fall harvest doesn't guarantee a profit unless expenses are curtailed throughout the year."

Santos stiffened, but the Wealthy Gardener seemed pleased by the answer. There was just something about this kid, he thought; he was different from all the others from the reform school.

At twenty-one years of age, Jimmy was a contented loner. He was smart, muscled, serious by nature, and mature beyond his years. He was also deeply private: ambitious to prove himself but dead silent on why he had spent time in a reformatory for troubled teens.

The Wealthy Gardener was a volunteer who taught weekly classes at the reform school. Jimmy became his best student. Eager to learn, he was teachable. Jimmy quickly absorbed the Wealthy Gardener's life lessons, and he seemed to have the capacity to apply them. It was only a matter of time, the Wealthy Gardener believed, before this ambitious kid overcame the demons of his past.

"That's easy for you to say," Santos snapped, "without any experience."

"It's more about math than experience," Jimmy said.

The Wealthy Gardener grinned, looking at Santos. "So let's discuss it. What if you maximized your earning capacity, but your business still couldn't meet its annual expenses? What would be the proper course of action?"

Santos was silent, his expression dumbfounded.

The Wealthy Gardener looked at Jimmy. "What would you do?"

"We meet expenses or we perish," Jimmy said, "and expenses walk on legs. When the profits vanish, the employees must go. It's as simple as that."

The Wealthy Gardener nodded without betraying his allegiance. He opened a folder and slid it across the table. Santos and Jimmy quickly scanned a hypothetical profit-and-loss statement in which total expenses amounted to $300,000.

"How much money is needed to run this business annually?" the Wealthy Gardener asked.

Santos blurted out, "Three hundred thousand!"

The Wealthy Gardener nodded, then cast a glance at Jimmy.

"I don't know for sure," Jimmy said. "I'd have to see where I could trim costs. But assuming that expenses are fixed, I'd need a lot more than three hundred thousand dollars annually. Only a fool would aim for survival in business without excess cash flow."

The Wealthy Gardener leaned back, unable to suppress his smile.

. . .

FINANCIAL EXCESS is surplus money, abundance, more than enough. After my initial financial struggles, I began to experience life with fewer money worries. I learned the dignity of working to provide for my family. I discovered a power within that offered true security. I found what success in a service profession felt like. And ultimately, I learned what it was like to be on a revolving treadmill with no financial direction.

After three years, I realized that I was only making ends meet. I worked six days a week and never took a vacation, but had acquired no savings. After the fourth year of a busy practice, I felt defeated by an empty bank account. I then realized that an income without more than enough is not nearly enough.

Only a fool aims for survival without excess.

Without a surplus of income beyond my living expenses, I would never be able to take my family on vacations. I would have to say no to helping my kids financially throughout their lives. I would be forced to decline assistance to my aging parents in their later years. I knew that thoughts of work would always nag me while I spent time with family and friends. And, most important, I would leave myself, and those who counted on me, vulnerable to the slightest economic setback.

On the other hand, I considered, having excess money would transform my family life. My wife and I could relax together. Our minds would be free to think and read in leisure. We could pursue nobler causes with more meaning. We could take dream vacations. We could pursue our interests. We could support our children and, when it became necessary, our parents in their later years. Our hopes would be greater, and our options would be exciting.

But since there was no income to save, what could I do? I was already working six days a week and was on call for emergencies on Sundays. My wife and I naturally examined our spending—even counting and tracking our expenses—but we found very little to cut. We didn't drive new cars and we didn't live in a showy neighborhood.

I had achieved a decent income level without any satisfaction for good reason: The cost of living was extremely high where we lived. Because the cost of living was so high, my respectable income left no excess to save. I was just getting by in a costly world.

Eventually my wife and I discussed our financial situation more deeply. We investigated our options to change our formula for profit— the equation of our personal income minus living expenses—and found no easy solutions. There was one viable option, but the plan would require the courage to uproot our lives.

After a lot of soul-searching and deliberation, we chose to sell my practice for $80,000 and change everything. We left Chicago and moved to my hometown, near Pittsburgh. This area was more rural, less metropolitan, and far less expensive. We saw less cement and more trees. And the equation for profitability was much better.

In this new location, I eventually opened a new clinic. I still worked six days a week, but Saturday was my "savings day." Every dollar earned on this weekend day was financial excess—money for savings that had been missing in my Chicago life.

In my new financial situation, I could provide for my family and protect them from future economic storms. And at last, I could breathe easier with more abundance. My new surplus income—cash that I saved and eventually invested into rental units—turned out to be necessary; it wouldn't be too long before health insurance cutbacks drastically reduced my income.

THE LIFE LESSON: FINANCIAL EXCESS

I learned that income equal to expenses is precarious,
And the pursuit of excess money is wise and necessary.

LESSON 2-4 · EXTRA SACRIFICE

Sacrifice: Something we give up for the sake of a better cause.

The garden with a purpose is free from weeds. So if you want to thrive, find your purpose and follow it until the very end of your life.

WALLACE HUEY

We pay the price for an extraordinary life, or the regrets of an average life, considered the Wealthy Gardener. The first requires a sacrifice of our hours, but the second requires a sacrifice of our dreams.

It was a sunny morning with pleasant weather, but the Wealthy Gardener was troubled as he peered through his window at Jared in the neighboring yard. Watering a flower bed, Jared seemed too settled with his abundant leisure. A life of ease leads nowhere, thought the Wealthy Gardener.

"Well, God, help me choose my words," he muttered under his breath, then walked out of the house and waved Jared over to meet him at the fence. They made small talk until the conversation stalled in an awkward silence.

"Do you mind if I ask a personal question?" began the Wealthy Gardener.

Jared shrugged. "Go right ahead."

"You have a lot of time on your hands now while you're between jobs, right?"

"That's an understatement." Jared laughed. "Too much time, really, especially since I'm living in the same house as my mom and dad."

"I figured you might say that," said the Wealthy Gardener, "and it got me thinking about what you said to me a while ago. You told me that when you work your butt off in life, things eventually turn out just fine for you."

"Yeah, that's how it works," Jared said. "I tend to succeed based on my work alone. I don't need any god or religion or delusional idea to help me."

"I won't argue philosophy with you," the Wealthy Gardener said. "But it leads me to ask the obvious question: Why don't you give some of your free time right now to make some money? I mean, why not find employment to tide you over between jobs?"

"You mean like work at a hardware store?"

The Wealthy Gardener chose a wise pause to remain calm. The dignity of work was sacred to him; his labor had given him everything he had in life.

"If you wish to save money, what's the downside of such a job?" pressed the Wealthy Gardener. "You may think an ordinary job is beneath you. This is a common delusion in your generation, and it is also the primary reason why so many of you remain broke."

Jared frowned. "I'm focused on finding an engineering job at this moment."

"Actually, you're focused on watering plants at this moment."

Jared exhaled audibly. "I guess that's true."

"You may want to consider that while you're living with your parents, you could save more money from an ordinary job than you've saved throughout your adult working life. You only need to fill your days with work and save every penny until something better comes along."

"Work for minimum wage?"

"It's more than you're earning by watering these flowers," the Wealthy Gardener said tersely, "and don't forget, it's all undiluted savings. More important, we're only talking about forty hours of your week. You have seventy more waking hours to call your own. You can surely formulate a plan to use those hours to search for a job."

Jared sighed. "I'll think about it."

"Think about what you want in your garden," said the Wealthy Gardener. "If you won't sacrifice your leisure, you'll need to settle for an ordinary life."

A SACRIFICE is something we give up for the sake of a better cause. We expect wealth to require sacrifice, but it is vital to be clear on the difference between extraordinary sacrifice and ordinary work. The distinction is illustrated by the parable of the gerbil farmer.

One winter's day, Bob and Sally, ordinary townsfolk without much ambition, purchased a modest farm. Rumors spread that they had received an inheritance and had spent the funds to try their hands at farming.

As the winter turned to spring and the land thawed, Bob went to work in a peculiar fashion. Day after day, he steadfastly erected wooden-post fences that divided the farmland into three distinct plots. Once the fencing was finally complete, Bob seeded and cultivated a crop in one section.

Neighbors watched with curiosity, but nobody approached Bob and Sally.

This bizarre farming routine continued for several years, and somehow Bob and Sally managed to survive on a third of the available land. Bob finished working at four thirty p.m. each day, keeping to a schedule he had known from his former job in town. Forty hours a week was more than enough work for Bob.

Finally an elderly neighbor, after watching for years from his farmhouse atop the hill, decided he needed to know what the heck was going on. Why was this crazy man farming only a third of his land?

He traipsed across the fields and met Bob, who was idling on his porch.

"I can't take it one second longer," the neighbor exclaimed, out of breath from the walk. "My curiosity is eating me alive. Why aren't you working all day like the rest of us?"

"I'm done working for the day. I finished my farming at four thirty."

The elderly neighbor choked aloud. "Okay, let me ask you this: Why did you separate your farmland into three sections and use only one of these sections?"

"So that's what this is all about." Bob grinned. "Why didn't you say so from the start? You sit down, old timer, and I'll be glad to share my secrets."

The neighbor sighed and eased into a rocking chair beside Bob.

"You work your life away, but I want a balanced life," Bob said. "And because I want balance, I divided my farmland into three equal sections."

"How does this give you balance?" the neighbor prodded.

Bob winked at him. "I bet you never knew that each section is labeled."

The neighbor's eyebrows furrowed, and he turned his head to examine the three sections. From this porch view, he could see that the plots were labeled "O," "E," and "G."

"Well, I'll be a son-of-a—"

"I know what you're thinking," Bob said. "It's pure genius, ain't it?"

"Well, uh, what the heck do the letters stand for?"

Bob stood as he proudly examined the farm. "The *O* stands for *ordinary*. If I stay within that plot of land, I get an ordinary life without too much work."

The neighbor's mouth fell open in incredulity. "And that's why you cultivate a third of your land each year?" he asked in a gasp.

"Damn right!" Bob said. "That plot labeled *O*, it keeps me and

Sally alive. It requires forty hours a week, and I can sit here while you work overtime."

The neighbor was stunned. "What the heck does the *E* stand for?"

"The *E* stands for *extra*-ordinary," Bob said, tapping his temple with a finger. "I keep out of that plot. It's above and beyond an ordinary workload. It's the extra work for *extra* money that uses a lot of *extra* time."

"But it's a full third of your acreage!" the neighbor said.

"Use your own land however you want, old timer. The extraordinary plot is no place for me. In my opinion, it's for the greedy without real priorities."

"How does a person with real priorities spend this time?"

"I reckon I can't always be sure."

The elderly neighbor groaned. "Okay, then—what's the *G* stand for?"

"That's my gerbil field," Bob said.

"Your *gerbil field*?" the old man shrieked. "What the heck is that?"

"It's where I go to escape," Bob said, as if his neighbor were an idiot. "I don't mind stepping into that land 'cause nobody tells me what to do. I can be the most mindless critter on the planet. I never stop moving, don't think much, and use up my time. It's the best place to go to forget my money worries."

"And so the point of it all?" the neighbor asked, stupefied.

"To keep my life in balance with an ordinary workload for survival income, while protecting my free time against extra work or extra demands, and then distracting myself with gerbil activity to avoid my persistent money worries."

The old neighbor rubbed his chin. "You know what I think the point is?"

"What's that?" snickered Bob.

"I think it's easier to work a little harder so you can worry a little less. And then you won't need to be spending your free time like a brainless rodent!"

It's a ludicrous tale, of course, but it subtly reminds us that the seeds of all future achievement are the hours planted in passing days.

If we plant only in the ordinary plot of a forty-hour workweek, we can expect to reap an ordinary harvest in our years. But if we plant in the ordinary plot *and* in the extraordinary plot—using the many free hours we have available each week—we give ourselves the best chance to reap an extraordinary crop in our lifetimes.

We pay the price for an extraordinary life, or we pay the regrets of an average life. An extraordinary life requires a sacrifice of our leisure hours, but an ordinary life requires a sacrifice of our cherished dreams. It depends on what is most wanted in the garden.

THE LIFE LESSON: EXTRA SACRIFICE

I learned that my days were the price of my aspirations,
And so I gave my life to avoid the regret of lost dreams.

Mental practices: Daily rituals of deep concentration.

The garden suggests there might be a place where we
can meet nature halfway.

MICHAEL POLLAN

Wealth requires hard work, the Wealthy Gardener pondered, but prosperity usually involves some lucky breaks. Only a superficial gardener takes all the credit, blind to the serendipity that harmonizes with one's aspirations. Did the Universal Intelligence aid his efforts, he often wondered, or was hard work the real force behind his fortunes?

The fall season was giving way to colder nights, shorter days, and oak leaves on the ground. Winter was on the way, noted the Wealthy Gardener, as he sipped hot tea and relished the sweeping view of the vineyards from his stone patio. Just then, he heard crunching gravel as a jeep steered up the winding driveway to his house.

Jimmy had called him late the night before and asked to arrange a meeting the following day, without explanation. The Wealthy Gardener had agreed; for the past five years, he and Jimmy had enjoyed a mentor-mentee relationship. The Wealthy Gardener had never had children, and Jimmy had no father.

Jimmy emerged from the jeep and walked over to the patio. They chatted over the progress of Santos's neighboring farm before getting down to business.

"I'm helping Santos get started," Jimmy began. "But I want it to be clear that I won't be staying in this apprenticeship for more than a year."

"It's a temporary position," said the Wealthy Gardener. "You should use the opportunity to learn about business in general, and cash flow in particular. Are you two not getting along?"

"It's nothing I can't handle," Jimmy said. "Santos has good intentions, and he now has a few cousins helping him, but he expects to open the farm in the spring and see the money roll in right away. I don't see any strategy."

"Are we meeting to talk about strategy?"

"It's about strategy in a way. I always wonder why things work out so well for you. Why are your business ventures immune to failure?"

The Wealthy Gardener chuckled quietly. "I must be very good at hiding my failures." He looked at his young friend and knew it was time for a serious talk. He trusted that Jimmy would be more open-minded than Jared, who refused to consider unfamiliar ideas.

"The older I get in this lifetime," said the Wealthy Gardener, "the humbler I am about the cause of my good fortune. On the one hand, I realize that without my hard work, none of my successes would have been possible," he said, studying the horizon. "On the other hand, I see others struggle just as hard without getting ahead financially. I'm not superior to them. The truth is, I have been blessed with many fortuitous breaks. Do you believe in good luck, Jimmy?"

Jimmy shook his head. "I see no value in thinking of luck."

"I, too, trust in cause and effect," said the Wealthy Gardener. "I've trusted hard work to earn my success. But in private, I've also trusted my daily mental practices to earn my good luck."

Jimmy looked curious but offered no response. The Wealthy Gardener eased up from his chair and stretched his legs. "Let's walk. It's a beautiful day."

Jimmy nodded and stood without speaking. He followed the Wealthy Gardener to a gravel path in the vineyards. Together they strolled silently.

"Native Americans used to walk this land," the Wealthy Gardener said, his hands behind his back, "and they believed a rain dance could invoke weather modifications. Rain dances were also common among populations in the Sahara Desert, Ethiopia, China, Africa, Thailand, and even in Europe. Today we dismiss this as a primitive ritual, and I'm not saying I trust a rain dance, but I do believe we still have a lot to learn about the powers of the mind when it is charged up and focused on a single purpose."

"Will you show me your rain dance?" Jimmy teased.

"In a sense," said the Wealthy Gardener. "We can speak honestly?"

Jimmy nodded. "I wouldn't have it any other way."

They walked the trail in silence for a minute. "I have witnessed unrewarded struggles for money, and it is as common as unanswered prayers for money. But I've found that my own success required hard work and daily mental practices. Both contributed to my economic fate."

Jimmy looked doubtful. "You command miracles to happen?"

"I have seen coincidences that appear as miracles," clarified the Wealthy Gardener. "And I believe these miracles are natural phenomena of a cause and effect that Nature has not yet revealed to us. I've seen evidence of an Unseen Force that responds to goals and faith."

"What exactly are your daily mental practices?"

"Whatever you see in my world," he said as they continued along the trail, "was first imagined long ago. In my quiet reveries, I focused on what I most wanted. And I performed a daily ritual of deep concentration on that goal. I gave daily attention to it. I saw it in my mind's eye. At first this ritual gave me strength for my work. The daily focus also restored my best attitude. Later, it seemed to connect me to an Intelligence that handed over ideas, plans, and lucky breaks."

Jimmy laughed. "Your beliefs are those of a rainmaker."

"Don't judge me too harshly," replied the Wealthy Gardener, chuckling. "Many people believe in the power of prayer. The rain in my life fell in the form of uncanny breaks, inspirations, coincidences, plans, and opportunities. My fortune was not all from my own hands. Then again, without the work of my own hands, my dreams would have surely been in vain. I needed both hard work and lucky breaks. And so I became the force that produced both."

Jimmy walked in contemplation. "How do I apply this in my own life?"

"Use your hours for impact every day," said the Wealthy Gardener, "but also concentrate daily on the outcomes you want most. When you connect with the inner experience of your desires, you will gain strength for the work. And you will discover your fullest powers. An inner wisdom will guide your ways if only you pause to listen to it."

MENTAL PRACTICES are daily rituals of deep concentration. Like prayer, the act of daily focusing sustains the attitude, fuels the determination, and perhaps even produces some lucky breaks in the accumulation of money. In the end, despite one's spiritual leanings, it seems that prayer positively affects the one who prays.

What I know for sure is that I gave daily time to mental practices, and I worked a lot. "God gives every bird its food," Josiah Gilbert Holland reminded us, "but He does not throw it into its nest." Hippocrates told us, "While calling on the gods a man should himself lend a hand."

I had witnessed the phenomenon of my business exploding in Chicago when I performed mental practices. Financial results came by harnessing my attention with a daily ritual of intense focus on outcomes. I didn't "kind of know what I wanted"—I knew my exact goals and wrote them repetitiously. And I made a practice of disciplined concentration on my central purpose to gain financial freedom.

Once I moved five hundred miles away from Chicago, I was starting from scratch again. The future was a vacuum. And it was my duty to fill this vacuum. I privately resumed my mental practices during my free hours.

In my house there was a cedar sauna that became my sanctuary for solitude. I retreated into this wooden box each night to do the mental work of deep concentration on my financial objectives.

On the walls of the sauna, I tacked pictures and drawings representing my goals. *What does financial success look like to me?* I would ponder that question and then use mental imagery with the aid of drawings. I recall drawing a clinic with a line of people waiting to enter the building. I drew a picture of my two children graduating from college debt-free. I scribbled a drawing of myself sitting under a cloud that was raining dollars—representing my own financial freedom.

I collected images online as well, printing them and hanging them in the sauna. I used this conceptualization technique as a daily ritual to crystallize my abstract desires into concrete shape and form.

My purpose for these sessions of deep concentration was to experience a state of financial freedom. My objective was to develop a burning faith in the fulfillment of my goals and aspirations by pretending and imagining that I had already achieved what I wanted in terms of money. And so during my sauna time, I strove to experience what these wishes would feel like after their actualization.

How exactly did I experience my wishes fulfilled?

I would enter the sauna and think of nothing for a minute, by which I mean *no words*. I would clear my mind, and I would audibly hum to refocus myself into the present moment.

Once I felt I had achieved peace, I would open my eyes and gaze at the images on the wall. I would then close my eyes again and feel the experience of those images. By doing so, I transported myself into my future dreams. If my thoughts drifted, I would open my eyes to look at the images again. I'd then refocus my attention on them. I'd concentrate on my goals and try again to experience their future realization.

Above the images, I had tacked a phrase on the wall: *FINANCIAL SECURITY: The power to "take a month" off without loss.* I repeated this statement: "In the future I will be collecting enough income, unrelated to my own hours and efforts, to vacation for a month and live off the cash flow without spending any savings." That is, my goal was to do as I pleased for thirty days without financial concerns.

The second phrase on the wall represented a higher long-term goal by age fifty: *FINANCIAL FREEDOM.* I repeated this statement: "By fifty years of age, I have a residual income that not only provides for my living expenses but also creates excess cash flow to reinvest and grow the business from its own profits. My goal is $220,000 in annual passive income from this business."

It is wise to observe that at the time I was repeating this statement, no business existed. As I imagined these conditions, I had no plan, no inspirational ideas, no savings, and no income. The future was a vacuum. It was my duty to fill that vacuum. I filled it with my future goals.

As the years progressed, my mental practices grew to include affirmations. I added the following assertions, tacked onto the sauna's wooden wall, to infuse my subconscious mind with self-confidence that would demand the achievement of prosperity. The capitalized phrases and underlined words are exactly as they appeared in my sauna. I would read these affirmations with as much emotion as I could muster. Without emotion, they're just words with no power:

> I ACT AS IF IT IS IMPOSSIBLE TO FAIL! Why NOT me? I earn my wealth through my service to others. I ALLOW good things. I am now awaiting better plans. I am a CHANNEL thru whom wealth circulates copiously and endlessly. WEALTH is MY WAY to impact the world. I do not expect or desire a PROBLEM-free existence. I seek strength and wisdom—not ease and comfort. I CAN & I WILL! I pay my living expenses with residual income. I use this ONE DAY for progress.

As a nightly ritual, I impressed these images and affirmations into my mind, burning them deeper through forced repetition. The words and images changed as I evolved through the years. My desires became clearer and the goals I imagined seemed more real to me.

If this ritual sounds exhausting, let me remind you that this work is merely the focusing of thought. It is the act of deep concentration—nothing more—on winning our dreams.

This nightly ritual, alone in solitude, was my sacred rain dance. It was the scene that occurred behind the curtain, the aspect of my inner life that nobody saw as I amassed growing financial advantages that led to my independence. I don't believe in miracles, but I do believe in results that look like miracles. I think it's possible that we know very little of our mental potential; I believe much is yet to be learned about the human mind fixated on a clear aim.

When I was at my best in this world, the skies opened and rained uncanny breaks, inspirations, coincidences, and rare opportunities upon me. My good fortune was not all from my own hands. But then again, without the work of my own hands, I would have surely died in a drought instead of prospering. I worked hard, but also sensed an Unseen Force working with me, beside me, and through me.

"According to your faith," said Jesus, "so shall it be done unto you."

In the end, by the time I was fifty, my children had graduated debt-free from college. I was able to live on residual income. And I now have a business with a perpetual income of over $220,000 that provides for my living expenses and increases in size from its own profits.

THE LIFE LESSON: MENTAL PRACTICES

I saw that wealth required hard work and lucky breaks,
And so I learned to be the force that produced both.

It is utterly forbidden to be half-hearted about
gardening. You have got to love your garden whether
you like it or not.

W. C. SELLAR

Striving for prosperity is the natural desire to be free, the Wealthy Gardener believed, but the greatest treasure of life is peace of mind. And he recalled when he had learned this lesson, the worst year of his life.

The tragedy had struck six years earlier. He would never forget that phone call at nine o'clock on a Saturday night. The caller had informed him that his wife had been involved in a head-on collision, in which she died instantly. Mary, a teacher, was sixty-three years old and about to retire.

He eventually learned that an underage drunk driver had swerved across the yellow lines, causing the accident. The teenager survived but was charged with a DUI and vehicular homicide; he was given a two-year jail term. After one year, the kid was transferred to a local reformatory for troubled teens.

In the aftermath of the accident, the Wealthy Gardener fell into a depression. He suddenly had nothing to look forward to, nothing to anticipate, and nothing to care about. This despair, he later said, was due to self-absorption. Mary had been his confidante, his best friend, and his lifelong companion. And her loss had stripped him of purpose.

After watching this downward spiral for a year, his neighbor Fred had finally intervened. Fred invited him to help with a weekly Sunday school. It was the start of his emotional recovery.

In time, the Wealthy Gardener regained his spirit by helping others. He started to engage in his businesses again and even expanded the winery to accommodate the growing weekend demand. With direction, he regained his sense of fulfillment. But deep in his soul, he knew he was not yet healed. He carried a sense of bitterness within him.

He learned about the boy who'd killed his wife in the accident. In seeking closure, he decided to confront this kid at the reformatory. He made an appointment and went to the school. When they met, he found a sobbing young man who was filled with remorse. The boy apologized repeatedly, and the Wealthy Gardener found healing in forgiveness.

He drove home and resumed his normal routines.

Life appeared the same, but now something was brewing deep within him. The familiar tug of the inner voice was pulling his mind back to the memory of the troubled teen. He knew this feeling—a slight uneasiness, a mild distress, an urge to action—all too well, but he wasn't yet sure of its message. He paused and meditated on the gut feeling, spent time with the urge, trying to decipher its meaning.

One day he awoke with an inspiration that felt right. He could always sense a right direction even when the destination was unknown. In this case, the right action was to volunteer his services and teach a class at the reformatory. He knew the teens at the reformatory had little chance to succeed, but maybe he could regain his own sense of purpose by helping them find their way.

These boys needed to prosper financially to overcome the desperate circumstances that led to a life of crime. And the reason to strive for prosperity and wealth, he told the kids, was to be able to one day pursue more important purposes than making money. The Wealthy Gardener's weekly classes were called the Eagle's Club, and the boys thrived in them.

His most coveted possession was a wrought-iron garden sign, a gift from the reformatory for his weekly volunteer work. The sign was planted in the ground cover of his backyard garden, where he could see it daily. On this plaque, he would occasionally read the mission statement that he handed out to every graduate of his class:

The Wealthiest Gardener

It's the one who shapes life with hours, who is master of attitude regardless of conditions, who feels entitled to nothing except that which is earned, who knows the pride of effort regardless of outcome, and who, instead of settling for less, asks quietly, "Why not me?"

It is the visionary who is impractical, who is even at times ridiculed, but who thinks independently and listens to the still inner voice to avoid the regrets of those who wonder what might have been if only they'd followed the pull of their soul.

It's the one who lives with purpose and intention; who shows up each day and does the hard task; who seeks satisfaction over pleasure; who strives to make a difference, to make the world a better place; but who, when actions fail to produce impact, will know that failure was never due to partial efforts.

It is finally the one who lies spent, exhausted, certain that there's nothing more that could have been offered on the altar of life, who meets the end with a clear conscience of having passed the ultimate test of giving one's best.

Chapter 3

WEALTH
PERSPECTIVES

LESSON 3-1 · CHALLENGES

Challenge: A problem or situation to be overcome.

A good garden may have some weeds.

THOMAS FULLER

An unprepared mind, reflected the Wealthy Gardener, invites suffering during the challenges of the day. But a battle-ready attitude leads to composure and poise in turbulent conditions.

It was well past dinnertime as he walked to the neighboring farm to check on Santos's progress. He found the grounds deserted, which struck him as odd, since there were two hours of daylight remaining. As he examined the lonely property, he heard muffled groans coming from behind the silo of the newly painted barn.

He walked toward the noise, but then stopped short and grinned at the sight: Jimmy was alone, but he was struggling, grumbling, and cursing the plants in a vegetable garden. The Wealthy Gardener silently watched the comical scene. A few months ago, he had suggested this gardening project to Jimmy to get him better acquainted with farming.

The Wealthy Gardener finally cleared his throat. "It's when the plants cuss back at you," he shouted, "that you need to be alarmed!"

Jimmy looked up, grinned, and wiped his face with his sleeve. "I swear to God—anyone who does this work for fun has got to have something wrong with them!"

"I take offense at that," replied the Wealthy Gardener, chuckling.

"You should take offense!" Jimmy retorted, walking toward him. "I mean, after long days of constant problems at work, I come back here and battle continuous problems in this damn garden! I pull weeds, and then new weeds pop up. I pick off the slugs and beetles, and new ones take their place. I put up a fence for rabbits, and then moles and mice tunnel under it. Plants get diseases, they get eaten, they get too much sun, they get too little sun. Why the hell does any sane person on this planet enjoy gardening?"

The Wealthy Gardener was now laughing. "Why do you think I told you to start a small vegetable garden?"

"You claimed it was to get better acquainted with farming."

"I duped you," he said frankly. "Within the borders of that little garden are the lessons you'll need for much bigger gardens."

Jimmy looked toward the small plot. "I'm honestly not learning too much beyond sweat and hard work in my free time."

"And that's an indispensable start to prosperity," said the Wealthy Gardener, his face now somber. "I wanted you to see that in a garden, you're at war against an opposing force. And in your life, it won't be too different. Problems are overcome for a day, but soon replaced with new problems. Life is hard, and it requires a lot of work. But you do have a choice in your work. You can resent your days of struggle, or you can work with the attitude of a master gardener."

"I need to learn to accept problems?"

"Not only accept problems, but embrace them," emphasized the Wealthy Gardener. "It's not problems that cause our suffering, but an unprepared mind that allows the suffering. The person who expects daily challenges will not become overwhelmed. This is the first lesson."

"What's the second lesson of my garden?"

"If you don't know it yet," chided the Wealthy Gardener, "you need more time in this small plot. For now it is enough to know that your problems are good for you. A useful life surmounts many problems, while the desire for ease causes suffering in your days."

DAILY CHALLENGES are problems or situations to be overcome. I wasted several naive years thinking I'd be happy only once I eliminated and overcame my daily problems.

When I was in my twenties, I read a book titled *Do What You Love, The Money Will Follow*. At the time, the book convinced me that job stress and struggle were abnormal and unnecessary. "Follow your bliss" is a common phrase along these lines. And nowadays we hear the expression "Follow your passion."

The trouble for me—and it seems to be a common trouble for others—is that this passion ideal led to the expectation of blissful and pleasurable work. My everyday problems felt like mountains when I expected my workdays to be without their fair share of frustration. For me, the famous book, and the advice of others like it, was not only wrong-headed but dangerous. It's better to expect problems as inevitable and normal, to expect all days to have challenges, and to maintain a problem-ready mind-set to surmount the trials that exist in every garden.

"Difficulties are meant to rouse, not discourage. The human spirit is to grow strong by conflict," said William Ellery Channing.

Later in my life, at the most hectic summit of my productive working years, I was running three small businesses, and each day was a war against problems. If running away had been a viable option, I would have laced up my shoes. But in a life of continual turmoil, I started using the term *stress-handling capacity*.

With constant exposure to stress and problems, one's ability to endure stress and problems grows stronger. We strengthen to handle the challenges that once overwhelmed us. We expand our boundaries, limitations, and capabilities through pressure and discomfort.

"A smooth sea never made a skillful mariner," an English proverb suggests. And as we endure, our challenges strengthen us.

But during exhausting weeks, I would cling to the mind-set that no matter the challenge, this too shall pass. It always did. I even found it useful to picture myself on the upcoming weekend after my current troubles had been fixed. I would mentally leap the hurdles and imagine the desired outcomes. This vision kept me sane and composed during weeks of unrelenting pressure and stress.

Regardless of our capabilities, there's no escaping from our problems. The only question is, do we have a vision of winning the day? Do we have the mind-set to stay the course and endure problems? Did we show up with a warrior's mentality to battle and maintain our direction? Without a prepared mind-set for the troubles of the day, our attitude can collapse under the weight of our problems. It's best to know work is a series of problems—and that all problems will pass.

I have found it useful to ask myself this question: What does success "look like" at the end of this week? What will life be like after my urgent problem has passed? I could always imagine my life on the other side of my immediate crisis. And if I could *not* imagine this better reality, it meant my problems had gained too much power.

Problems of the day are no match for impact hours. At times, the wish for an "easy day" may be normal and signal that rest is much needed. But the wish for an "easy life" invites delusion and unhappiness.

"Do not pray for easy lives. Pray to be stronger men!" said Reverend Phillips Brooks. "Do not pray for tasks equal to your powers. Pray for powers equal to your tasks." It is our strength in life that varies, not the burdens of living. "Do not pray for lighter burdens," Theodore Roosevelt said, "but for stronger backs."

A good garden will always have weeds that keep us working. Happiness is not found in a life without problems, but in a life of overcoming problems. We need only to maintain an upbeat attitude to face challenges and do our work of sowing to reap a harvest. A life without challenge is a life without a worthy contribution.

THE LIFE LESSON: CHALLENGES

I learned that a useful life was a challenging life,
And a battle-ready mind-set was critical to win the day.

LESSON 3-2 · CRISIS

Crisis: A time of intense difficulty, trouble, or danger.

A garden is always a series of losses set against a few
triumphs, like life itself.

MAY SARTON

Wicked storms and financial setbacks happen, mused the Wealthy Gardener, but the real problems occur when misfortunes become excuses. Adversity can lead to darkness, or it can lead to the Inner Light.

The Wealthy Gardener had gathered Santos and Jimmy in his small office for their weekly business meeting to discuss the dangers of farming and how to prevent future calamities. Santos was in one chair. Jimmy was in the other. Within five minutes, they were arguing.

"I have a question," Jimmy said, not looking at Santos.

"Okay, let's hear it," said the Wealthy Gardener.

"So about the threats to survival—we've been using your operation as a model. Santos claims that your worst setback was a tornado twenty years ago that devastated the crops, leveled the barns, and almost ruined you."

"There is no doubt that that was a tough year," the Wealthy Gardener said slowly. "And it caused many more difficult years in the fight for profitability. Who expects such a thing to take everything you possess and level it in a single moment?"

"So natural catastrophes are the greatest threat?" asked Jimmy.

"Well, you must not forget," said the Wealthy Gardener, "that I had an emergency fund, and I carried property insurance. I was confident that I'd be okay. I still had my health, my mind, and the knowledge of how to build a business. I had the ability to make plans. I had the resolve to recover. The storm didn't take those intangibles from me. With my ambition and focus and confidence intact, I could rebuild from scratch. I did it once, and so I knew I could do it again."

Santos sighed, his expression sullen. The Wealthy Gardener paused, his eyes drifting to a window overlooking the lush grounds of the vineyard.

"No, that wasn't the worst threat to my business," he said softly. "The worst setback was about fifteen years after that bad storm. It was when Mary died in the accident. The tornado wiped out my physical assets, but Mary's death almost wiped out the important stuff."

Santos was dead silent; Jimmy looked at the floor.

"Some phases of life we just endure, and there is nothing more to say of them," the Wealthy Gardener continued. "No silver linings, no deep meaning to make it okay. It's just a crisis. Time doesn't heal the wound, but we can grow a scar. And with a scar on the wound, we learn to function in the world. We limp on and make the best of it."

The Wealthy Gardener leaned forward. "The greatest threats are the ones that affect our courage and drive. But it is our duty to function again, if not for ourselves, then for others. We can recover from anything, and we must." He and Jimmy locked eyes for a moment.

A CRISIS is a time of intense difficulty, trouble, or danger. There is no escaping the catastrophes of life, but all storms pass, and we must ultimately move on and reestablish direction. We must use the days.

"The first and final thing you have to do in this world is last in it and not be smashed by it," wrote Ernest Hemingway. "Misfortune comes to all men," a Chinese proverb reminds us.

What tornadoes will sweep into our landscapes? If we live long enough, we will attend the funerals of our parents, siblings, close friends, and sometimes even our children. We may face the loss of a job and income. Betrayal by others in business or even marriage is possible. We may face financial setbacks due to a physical injury.

This is not reason to brood, but to prepare. It is delusional to expect a life of ease and comfort. A more empowering approach is to seek inner strength and wisdom to weather the inevitable trials with grace and self-possession. A tragedy is only tragic when it becomes an excuse.

"Endure, and preserve yourselves for better things," Virgil said wisely. So how do we prepare for the difficulties in this world?

I will describe my worst financial crisis in a later chapter. This tornado swept into my landscape and tested me beyond my physical capacity. I even suffered from alopecia, with bald spots on my face, eyebrows, and head. I couldn't sleep without pills, and even then, anxiety would wake me from my drugged stupor in the middle of the night. But this greatest crisis of my life, which stripped me of nonessential concerns, isolated a life lesson that towers above all others.

I learned that no catastrophe has the power to take away my Inner Light. Inside each of us is a central, spiritual presence that we feel most when we are left with nothing else. When my situation was most grim, during the bleakest moments of the darkest months, this one lesson shone brightly. I could lose my job, my income, my kids' college funds . . . but no person and no event could take my Inner Light. It was mine alone.

And it was all I had at the time.

When you find yourself in a crisis, be like a strong oak tree in a northern winter. The cold weather sweeps in and stays for long months, the wind howls, the days get shorter, and the darkness grows longer. The lifeless tree is frozen like a towering ice statue. In the worst of times, there is nothing to do but outlast the elements. The tree stands erect and takes it. It accepts and endures the pain. But the tree, frozen or not, survives until spring. It's sometimes missing a branch when the weather finally warms, but it is alive.

"I bend, but I do not break," Jean de la Fontaine said. The breaking of which he speaks refers to the spirit, and leaves a person worsened, bitter, and without joy. It is far better to bend with the howling wind by accepting that some problems just are, and while they feel unfair, we can learn to suffer and endure them without breaking.

"If you want to see the sunshine," Frank Lane said, "you have to weather the storm." The sunshine will always come. Just as a garden can endure wicked storms, so, too, can a human being. We are resilient creatures if we choose to be. Despite death and pain, failures and setbacks, we can always recover.

It is our reaction to tragedy, our resolution in the storm, that defines our lifetime. We can carry heavy burdens without complaints. Dwight D. Eisenhower was named Gallup's most admired man of his generation twelve times. He was the leader of the Allied forces in Europe during World War II; he became president of Columbia University; he was the supreme commander of NATO; he was a two-term US president who ended the Korean War, initiated the US highway system, and signed off on NASA. He spent his final years as a peacetime ambassador. He achieved a life of global impact despite personal tragedy. "The death of our four-year-old son," he said at the end of his illustrious life, "We never did get over that."

Ike didn't get over it, but he grew a scar and learned to live. The crisis passed, and it surely left him worse off. But it could not extinguish his light.

"In the depths of winter, I finally learned that within me there lay an invincible summer," said Albert Camus. We must only outlast the season.

THE LIFE LESSON: CRISIS
....

I saw that even the most enviable lives include tragedy,
But tragedies are only tragic when they become excuses.

LESSON 3-3 · PROCRASTINATION

Procrastination: The delay of an action or decision.

A man of words and not of deeds is like a garden full of
weeks.

ENGLISH NURSERY RHYME

The Wealthy Gardener raked leaves on an invigorating autumn afternoon. Gardens don't respond to future intentions, he considered pen-
sively, and dreams don't respond to the actions of someday.

His thoughts were interrupted by his neighbor Fred, who sauntered
over and leaned on the fence between the two properties. Recently retired, Fred was growing worried over his idling son Jared's lack of direction. Of course, Fred seemed to be mired in his own procrastination.

"Don't you ever stop working?" Fred joked. "I used to think you were
retired, but since I've been home, I get weary just watching you."

The Wealthy Gardener chuckled as he approached the fence.

"This is retirement to me," he said, smiling broadly. "I like to stay
moving, doing the things I enjoy. The simple pleasures are the key to a
happy retirement."

Fred nodded, then was silent for a long moment. "I'm learning the
same thing," he said. "I thought I'd be happier without my daily work
responsibilities."

"I have an extra rake for you."

"No thanks, I have my own rake—and my own leaves."

They both laughed, but then another long pause ensued.

"Don't take this the wrong way," said the Wealthy Gardener. "It's just
that I know you, Fred. And you were happiest and most fulfilled when
you had great responsibilities. I think maybe retirement might just take
some time for you to get used to."

"I should talk to Jared," Fred quipped. "He seems to enjoy retirement."

They both chuckled at this wisecrack for a minute. But slowly Fred's expression grew serious. "I just don't know how to help him."

"I've tried to talk to him," said the Wealthy Gardener. "I'll keep trying, though, if only for your sake."

"I'll accept your aid," Fred said, "and don't be afraid to be blunt."

"Done that already," replied the Wealthy Gardener. "What about your own plans, Fred? Have you given any thought to what you want to do?"

"What do you mean?"

"I mean, you now have unlimited opportunities. You've earned the freedom to do as you please. What's your dream for the remaining years?"

Fred pondered the question in silence. "I see what you're up to, you old rascal. I'm complaining about Jared's lack of direction while you're drawing my attention to my own. I get it. And trust me—I'm trying to figure it out."

"I'm sure you'll be fine. Are we still on for cards tonight?"

"Of course," Fred said. "And don't forget your quarters. I'm starting to rely on your weekly donation for my coffee money."

They laughed as they parted ways. But in his gut, the Wealthy Gardener didn't feel as certain about Fred's future as he had claimed. Some retirees never figure out that they can still seek adventure. Inactivity can grow into a habit, and courage can wane without urgency.

PROCRASTINATION IS THE DELAYING or postponing of an action or decision to *someday*. Achievers accept the transitions of change, while procrastinators never step into the action phase of dreams.

"I know you will work hard," the Unseen Power seems to taunt us, "but can you make the hard choices, and will you accept the known discomforts that are demanded for wealth? Will you willingly choose to walk into unfamiliar places to get to your cherished dreams?"

In my life, there was a crucial day when I stopped learning and talking about real estate and instead set out in the direction of doing it.

I called a real estate agent to walk me through two investment properties. I moved past the decision and into the action. I entered a foreign world of risking my savings, meeting contractors, managing renovations, controlling costs, landlording, and reorganizing a weekly schedule that already contained no free hours.

Behind the defining moments of our lives, we will surely look back at a decision when we once took a risk and walked directly into uncertainty. We chose to accept whatever trials we had to endure, and we were willing to bet on ourselves to handle the adversity. Then again, maybe we'll recall failing to stand up for our dreams.

One of my great friendships occurred during my thirties. Greg was an accountant at a lumber company. He was married with a daughter and owned a house with a pool. Greg was the guy with a daily joke.

One day, in the middle of a cold winter, Greg stopped by my clinic for a chiropractic treatment. After we spoke for a few minutes, he excused himself to use the restroom. It was a small lavatory without heat, and its position on an exterior wall sometimes turned the room into a frigid icebox.

It was the busiest hour of the day at the clinic, with patients everywhere, and during the madness Greg came flying out of the bathroom in an animated frenzy.

"Hey, Doc!" he shouted, his voice booming loud enough for all to hear. "Do you know what it's like to take a shit on a block of ice in the pitch dark?"

I shook my head and grinned. "No, I don't, actually."

"Why don't you sit on your toilet and find out?"

I walked back to the frigid little restroom and found that the lightbulb had burned out.

Every time Greg told a joke, he'd laugh until he couldn't breathe and his face turned purple. By the time I returned to the reception room,

Greg was suffocating from convulsive laughter. All the other patients were howling!

But in his serious moments, this friend encouraged me to pursue real estate. His brother-in-law was a dentist who owned thirty-two rental units, and those units provided extra income that paid for two amazing vacation houses.

Greg also shared his dream to return to Florida. He had lived there before moving up north, but his heart never left the Sunshine State. Someday he'd have a small business in St. Petersburg, maybe rent wet bikes or run a fishing charter business. He told me stories of his time spent on the water. He even told me of an adventure when he lived out of his car and slept on the beach for an entire summer during his twenties, just for the heck of it.

But with age came responsibilities.

Greg now had a family, a mortgage, three cars, a job, and a solid life. His daughter was in high school, and he didn't want to uproot her. His wife's family was in the area, but she was a true sweetheart and was willing to move.

I encouraged his dream, and he encouraged mine. Over time, we bonded like brothers.

"Why not return to Florida?" I asked. He could try those business ventures he'd described, and he also had an easy fallback plan. In the worst-case scenario, he could find an accounting position near Tampa.

He promised he would do it.

But always, he would do it *someday*. It was the little lie that kept him sane. Greg would have been crushed if he had to say no to the dream. Instead, he didn't say no—he just pushed the dream back. He always delayed it to "someday."

His daughter graduated from high school and received a scholarship to attend college. Now she only visited her parents on breaks between semesters.

"It's now or never," I reminded him. "You're fifty years old, pal."

"I know, you're right," he said. "I'll do it after my daughter graduates."

His daughter graduated from college, and I stopped badgering him. It seemed that the conversation now made him feel uncomfortable. In the end, Greg was unable to pull the trigger. And he just kept going to work each day while the dream slowly faded and died. The days passed and turned into years.

Few of us can accept the pain of saying no to our dreams, so we cleverly deceive ourselves with the thought of going for it *someday*. *Someday* is an excuse to avoid the immediate discomfort and anxiety of change. *Someday* leads to passive inaction, so the regrets of abandoning our dreams are not immediate.

In time, Greg seemed to grow lethargic, though he'd still tell the same terrible jokes. But the laughter ended with the news that Greg had a rare form of cancer and had two months to live.

I called his house when I learned of it. He wasn't home. He had left the area and wouldn't be returning. He would spend those final two months with his wife in Florida.

Greg faced the ultimate price of procrastination. What were his reflections during those last months, experiencing the short-lived dream too late? I'll never know. We never said goodbye. I can't imagine his tortured regrets.

"Somebody should tell us, right at the start of our lives, that we are dying," said Pope Paul VI. "Then we might live life to the limit, every minute of every day. Do it! I say. Whatever you want to do, do it now! There are only so many tomorrows." We must not allow our dreams to turn into our regrets.

THE LIFE LESSON: PROCRASTINATION

I saw that dreams don't respond to thoughts of someday,
But only to brave actions and turbulent transitions.

Intangible: Unable to be touched or grasped;
not having physical presence.

The garden is a love song, a duet between a human
being and Mother Nature.

JEFF COX

All prosperity begins with desire, opined the Wealthy Gardener, and
grows in the most mysterious ways. We gain the cooperation of a Silent
Partner in the quest for wealth if we know what we want, maintain absolute faith, offer many impact hours, and heed the whispers.

On a warm Saturday in autumn, the Wealthy Gardener was at the
winery, intermingling with patrons who sipped wine and listened to live
jazz. He approached a table where he found Jared with several friends.
Jared and the Wealthy Gardener hadn't spoken since Jared started working at a packaging company one month earlier. Greetings were exchanged,
and the Wealthy Gardener invited Jared to stop by his office later.

Three hours later, Jared found a seat near the Wealthy Gardener's
desk. Catching him up on the job situation, Jared explained how he'd
started his new work at the factory, loading boxes onto trucks, but then,
within just the first month, he had been promoted to a supervisory job
overseeing a small group of packers. He appeared confident as he spoke.

"That's progress," the Wealthy Gardener said. "You're now using
your hours with more impact than when you were watering flowers. And
it seems you're clearly more satisfied with your new situation."

Jared paused before he spoke. "My life's not too bad, I guess. But let's
face it—a year ago I was an engineer in an air-conditioned office earning
twice my current salary. I wasn't living with my parents, either," he said,
sighing. "So no, I'm not completely satisfied. I'd like much more out of

life. But because I don't have time outside of work, I'm making no progress on my search for an engineering job."

The Wealthy Gardener considered Jared's position. The current situation allowed him to save money, enjoy friendships, and live with financial dignity. But he was also ignoring the silent whisper of discontentment. When we ignore our inner wisdom, we will come to regret it.

"It's good that you're now earning an income and saving money," said the Wealthy Gardener, carefully measuring his words, "but you may be in a very dangerous place in your life right now."

Jared was taken aback. "I'm in a dangerous place?"

"There's nothing wrong with your situation," said the Wealthy Gardener, "unless you're ignoring a sense of discontentment. It's a 'comfort trap,' when things aren't too bad, but they aren't great, either. We ignore the whisper of the soul in the comfortable life."

Jared exhaled. "Here we go again with your 'God of the Garden' talk."

The Wealthy Gardener stood and walked Jared to the window. "I tell you this for your own benefit," he said. "Do you see all those people now enjoying this day on my property? They all want more out of life, but they don't want it bad enough to trade their comfort for it. And so instead of pausing to pay attention to the pull of their souls, they're escaping their lives today."

"They look happy to me." Jared laughed.

"And so they are," agreed the Wealthy Gardener, "as their hours pass . . ."

They walked back to the desk and sat down. "You're doing okay," the Wealthy Gardener said carefully, "but what is your direction? And are you expressing your fullest potential in your current life?"

"It's a temporary situation," Jared said simply.

"You may learn otherwise," responded the Wealthy Gardener, "if you ignore your inner wisdom. The Unseen Force of which you speak lightly is Universal Intelligence, and it works to aid the fullest expression of life. You can use this power, or you can struggle alone."

Jared glared across the desk. "I'll struggle alone."

There was a tense silence as the Wealthy Gardener leaned forward and picked up an acorn from his desk. "Do you know why I keep this acorn in front of me each day?"

Jared shrugged.

"It's to remind myself to never be so arrogant as to think I know it all," the Wealthy Gardener said calmly. "When I look at this tiny acorn, I am reminded of its potential, and I am humbled by the mysteries beyond my understanding. Only Nature can produce a seed and make it grow."

Jared eyed the acorn. "I suppose this all leads into a lecture?"

"Our fullest potential requires a mind open to unknown possibilities. We must consider the wonders of life that we can't fully understand— like the stupendous potential of an acorn."

Jared laughed condescendingly. "I can understand an acorn!"

"Your mind is now like this acorn," snapped the Wealthy Gardener. "On my desk, it has the potential within it to be a great tree. But this acorn has been on my desk for more than ten years, and what has become of its potential over that time?"

Jared looked thoughtful, but didn't answer the question.

"Now consider the mystery of it," the Wealthy Gardener continued. "If we put this seed in fertile soil, it somehow comes to life. A seed that was dormant for ten years will mysteriously grow into a great oak tree. And this tree will produce thousands of acorns like the one on my desk."

Jared breathed deeply and exhaled. "And the point is?"

"Don't ever speak lightly of Intangible Forces. When you doubt the unknown, you doubt yourself. You have more potential within you than a tiny acorn, and the Unseen Power is available to help grow your individuality into its fullest expression."

"I have just one question," Jared countered. "What if that's all bullshit?"

"I like to err on the side of caution in spiritual matters," confessed the Wealthy Gardener. "But to answer your perfectly rational question, if

Universal Intelligence is a delusion, then focusing on goals, cultivating faith, developing plans, offering hours, and living with purpose can only help us achieve our dreams. And we may observe a few coincidences that expand our minds."

INTANGIBLE: UNABLE TO BE touched or grasped; not having physical presence. We gain the cooperation of Intangible Forces when we emotionally feel an outcome in our imagination. We produce serendipity and synchronicity according to the depth of our faith. I've stated that when I have been at my best in this world, the skies have opened and rained inspirations, coincidences, and rare opportunities upon me.

I will now share a personal incident when mental practices coincided with a serendipitous event that drastically shaped my current life. I have learned through experience that Universal Intelligence is working when inspirations begin to flow and uncanny coincidences start to show up in harmony with my most dominant thoughts.

By fifty, I'd attained my financial ambitions. Having reached the mountaintop after climbing for so long, I was surprised to find little euphoria. In fact, I felt only a sense of relief and an unexpected familiarity with a condition I'd envisioned many times in my mind.

I was grateful beyond words, for sure, but I was also aware of a new melancholy, one that I could not comprehend. I had it all, but I was not elated. I have come to know this state of benevolent melancholy as the whisper of an inner wisdom. It is a signal for me to *pause*.

I believe in Universal Intelligence. When I feel something isn't quite right in life, I meditate for an answer. I imagine that my limited intelligence can gain access to an infinite intelligence. After achieving financial freedom, I sought an answer for my vague discontentment.

At the time, my son, Mike, was in his final year of college and would soon begin his own quest for financial achievement. In my quiet moments, I felt a pull to share with him the knowledge that I'd gained over the past thirty years. This inspiration came in the silence, and it energized me.

As I contemplated what I would like to convey to my son, the strange new melancholy lifted. When I backed away from the inspiration to act, the melancholy returned.

Let us slow down this story here to examine the Intangible Force in this event. A feeling of melancholy got my attention; it lifted when I considered a new activity. When it came, I paused and searched within. I didn't distract myself or escape the unpleasant feeling. In the pauses, within the odd moments of the day, I sought its meaning.

I paused for several seconds and questioned what to do. We all have a sixth sense—our inner wisdom—that exists in stillness and silence. And if we pause, we can access this guidance.

I set aside all reason and decided to go for it.

I wrote the first wealth missive in secret, developing it in the privacy of my home office. I agonized over this message in my free hours for a month. Finally, after forty hours, I was too exhausted to edit another word or move another comma. I was done—it was ten pages.

I attached the life lesson to an email and sent it to my unsuspecting son at college. I explained in the email that I might write a book about prosperity, and I wanted his brutally honest feedback on chapter one.

I then waited in a vulnerable state of self-exposure. Mike called me later that night, and his supportive words caused tears, unseen by him. We discussed the missive. I hung up the phone, and it felt right. We had had a genuine dialogue between father and son.

I then started my book of lessons on prosperity in earnest. I'd finish one or two a week and email them to Mike. He would return them to me with comments, arguments, and suggestions. And we'd talk about them.

But over the course of six months, I once again started to feel the sense of melancholy. It was my inner voice guiding me to change. Something was not quite right, and I once again meditated to try to understand what the inner wisdom was trying to tell me.

At that time, I still worked three days at my clinic while managing my sixty-five rental units. If I could only leave the clinic for just *three months*, I believed, it would be enough time to outline the many lessons I wanted to share with my son—and maybe even with the public.

I was tempted to close the clinic temporarily since I didn't need the income and the book project seemed to have a growing purpose for me. I was compelled in this direction but still struggled with indecision, unable to pull the trigger, forever reluctant to leave my patients.

I was at an impasse. Since I didn't change my life to gain time to write and think, I endured a mild state of melancholy. I felt my own inner voice, the whisper of Universal Intelligence. But I didn't follow it. I wouldn't step boldly into the unknown—not by my own free will.

"Life always whispers to you first," Oprah Winfrey said, "but if you ignore the whisper, sooner or later you'll get a scream."

I was about to learn this truth.

One day, as I was finishing up at the clinic, my wife called to say that the sewer line at our home was clogged. I called three plumbers that I regularly used for sewer-line issues. Each was unavailable. But one of the plumbers offered to lend me his drain snake if I'd swing by his house. I thanked him, jumped in my truck, picked up the snake, and transported the machine to my house.

A drain snake is a metal coil about an inch thick that rotates by the force of a power motor. Wearing a pair of thin gloves, I fed this snake into the basement drain. Suddenly, the glove on my left hand snagged on the rotating coil, which pulled my hand into the machine.

I felt an explosion of fire in my hand. Instantly, I saw blood and skin and realized that half my left pinkie finger was gone. I grabbed a towel, wrapped it around my hand, and squeezed. After I'd exhausted my vocabulary of curse words, my son drove me to the ER. There they stabilized the injury and sent me to a trauma hospital for surgery under anesthesia.

Why am I telling my mutilated-finger story?

Because when I returned to the doctor for a postoperative visit, he informed me that, due to the six broken bones in my hand and my missing finger, I would need to be off work for *three months*. I could do nothing physical during this respite.

It was surely a coincidence, you say, that I wanted precisely three months of solitude to organize and outline this book. It is always easy to discredit the uncanny events that show up in harmony with our ambitions. But Universal Intelligence operates through serendipity.

You may think it odd to view such an injury as a blessing, but this unlikely series of events may have been the only way to extricate me from my duties at the clinic. As for the doubter who needs further proof, take a closer look at my picture in the final pages of this book. You will want to focus on my left hand, and then examine the little finger. Who needs a pinkie, anyway?

THE LIFE LESSON: INTANGIBLE FORCES

I found that the inner voice whispers in the silence,
And that Universal Intelligence will aid financial ambitions.

LESSON 3-5 · WEALTH SEASONS

Season: A period marked by particular conditions or activities.

A garden is where you can find a whole spectrum of life, birth and death.

TIFFANY BAKER

"The first thirty years are for the learning of money," the Wealthy Gardener wrote in his book, chuckling. "The next thirty years are for the earning of money, and the final thirty years, if done correctly, are for the burning of money."

He grinned and stood, spotting Jared next door, sitting in an Adirondack chair beside a birdfeeder, a full beer in one hand and five empty bottles lying in the grass. The Wealthy Gardener walked to the fence, and their eyes met.

"You must be pretty thirsty," joked the Wealthy Gardener.

Jared swigged from the bottle and walked to the fence. "I've been thinking about what you said last weekend. And you're right—my life is pathetic."

"I never said such a thing. But now you're getting drunk?"

"I'm thirty-two years old, divorced, and have nothing to my name. My friends have houses and families, and I'm living with my parents. I don't even have a career anymore. When I was young, I thought I'd be a tremendous success by now."

"But now you're over the hill?"

Jared shrugged. "In eight years, I'll be halfway done with my life."

The Wealthy Gardener laughed aloud at the remark.

"What's so funny?"

"I evidently got your attention with my acorn lecture," said the

Wealthy Gardener, "but I suppose I didn't tell you the full story of the tiny seed."

Jared scoffed. "I'm sure you're about to tell it now."

"As a matter of fact, that's what I'll do," said the Wealthy Gardener. "Do you realize that at this moment, we are standing under a northern red oak?"

Jared looked up at the big tree, its branches sprawling overhead.

"I planted this tree myself about forty-five years ago," the Wealthy Gardener said, "by burying a tiny acorn in the fertile soil. So anyway, just last year, this tree started to consistently produce acorns. Do you know what that means, Jared?"

Jared took another swig, looking bewildered. "I haven't a clue."

"The tree is a total loser," said the Wealthy Gardener. "Northern oaks live to be two hundred years old on average, but so far this pathetic tree has only managed to grow tall, survive the winters, and develop extremely deep roots."

Jared understood. "It hasn't produced much yet."

"And isn't it interesting?" asked the Wealthy Gardener. "The tree hasn't produced much yet, but it's right on schedule. You must be aware of the seasons of your life. When it comes to wealth, there are seasons and cycles just as there are seasons for the growth of a great tree. You're being too hard on yourself at your stage of life. You're just entering your summer season of prosperity."

"What's the summer season?"

"It's the middle phase of your financial life cycle," said the Wealthy Gardener. "At thirty-two, you are leaving the survival season and entering the accumulation season. I never said that your life was pathetic. But I did intend to wake you up. You need to focus on your direction and use your potential. You may now be entering the summer season, but unlike a tree that grows on its own, your wealth tree is happy to not grow at all. Money grows from the seed of desire backed by faith and ever-changing plans. And it must be kept growing with daily impact hours, or it will eventually wither and die."

A SEASON is a period of time marked by particular conditions or activities. Building wealth is a drama that unfolds in three distinct acts. The growth of financial prosperity has a spring, a summer, and a fall. When we're impatient to reach our financial goals, grasping the truth of the wealth seasons will help to ease our stress.

On an uneventful summer day, my wife and I strolled hand in hand through a middle-class neighborhood. We were in our mid-twenties. As we walked, I observed the houses on the street, thinking that behind each house was an owner. And each owner had a job, and each job provided enough income to afford each of those houses. I was a young renter at the time, barely able to pay the bills. It was the spring season of my financial life cycle. I was learning about the work of earning.

By the age of thirty, I was still nowhere near reaching my expectations. I was working hard and using my time. I'd figured out how to survive, but I had not yet figured out how to accumulate money. I now had a home, but I could not amass great savings. The seasons were changing, and I was changing, too.

"Look deep into nature," said Albert Einstein, "and then you will understand everything better." All of nature grows inexorably with direction and patience. Large trees emerge slowly from small beginnings. Our financial life cycle unfolds in patterns that align with predictable seasons.

ACT ONE: 0 TO 30 YEARS—FINANCIAL STABILITY
This first act consists of learning to survive. We absorb and adopt the money ideas of our families. We are ingrained with cultural biases about finances. We become educated, then employed, and begin trading our hours for dollars. We learn to be financial grown-ups. We learn about

banks, credit, and expenses. We find spending to be thrilling at times, but we learn that it decreases financial stability. During the spring of our financial life cycle, the future is bright with an expansive time horizon. In the spring, optimism is highest.

"April hath put a spirit of youth in everything," wrote Shakespeare.

As we approach the age of thirty, however, our financial conditions get more serious. We see differences in life conditions based solely on one's finances.

ACT TWO: 30 TO 60 YEARS—FINANCIAL ACCUMULATION

The second act consists of accumulating money. We have lost our youthful idealism and realize that money is critical. We want a comfortable life, or at least enough money to not have to worry about our finances.

It's the summer season of the financial life cycle.

"Look, here is a tree in the garden and every summer it produces apples," wrote Alan Watts, "and we call it an apple tree because the tree 'apples.' That's what it does." We bear the most fruit in the middle season.

In the summer season, we become more competent adults. We set financial goals, even if we don't know how to achieve our aims, and we think about saving money. Our earning potential is at its peak, but we also acquire more expenses. We gain a family and dependents. We get promoted, we receive bonuses, and we upgrade our education.

We discover it's not about how much money we *earn* that counts, but how much we *save*. We amass savings. And we learn to invest savings so that our money earns money and compounds.

ACT THREE: 60 TO 90—FINANCIAL INDEPENDENCE

The final act consists of the fall harvest—the comfortable retirement that we have earned during our accumulating years. Our lifestyle in the fall is based on the amount of wealth we have amassed and how much of that wealth we are able to access. If we've failed to accumulate, we may be required to continue the work of earning. In the fall, our experience varies greatly due to our accumulation of money.

"There is a harmony in autumn, and a lustre in its sky," wrote Percy Bysshe Shelley, "which through the summer is not heard or seen."

The financial life cycle is as predictable as the seasons. "Adopt the pace of nature," said Emerson, "her secret is patience." Lao Tzu said, "Nature does not hurry, yet everything is accomplished." Be in no hurry.

It's best to know that wealth unfolds in its own season.

THE LIFE LESSON: WEALTH SEASONS

I learned that wealth emerges like a theater drama,
With three acts, not two halves, that require patience.

Personal growth: The process of improving, getting better.

When gardeners garden, it is not just plants that grow,
but the gardeners themselves.

KEN DRUSE

The impossibilities of today, the Wealthy Gardener reflected, can become the realities of tomorrow. With clarity of thought, persistence, dedication, and sacrifice, a novice gardener can grow into a master gardener within an inconceivably short amount of time.

At a botanical society meeting, the Wealthy Gardener lectured on new diseases affecting local flora, and then presented the history of the name *marigold*, a golden flower which was originally called Mary's Gold, in reference to the mother of Jesus.

Among this circle of serious-minded master horticulturists, the Wealthy Gardener had won the Garden of the Year Award in a recent competition. Jimmy had tagged along to the meeting that night, and now they drove home together in the Wealthy Gardener's truck.

"I never knew gardening was so complicated," said Jimmy, gazing out a window.

"It's not really complex," said the Wealthy Gardener. "It's simple at the core. But those were master gardeners in that room, and they like to be challenged."

"It sounded complicated to me."

"You mean it sounded unfamiliar," clarified the Wealthy Gardener.

Jimmy smiled. "Yeah, I guess that's true."

"But you're already familiar with one lesson of the garden."

"That it's a royal burden?" Jimmy quipped. "I found that it's an endless struggle of me against nature—with me trying to keep up."

"That's too true," agreed the Wealthy Gardener. "The work is fighting the daily forces of entropy, chaos, and disorder. But master gardeners know that gardening is about the satisfaction of labor. It's about staying engaged in a pursuit that pleases the soul, despite its many problems."

"Master gardening requires a lot of learning."

"I suppose it's just that we all want to grow," said the Wealthy Gardener. "Wouldn't it be boring if we planted the same exact garden every year and never faced a problem? How would you like to stay in your little garden all your life? Can you imagine a life without direction and change?"

"I think I'd rather die," Jimmy quipped.

"And yet people do it," said the Wealthy Gardener. "They may not choose to do it, but they will allow it by procrastination or fear of the unknown. People end up where they start in life when they fail to pause and listen to their inner wisdom. There's no evolution in a hectic life, and too many people exist to maintain their little gardens."

"I can't even imagine that confinement."

The Wealthy Gardener shook his head as he drove. "Have you figured out the next lesson of your vegetable garden yet?"

Jimmy sighed. "I must be dense, because I haven't found much meaning beyond the sweat and work. It's actually become a boring chore."

The Wealthy Gardener drove in silence for a long minute. "Have you ever considered," he said softly, "that within your boredom lies the lesson? And this boredom comes from your inner wisdom?"

Jimmy thought about it. "So I'm bored without growth in the garden, and this feeling is a sign from within that I need to change?"

"Drudgery can have meaning if it's done for a reason that advances you in some way. But you view working in your garden as just a dull chore with no growth in it for you. And this arduous chore causes no clear direction in your life."

"That's what sucks about it."

"What is good for a plant is good for the gardener. As plants grow toward the sun, human beings should always grow toward their fullest potential. When a change is needed, we know it through a sixth sense."

"How do I grow into my fullest potential?"

The Wealthy Gardener smiled. "I've been thinking about that subject a lot. There's no simple answer, but I'm working on it."

The truck meandered along the farm's lengthy driveway and came to a stop near the house. They went inside, and the Wealthy Gardener prepared tea for Jimmy and himself.

"There's one more lesson in your garden," said the Wealthy Gardener, sitting in a rocking chair opposite Jimmy. He had a twinkle in his eye. "I intentionally made your garden the exact size of the vegetable garden I had when I was but a youngster."

Jimmy looked bewildered. "Why did you do that?"

"As a teenager, I was given a small plot on my uncle's land. I had then what you have now. But I also had a willingness to grow my garden into something more during my lifetime," he replied. "I gave you this task so you would know my own start in life and could begin as I once began."

Jimmy sat up straighter. "How did you do it?"

"I expanded the borders of the garden," said the Wealthy Gardener, "by expanding the boundaries of my mind. Few goals are impossible for someone who will devote time to lifelong learning and continual self-mastery."

Jimmy frowned. "I'd like to hear the story of your success."

"I can tell you what was true for me," the Wealthy Gardener said at last, leaning back in his chair. "I started exactly as you have, with a small vegetable garden. In a short time, I came to see that I could stay in this small garden for my entire life. Unless, of course, I changed."

Jimmy nodded, without speaking.

"It didn't take a genius to see that a bigger garden was better," he continued softly, "and I knew this truth even as a teenager. I was from an uneducated family, but I got hooked on reading. Horatio Alger's stories changed the way I viewed things. In those stories, I entered a world where poor boys with ambition could prosper in this life."

"But still, you started with just a vegetable garden?"

"Oh, but I had much more," corrected the Wealthy Gardener. "I had a brain, lots of time, few living expenses, and an eagerness to learn and to work. I had nothing to risk because I had nothing to lose. And so I took chances. Some might say I had a disadvantaged childhood like yourself, but I was born in the best country on this planet to rise by my own merit."

"Okay, I get it. But how did you begin to rise?"

"Can you imagine a little garden turning into my current operations?"

"No, I can't imagine it."

"I guess you'd say it was then impossible."

"What do you mean?"

"I couldn't imagine the ending, either. It wasn't possible. I just chose one goal beyond my grasp, and I grew into it. Then I chose another goal beyond my grasp and grew into that one. And in this way, I expanded my powers."

"I get it," Jimmy said. "You challenged yourself and grew yourself, and then the impossible goals became possible due to your continual advances."

"It was that and more," the Wealthy Gardener said thoughtfully. "I used my hours, and those hours were the key to using my full potential. In addition to my own efforts, I discovered powers of my mind, and this skill catapulted me in big leaps. I worked with the Unseen Force that aided my efforts according to my faith."

Jimmy sighed. "And now I'm starting out the same as you."

"Start with a goal of prosperity—and I mean an exact amount of money—and give it a completion date. Then grow to be worthy of it. Expand your mind until you no longer fit into your current environment. You will then witness that all gardens grow from the mind of the gardener. The way to a larger garden," said the Wealthy Gardener, "is to outgrow the one you've got. Set impossible goals, and then apply yourself to activities that impact the realization of those goals."

"So you became wealthy by going after goals beyond your abilities?"

"Yes, beyond my *current* abilities. The way of nature is growth or death. When a plant stops growing, it then starts to die. We should always be growing ourselves."

"But what if I reach my ultimate goals?"

"Then you, my young friend, have a wonderful problem," said the Wealthy Gardener, smiling. "Master gardeners always evolve, and so do their dreams."

Jimmy grinned. "So we may never reach our full potential?"

"Now, *that* is a question I've never been able to answer to my own satisfaction," said the Wealthy Gardener, leaning forward in his chair. "How can we know our fullest potential? I believe I was at the edge of my capacity when I almost wasn't smart enough to meet a goal, when I almost wasn't strong enough for the work, and when I almost failed despite my fullest struggle. But given enough desire and faith, we find that we are smart enough and strong enough to earn our dreams. We can learn, and we can grow as we work to achieve our goals."

Jimmy sat quiet, considering this.

"This I know for sure," the Wealthy Gardener continued in an even tone. "Reaching your fullest potential is a duty. It is your assignment, and it is usually beyond the edge of your current capacity."

Jimmy said goodbye shortly afterward, and the Wealthy Gardener retreated to his study. The realization of wealth had been a lifelong quest of actualizing his full potential. His success had required learning, discovering, and using the powers of the mind, then making an impact in the steady parade of passing days.

In a reflective state, he recounted the personal growth he had enjoyed due to his ambition. It was true, as he had told Jimmy, that he had outgrown many gardens during his lifetime.

But exactly *how* had he outgrown these gardens?

Now this was the question that plagued him. He knew that his wealth had grown in stride with his competence. Indeed, wealth seemed to be attracted only to those with substantial personal power.

Late into the night, he reviewed the powers that he believed were behind his own wealth. And he wondered if these powers for wealth could be taught to and mastered by others with financial ambition.

THE LIFE LESSON: PERSONAL GROWTH

I found that impossible goals led to personal growth,
And my powers always stretched to meet the demands.

PART II

Wealthy Gardening

God sure has blessed you with a beautiful farm," said the preacher. *"Yes, he has, and I am grateful,"* replied the farmer, *"but you should have seen this place when He had it all to Himself!*

EARL NIGHTINGALE

Chapter 4

THE 55 POWERS
FOR WEALTH

Purpose: A goal or aim, especially one that
transcends selfish ends.

I like gardening—it's a place where I find myself when I
need to lose myself.

ALICE SEBOLD

The storybook fantasy of financial success, thought the Wealthy Gardener, is that the climb to wealth is a glamorous ascent. The reality is a journey of sacrifice and inconvenience backed by a cause more important than personal comforts.

They played cards on a Wednesday evening, a couple of old guys repeating stories from long ago and laughing at every one. The Wealthy Gardener enjoyed the company, and Fred seemed to find comfort in the weekly ritual. Such relationships were important in these years. Fred had been running the table, and the Wealthy Gardener was nearly broke.

Then the conversation turned serious. "To be honest with you," Fred admitted, "I never would have believed I'd be feeling so lost in retirement. It's not that I miss the work, because I don't. It's just an empty feeling, like something's missing. When I had a job, I knew why I was getting out of bed in the morning. It wasn't fun, but the work gave me a routine."

The Wealthy Gardener studied his neighbor across the card table. Fred had been retired for over a year now and was still having a tough time adjusting.

"Some transitions take time," answered the Wealthy Gardener. "You've been working hard ever since you were out of high school. It will get better."

"I've had enough time." Fred picked a card from the stack and laid one down. "Connie thinks I need to take up golf or start gardening, but I never did like chasing a little ball in the heat or pulling weeds in the dirt. I'm just not too excited despite all this freedom."

The Wealthy Gardener nodded with compassion, considering his next words carefully. "Do you remember what you told me after Mary died?" he asked at last.

Fred exhaled deeply. "I told you to find a worthy cause."

"You did tell me that. And you know, at the time, I kind of resented you for saying it. You had a wife and family. You were the general manager at the plant. You had everything going for you. It seemed to me that I had nothing. I was self-absorbed in my misery. I was paralyzed by the pain. It's natural to mourn, but I'd stopped living and giving. And that was a terrible mistake."

Fred thought about these words without responding.

"Do you recall what else you told me back then?" the Wealthy Gardener asked.

Fred nodded slowly. "I thought you needed to engage in life. You needed to get off your butt and get moving. You needed something to live for."

"I needed something to get out of bed for," agreed the Wealthy Gardener. He pulled a card from the stack and discarded. "I needed a purpose in my life other than myself. That's what you told me. And it was life-saving advice."

Fred didn't speak as he studied his cards. Finally, his gaze lifted and he looked at his friend. "I hear what you're saying, and I appreciate it. But the death of your wife is not the same as my retirement struggles. I didn't lose what you lost. I don't think it's really an apples-to-apples comparison."

"You may be right," said the Wealthy Gardener. "But I lost my purpose for getting out of bed in the morning. And, in your words, I simply needed to get my butt moving and engage myself in a worthy cause. Your advice was spot on, and I found my reason to continue at the reform school."

Fred smiled reluctantly, accepting the message without a response.

A PURPOSE is a goal or aim, especially one that transcends selfish ends. A purpose for wealth, beyond hoarding it, is vital to sustain the ongoing persistence needed to acquire it.

What drives us to sacrifice for wealth? For me, I wanted to live without a job so I could use my time for other pursuits, and I also felt a deep need to provide financial security for my wife and kids.

These purposes were my driving forces. I would sacrifice every comfort for personal freedom and for the welfare of my loved ones. I would have quit countless times without these causes for amassing money. When you're starting from scratch in the middle class, upward mobility requires overtime hours and uncommon frugality.

It is tempting to say, like the masses believe, that I sacrificed my time at a job to provide for my family. This is a delusion. The daily job is not a sacrifice because it is mandatory to one's basic survival. We must do it, even without a great cause, because we have no choice. The forty-hour workweek, like it or not, is a requirement of staying alive in a free-market society—not a personal sacrifice.

The price of financial prosperity—the real sacrifices for abundance— is our free hours. During my evenings and weekends, I gravitated into real estate rentals and flipping houses when I could have done other things. I recall sunny Saturday afternoons spent in renovation projects. I started to wonder if it was all worth it. Why was I killing myself with all that work?

I thought of my small children. If I didn't sacrifice those extra hours, they'd be buried under overwhelming college debt. I'd never be able to help them when they grew older. How could I tell them that hard work pays off if they witnessed that my own life—without extra sacrifice—was merely a survival trap?

I resumed my work, stayed the course, and pursued wealth for a worthy cause outside myself. Since those challenging days in the middle years, I've realized my other goal for financial prosperity: Now that I'm free to do as I please, I can devote my days to greater purposes, since I no longer spend my waking hours earning a living.

Another example to clarify the importance of a cause behind our sacrifices is writing this book. If not for my son and our weekly talks, I doubt I would have endured or even been able to survive three years of full-time effort in this solitary endeavor.

Isn't it paradoxical that a purpose outside ourselves motivates our most sacred efforts, which in turn provides a sense of fulfillment? "Life becomes harder for us when we live for others," said Albert Schweitzer, "but it also becomes richer and happier."

Money itself may not be enough to motivate us to sacrifice, but sending our kids to college may get us moving. Escaping poverty or debt may be reason enough to give up our leisure time. The dream of freedom can inspire us to work harder and amass wealth. We are wired to seek a life of purpose and forward direction. When we discover what makes us tick, we discover our full power. A deeper cause fuels the persistence behind the sacrifices of achievement.

THE LIFE LESSON: PURPOSE

I saw that prosperity required sustained inconveniences,
But I was driven by causes greater than my comfort.

LESSON 4-2 · COMPENSATION

Compensation: Something we get for something we give;
repayment for a contribution that is needed and useful.

My green thumb came only as a result of the mistakes
made while learning to see things from the plant's point
of view.

H. FRED DALE

An important income, mused the Wealthy Gardener, results from important contributions. In a free market society, we receive an income only by offering a valuable service or product to help others.

The Wealthy Gardener stood behind a podium to address a classroom of delinquent boys. For the past six years, he'd been volunteering his time at this reformatory for troubled teens with his weekly Eagle's Club class. Today he was reviewing the four laws behind the work of earning money.

On a chalkboard behind him, he had scrawled four laws as an introductory lesson; they were all his students needed to know for now—but of course, this income formula was just a start:

THE INCOME FORMULA
The need for what you do
How well you do what you do
How difficult it would be to replace you
How many people you serve

"And so, if you're not getting the income you want in life," he said, "you must think about your service in terms of these four variables. Your income always reflects the world's view of your contribution."

Jimmy watched quietly from a side chair. The boys who were currently in the room didn't know that he had been a student in this same classroom not too long ago.

A kid spoke up: "What if I don't want to serve nobody?"

"Well, I have bad news for you," said the Wealthy Gardener. These kids only seemed to understand straight talk. "The world doesn't really care what you want. In fact, it doesn't even care that you exist. You must earn what you get, and your rewards will always be a true indicator of the service you give."

"So to make money," the kid pressed, "I have to sacrifice for others?"

"The reason you are paid by any employer," said the Wealthy Gardener, "is to serve his or her interests. That's the reality. Most work is such that you wouldn't do it for free. You get paid to perform and to function. If you refuse to serve, you'll need to get used to hunger."

"My old man slaved all his life," another kid said. "He broke his back for a company, earned enough to stay broke, and lost his job. That ain't for me."

"Don't be too harsh on your old man," advised the Wealthy Gardener. "He may have been thinking of you while he was doing the work of earning. But let's get back to the formula to learn from his example. Was there a need for his service?"

"He worked on an assembly line for thirty years."

"So he was useful for a long time," the Wealthy Gardener said. He then went through the income formula to show that the vulnerability of this type of job—working on an assembly line—was the ease of replacing the worker. "The problem with most people is that they think they're irreplaceable. When they think so, they're usually wrong."

A kid at the front of the class raised his hand. "My mom says that we all have unique talents and interests, and if we use them, money will take care of itself."

The Wealthy Gardener studied him. "What does your mom do for a living?"

"She's a piano teacher."

"Okay, let's consider this example according to the formula." The class collectively agreed that (1) there was a limited need for this service; (2) the mom may have been a good piano teacher, but (3) it sadly wouldn't be too hard to replace her; and (4) she served only fifteen students per week.

"So we can agree that piano lessons may add to quality of life," said the Wealthy Gardener, "but they're a luxury for most people—not a need. And it's unlikely that this profession will generate a substantial primary income."

The class was silent. "It is good to find work that you love," he continued, "but the work should love you back. It's like any relationship: If you do all the giving and you receive no love in return, then you will become resentful."

"How can work love me back?" asked a kid from the back row.

"It should reward you with satisfaction, it should fulfill a need within you to contribute in your own way, and it should pay you enough money to support the lifestyle you desire," said the Wealthy Gardener. "Over time, unrewarded effort breeds resentment. The right service for you is the one that loves you back."

COMPENSATION IS SOMETHING we get for something we give; repayment for a contribution that is needed and useful. And we must never forget that our income reflects the need for our service, how well we perform it, how difficult it would be to replace us, and how many people we serve.

Before any other factor, financial prosperity requires adequate compensation. "Money is a headache," said Terri Guillemets, "and money is the cure." We need to earn a financial surplus.

I didn't always understand the income formula, but I got it right in the end. Flipping houses in rural Pennsylvania became a means of compensation for me, but the margins were tight. This was not luxurious California, with $200,000 spreads between buy price and sell price. I was aiming for $15,000 of profit per house, before taxes.

Using the income formula, why did I make money in flipping real estate?

1. I served a need. In my local area, I saw that homebuyers spent all their money on down payments. They had no savings left over for repairs, updates, new appliances, roofs, or landscaping. Due to this situation, I offered turnkey properties. *Just buy groceries*, I advertised.

2. I provided rare quality. I believed in perfection, and I demanded it from the workers repairing the homes I was flipping. And then to sell the product, I promoted the houses better than other sellers.

3. I was difficult to replace. I had the cash savings to acquire the properties I wanted, and most others who wanted to compete for those houses did not. My money was a growing snowball that empowered me to do business. The need for initial capital created a moat that limited the competition. The millionaire investors were interested in apartments and commercial real estate, not my small scraps at the table. It all added up to a niche market.

4. I flipped five houses per year. This was a small service to humanity compared to the busiest professionals, who churn out a hundred flips every year. Still, my little operation was enough to increase my savings, since I was also operating two other businesses.

Of course, the real estate flipping business was full of constant stress and problems, which I willingly endured for the earning of money. Where's the fulfillment in this line of work? It's *in the bank*. "Never complain about your troubles; they are responsible for more than half of your income," said Robert R. Updegraff.

With no pressure, we get no diamonds.

"One thing I do know for sure is that your rewards in life will be in exact proportion to your human services," said Earl Nightingale. "If you want more rewards, you'd better throw more logs on the fire in the form of more service." We may need to offer more service, or we may need better strategies, more training, or even a new career altogether to produce more heat from the same fire.

When we pursue the aim of monetary accumulation, our service to others must answer two questions: (1) "How can I help?" and (2) "What's in it for me?" When we figure out the proper balance between these two questions, fulfill a human need, then use the hours of our days, we find a way of life that leads to financial power.

"We each serve a portion of humanity—our inner contacts, family, friends, neighbors, coworkers, customers, prospects, and employers," Nightingale said. "Wishing for more tangible or intangible rewards without giving more or better service to others leads to frustrations, failure, demoralization, and surrender." Wealth flows from a useful service that loves us back.

THE LIFE LESSON: COMPENSATION

I found that my income equals the need for what I did, how well I did it,
How difficult it would be to replace me, and how many I served.

Crusade: A vigorous, life-changing movement
to advance a cause.

There is no spot of ground, however arid, bare or ugly,
that cannot be tamed into such a state as may give an
impression of beauty and delight.

GERTRUDE JEKYLL

When he met Jimmy at the reform school five years earlier, the Wealthy
Gardener recalled, he had seen only a lost young boy with little hope or
direction. Jimmy's potential was dormant, but he was now the graduate
with the most promise. Anything and everything is possible with the
steady use of days in a five-year crusade.

They were sitting in front of a roaring fire in the Wealthy Gardener's
family room on a Saturday morning. There was snow falling outside.

"Knowing what you know now," Jimmy asked, "if you were in my
shoes at my age, what would you be most concerned about in life?"

The Wealthy Gardener smiled. "I've confessed my abiding belief in
the Universal Intelligence," he answered. "And you're aware of my daily
ritual of mental practices and deep concentration—so if I was your age
now, I think I'd spend the next five years mastering these skills. After
these years pass, just think of the life ahead of you."

Jimmy seemed taken aback. "Why would it take five years?"

"An oak tree grows two feet a year," said the Wealthy Gardener, "and
the change is barely perceptible. But after five years, the oak will have
advanced its cause by ten feet. People want to be mighty oaks without a
stretch of time, but that's not the way Nature works. Every worthwhile
reward or mastery of a skill grows over many years."

"I can be patient." Jimmy exhaled. "What do I need to do?"

"There are a lot of things. The foremost is clarifying what you want most. You must also learn to engage your hours and give your best effort every day. You need to develop a cause, a meaning, to keep you going through hard times. And you must learn to live in a world that you can't see but can sense, forever knowing that you are never alone because you're a part of the Universal Intelligence."

Jimmy laughed aloud in exasperation. "Is that all?"

The Wealthy Gardener chuckled. "It may sound like a lot initially, but it's nothing more than converting wasted hours into purposeful hours each day—and concentrating on your goals."

Jimmy gazed thoughtfully out the window at the falling snow. He was sure his life would work out somehow. There was nothing but time, hope, and positive expectations for the future. But now he felt an inner pull to secure a direction by using his daily free hours.

"When you were young," Jimmy asked, "did you plan your life?"

"As I explained not too long ago," said the Wealthy Gardener, "I set smaller goals and grew into them. What I have found is that every five years, life changes so much that we can rarely predict what we'll want after those years have passed. I've learned to plan my life in five-year crusades or causes—what I call *magnificent bridges*. Five years is the furthest out I plan now. It's long enough for our actions to change everything, and it's a short enough span of time to manage."

Jimmy was silent for a moment. "Where do I start?"

"Sit in solitude every day. Be quiet and be still. Calm your thoughts and get to know your inner voice. In the silence, concentrate on the things you want. If you can't narrow your focus, you'll forever dissipate your potential during the crowded days of an ordinary life."

A CRUSADE is a vigorous, life-changing movement to advance a cause. And five years is short enough to be manageable but long enough to transform every unwanted condition of our lives.

A friend of mine had fallen into the trap of massive debt. Student loans plagued him during his twenties, and when he married, his wife's student loans matched his own. They had a child, bought a house, and leased two new cars. Step by step, they fell deeper into debt.

By the time he turned thirty, they were helpless and depressed over the prospect of working only to pay their lenders. They had racked up credit card debt of $35,000; a mortgage of $150,000; car loans over $60,000; and combined student loans over $110,000. I know all this because the information showed up on his credit report when he applied to rent one of my apartments.

"The hardest part was just getting started in reducing the debt," he told me, "because it just looked so overwhelming. I couldn't attack the huge debt all at once, but I could pay off my smallest credit card, I could trade in my cars, and I could sell my house."

I witnessed the changes in their life over the following years. They swallowed their pride and moved into one of my rental units. I watched this family with admiration. She worked forty hours a week, and he did the same. But in their free hours, they started building a network marketing business. Within five years, they had achieved complete freedom from debt.

"When patterns are broken, new worlds emerge," said Tuli Kupferberg. But what will those new worlds be? For better or worse, we need to take a step of faith into a world we do not know and have never experienced.

Another friend overcame tragedy within a five-year time span.

Angie was married with two young children when her husband died from a sudden brain aneurysm. Within a year, she had sold their house and moved in with her parents. Angie worked full time to pay their bills, but she enrolled in a community college program for nursing and worked toward her degree in her free hours.

When I saw her during that time, she looked pale and exhausted. But after five years, Angie had become a full-time registered nurse and was buying the house next to her parents'.

"Most people overestimate what they can do in one year," said Bill Gates, "and underestimate what they can do in ten years." But the possibilities within a five-year crusade are life-changing. Why is it a crusade? Because it is a vigorous movement that transforms all.

"Nothing worthwhile comes easily," wrote Hamilton Holt. "Half effort does not produce half results. It produces no results. Work, continuous work and hard work, is the only way to accomplish results that last." Winston Churchill told us, "Continuous effort—not strength or intelligence—is the key to unlocking our potential."

We always have a new life every five years. And we can always choose the direction of the next five years. We cannot always change our unwanted condition instantly, but we can always begin to steer in a new direction. Our destination is decided by the slightest turns.

Like a cruise ship at sea that alters direction by a slight rotation of its steering wheel, we, too, can begin a slow, arcing turn toward a new life with a single decision followed by steady action in a new direction.

We can sign up for one class and aim toward a career. We can pay down one credit card and veer toward freedom from debt. We can save one dollar and steer toward prosperity. We can always do one thing. Crusades are made of direction, momentum, and deeper causes.

"Every worthwhile accomplishment, big or little," said Mahatma Gandhi, "has its stages of drudgery and triumph: a beginning, a struggle, and a victory." Anything and everything is possible with a five-year crusade.

THE LIFE LESSON: FIVE-YEAR CRUSADES

....

I found that wanting fast results led only to despair,
But a steady effort over five years transforms all of life.

LESSON 4-4 · RESISTANCE

Resistance: An opposing or oppressive force.

Successful gardening is doing what has to be done when
it has to be done the way it ought to be done whether
you want to do it or not.

JERRY BAKER

The daily challenge of work, thought the Wealthy Gardener, is the start
of each task. A body in motion tends to stay in motion, but a body at rest
tends to come up with a lot of excuses.

Jared sat at the indoor bar of the winery with a glass of wine at six p.m.
on a Friday. The Wealthy Gardener caught a glimpse of him and walked
over to sit on the adjacent stool. They exchanged greetings, and Jared
explained that he was there that evening to meet a girl.

"So how is life working out for you?" asked the Wealthy Gardener,
obviously referring to their ongoing discussion about Jared's current job
situation. The last time they talked, Jared had been drunk and disconso-
late on a weekday afternoon in his parent's backyard.

"Not too bad, I guess," Jared said casually.

It was a curious answer, thought the Wealthy Gardener. Jared's vague
response was a total dismissal of the question, showing little regard for
their recent conversations.

"So who is this new girl?" the Wealthy Gardener asked, moving
toward safer ground.

"She's pretty special." Jared beamed. "I never met anyone like her. It's
like when we're together, there is no great effort. It's just easy to be myself."

"That is special," agreed the Wealthy Gardener. "And how does she
feel about you searching for a job elsewhere in the country?"

Jared picked up his wineglass and took a sip. "She gets quiet every time I mention it. So you can only imagine what that means."

"It means she's giving you silent resistance," he answered. "But I must ask: Are you actively searching to find the job?"

"I work a lot of overtime now at the company," Jared said, "and it pays time and a half. My days are so full, I don't have any free time."

The Wealthy Gardener thought about this: Jared's search for an engineering job was on hold, he was smitten with a local girl, and he excused his lack of effort with his lack of free time.

"So you're happy with the way things are?"

Jared smiled slowly. "I'm not as demoralized as I was the last time we talked."

The Wealthy Gardener was silent for a moment.

"Is that a bad thing?" Jared asked.

"Not at all," said the Wealthy Gardener. "Desires can change in life as the people and circumstances change around us. But it's important not to settle, that's all."

"You think I'm settling?"

"It's not my aim to judge. I'm just going by what you tell me. Last time we talked, you were demoralized by your life's progress. I told you that at thirty-two, you were just starting the summer of your financial life cycle. Now it's a whole new story."

"Yeah, you're right. I didn't mean to be defensive."

"There's nothing wrong with being comfortable in life," said the Wealthy Gardener. "If you choose your life, and get what you want, that's good."

They were silent, each deep in their own thoughts. It was always interesting, mused the Wealthy Gardener, to observe words versus deeds. It is easy for people to take just a few daily actions, but it is even easier to take no action at all. And it's easy to make excuses.

Just then, a striking girl in a miniskirt approached, sat beside Jared, and crossed her legs. Introductions were made, and she ordered a drink.

As the Wealthy Gardener excused himself to leave, he knew that he had just come face-to-face with Jared's resistance.

And Jared was in way over his head.

RESISTANCE IS AN OPPOSING or oppressive force against goals. It is our inherent human laziness, procrastination, distraction, excuses, and the desire to be doing anything but the day's productive work. Resistance is the reluctance to engage in action and sacrifice our free hours.

"Any idiot can face a crisis; it's that everyday living that's rough," wrote Clifford Odets. "Rule of thumb: The more important a call or action is to our soul's evolution," wrote Steven Pressfield, "the more Resistance we will feel toward pursuing it." Urgent tasks get our attention, while important tasks get our resistance.

A good friend of mine worked in the executive offices of an international coal company. Of all businesspeople, he was one who had my fullest respect. But in 2015, coal prices plummeted. Worse, there was decreasing demand for coal, and the situation looked bleak for the industry. Most coal companies declared bankruptcy.

"Bill, have you considered a new company or industry?" I asked when I couldn't take it anymore. His job was in jeopardy. "Consider your options."

"Yeah, you're probably right," he said. "I know I should be looking."

He never looked for a new job, and he eventually lost his income due to his company's inevitable bankruptcy. It wasn't fear that stopped him. It wasn't inability or stupidity. He just didn't do what he knew he should have been doing. What lies in our power to do, we learn, often lies in our power not to do.

How do we beat resistance? Marie de Vichy-Chamrond, marquise du Deffand, said, "The distance is nothing; it is only the first step that is difficult." The first step out the door is more challenging than the two-mile walk that follows it. The same rule holds true in every dreaded exertion of our work—it's always about the first step. In all duties, it is the beginning that tests our resolve. What we begin, we tend to continue.

"Make it a point to do something every day that you don't want to do," said Mark Twain. "This is the golden rule for acquiring the habit of doing your duty without pain." Alistair Cooke told us, "A professional is someone who can do his best work when he doesn't feel like it."

At the start of every day, I perform 150 push-ups. It is easy to do, but it's even easier *not* to do. To beat resistance, I force myself to do one push-up, followed by twenty-nine more. Then I pause for a minute, followed by another set of thirty push-ups. After fifteen minutes, I've completed all 150. It's simple enough, but it's a ridiculous mental challenge.

I rank this push-up ritual among my most difficult daily tasks not because it is hard to perform but because it is hard to begin.

And every task of the day, especially tasks that can be easily postponed, seems to have a similar degree of resistance.

We beat resistance by taking one step of action.

Brian Tracy advises doing the most undesirable task of each day first. If you must "eat a frog" during the day, he says, it's best to eat the frog first—before all the other actions on your list. And if you must eat two frogs in one day, he suggests eating the ugliest one first.

A body in motion tends to stay in motion, while a body at rest tends to come up with a lot of excuses. A task begun is nearly half-done.

THE LIFE LESSON: RESISTANCE

I felt steady resistance against doing the hard work of the day,
But learned to conquer each task by just getting started on it.

Productivity: The quality of being consistently effective.

The best fertilizer is the gardener's shadow.

ANONYMOUS

Behind every abundant harvest, mused the Wealthy Gardener, is a tired farmer with a smile of satisfaction due to consistent productivity.

A few miles down the road, Jimmy sat in his bedroom in the dim light of a desk lamp. He was reflecting over a recent conversation he'd had with the Wealthy Gardener in which he'd stated that a productive life was the result of a lot of sowing in the passing days. He'd claimed that impact hours were like cement blocks that formed the foundation of all worthy achievements. Jimmy liked the way he had explained the concept of consistent productivity through the parable of the oak forest.

"Imagine that your goal is to create a thousand-acre oak forest where now there is only barren soil," the Wealthy Gardener had said. "The task will be the enduring legacy of your life, serving the birds, squirrels, deer, raccoons, and insects long after you are gone. But the one condition is that you can only do this work in your free time during the next ten years. How can you accomplish this feat?"

Jimmy had laughed at the preposterous undertaking. "It would take ten thousand acorns," he said, "and I would just start planting daily."

"Just start planting and see what happens?"

Jimmy thought about it. "Okay, I could give the task an hour each day," he said at last. "And then maybe ten hours of planting each weekend. If I did nothing but plant seeds in those hours, I'd be able to cover several acres each hour. This would add up to a hundred acres every month. And then I could complete it all within a year."

"And that is the effect of small efforts when you know what is wanted and then engage consistent hours for a clear purpose," said the Wealthy Gardener. "The impact of a productive life always reflects the impact of its collective hours. We just break the big achievement into smaller pieces and stay consistent in our actions. A plan of action helps us stay the course during the longest journey."

"But isn't success more complicated than planting acorns?"

"Is it really?" asked the Wealthy Gardener. "Or is that just an excuse? Success is always an organized plan and consistent effort."

"I think planting seeds is simpler than growing wealthy."

"And by saying so, many people give themselves a pass for being careless with their hours. But in the example of planting an oak forest, you will notice that you gave almost all your free hours to the task. Productivity comes from following a plan, and a plan comes from a clear goal. It's knowing what you want and then staying the course."

Jimmy sighed. "What if I don't know what I want yet?"

The Wealthy Gardener chuckled. "Then you should have plenty of time to ponder it. And the most productive hour of every day is the one you use to think about, imagine, dream, plan, and clarify your goals. This one hour elevates all your other hours."

Now, alone in his bedroom, Jimmy sat and contemplated their conversation. How could he put his free hours to best use? He decided that every night, he would sit alone and spend time thinking, dreaming, and imagining his best future.

After three weeks of this ritual, Jimmy started to appreciate the private retreat. He could see how this time alone affected all his other hours. He was realizing how much free time was available in his life. And he was becoming more focused during every waking hour.

PRODUCTIVITY IS THE QUALITY of being consistently effective. Wealth is earned by productive action in the passing days, which turn into weeks, which morph into years. What daily rituals can ensure the right attitude that leads to consistent, ongoing productivity?

We clearly must stay motivated to meet the daily demands.

In my own life, the time I've spent thinking, dreaming, planning, strategizing, reviewing problems, and picturing outcomes has reset my mind and helped me maintain continuous, daily productivity. In other words, if I focused my attention on my goals every day, the proper attitude and actions filled up my hours.

"An earnest purpose finds time, or makes it," wrote William Ellery Channing. "It seizes on spare moments, and turns fragments to golden account." Charles Caleb Colton said, "Much may be done in those little shreds and patches of time which every day produces, and which most men throw away."

Emerson stated the following on productivity: "Guard well your spare moments. They are like uncut diamonds. Discard them and their value will never be known. Improve them and they will become the brightest gems in a useful life."

To control my own behaviors, I claimed spare moments to re-center my attention on what I wanted in life and why I wanted it. What was my intention? I used the odd moments to maintain a sense of being successful. And I also tracked my daily hours of productivity.

Mel Robbins, author of *The 5 Second Rule*, speaks of an inner wisdom that we can sense throughout the day in times of decision or negative tendencies. By counting 5 . . . 4 . . . 3 . . . 2 . . . 1 at vulnerable times during the day, we can pause to stay in touch with our inner wisdom, which leads to better decisions.

With stillness in the odd moment, we stay on course.

But in every day, there was always one bright gem that influenced the other hours. At the risk of repetition, I will emphasize again that my steady productivity was assured by a daily ritual. I reset my thoughts on my goals by engaging in these daily mental practices:

1. Affirmations. I repeated words and phrases to build my inner character and convictions. In addition to specific affirmations, I repeated the general Émile Coué phrase: "Every day, in every way, I'm getting better and better." It may sound foolish, but this vague assertion set a course for better days ahead through anticipation.

2. Visualization. I visualized weekly outcomes and final achievements of long-term goals. I am currently imagining myself sitting alone on a beach and feeling the pride of a quality manuscript that satisfies me. I foreshadow my life with a vision of the future.

3. Action goals. I wrote action goals, and I followed a plan of actions every day. An action goal is to run three miles or to eat fewer than 2,000 calories a day; it is not to lose five pounds (that is an end goal). To gain upward mobility, I had action goals and tracked impact activities.

In terms of gaining productivity, we must always confront our weekly schedule, constantly revising plans that aren't moving us forward and always seeking more effective hours in our days. We must always beat the voice of defeat that whispers in our heads.

When I maintained a success mind-set throughout my days, everything else took care of itself. These mental practices compelled my daily actions, fueled my motivation, restored my strength, and attracted uncanny coincidences that harmonized with my financial goals.

A productive life involves a lot of sowing in the passing days. Behind an abundant harvest is an exhausted farmer with a smile of satisfaction from consistent productivity. We reap what we sow.

THE LIFE LESSON: PRODUCTIVITY

I learned that a prosperous life is a productive life,
And that productivity leads to a smile of satisfaction.

LESSON 4-6 · PEAK STATE

Peak state: An optimal mode or condition of being.

Early to bed, early to rise, Work like hell and fertilize.

EMILY WHALEY

Exertion turns worry into confidence and fatigue into vitality, pondered the Wealthy Gardener. No other remedy does more for the spirit.

Jimmy had just arrived for an early morning jog. "Are you sure you're up for this?" the Wealthy Gardener taunted, lacing up his running shoes.

"No offense," Jimmy said condescendingly, "but I'm pretty sure I can keep pace with a senior citizen."

The Wealthy Gardener laughed heartily as he headed for the door. They were soon running at an eight-minute-mile pace. The temperature was inviting on this late March morning. They finished a three-mile loop that ended at the Wealthy Gardener's office.

"You were quiet out there," said the Wealthy Gardener, chuckling.

Soaked in sweat, Jimmy gasped audibly. "It's . . . not . . . fair," he said, wheezing between words. "You've been training for nearly a century."

The Wealthy Gardener laughed again and invited him inside. Five minutes later they were seated at the kitchen table, each with a bowl of ice cream.

Jimmy spoke up. "So, knowing you, I assume there's a lesson in today's forced torture session. So let's hear it . . . What am I supposed to learn from this agony?"

"Have you ever heard the parable of the lumberjack?"

"Nope," Jimmy said, "but I bet I'm about to."

"There was once a lumberjack," said the Wealthy Gardener, "who chopped trees every day for years. As you can imagine, he initially grew strong due to the strain of his work. After several years, however, his strength started to fail him. He felt overwhelmed by fatigue during his long days—and in this tired state, he started to doubt himself.

"One day, as he sat on a stump, exhausted and demoralized, a smaller lumberjack came along and asked him what was wrong. The tired lumberjack said he was about to pack it all in and try his hand at a new trade. The newcomer considered the situation thoughtfully, then asked, 'Have you ever sharpened your ax?' The lumberjack was dumbstruck, realizing the foolishness of his neglect."

The Wealthy Gardener grinned. "We must keep the body and mind strong, or we'll find ourselves swinging at trees with a dull blade."

Jimmy thought about it. "You're suggesting daily exercise?"

"Just as a lumberjack must sharpen his ax, we, too, must sharpen our own physical tools," said the Wealthy Gardener. "Get a daily workout, and you'll naturally eat and sleep better. You'll be a different person. Exercise will enhance your performance in your daily hours."

"It sounds easy enough."

"What is easy to do is easy to not do. It will take a few weeks, but exercise becomes a positive addiction," the Wealthy Gardener said matter-of-factly. "Why do you think I'm telling you this now?"

"To sharpen the mind for the challenges of the day," Jimmy said slowly, "because hard tasks are easy with enough energy, and the easiest tasks are difficult without energy."

The Wealthy Gardener nodded. "The better your state, the more you can accomplish in your hours. And the more you can accomplish, the more you'll enjoy your workdays."

A PEAK STATE is an optimal condition of being. At the mid-stage of life, when financial responsibilities are greatest and family demands are exhausting, we're most likely to neglect the care of ourselves. In my early thirties, a friend and I were in very similar situations.

My friend had a promising career and a loving family. He was obviously working his way up the corporate ladder, but mysteriously he started sinking into a dark pit. Without any clear cause, he grew physically tired, lethargic, unmotivated, and unenthused about life; in fact, he was visibly disengaging from his work and family.

"I have everything in the world that's supposed to make me happy," he once confided in me, "but I honestly no longer give a shit about any of it."

At such times, many people come to the wrongheaded conclusion that success or materialism is the cause of their unhappiness. But there are many possible causes of listlessness, not the least of which is neglecting your physical body.

My friend went to doctors, increased his caffeine intake, attempted counseling, started attending church, and even tried Zoloft and Prozac. Nothing worked; his decline couldn't be stopped. But then one day at the gym, I saw him, drenched in sweat, running on a treadmill. He told me that he had started working out and was beginning to feel better.

Only months later did I learn the whole truth, when he confessed that on his worst day, he had contemplated suicide. "And that," he admitted, "was when I knew I had to change drastically."

I saw that nothing in the world around him had changed, but he had *changed himself* in the world. He began every day with vigorous exercise. He started by walking, then progressed to jogging, and finally to running. He set a goal to finish a half marathon and accomplished it. He slowly restored his physical strength, his mental energy, and his spiritual vibrancy.

He didn't need a new career, but he did require a stronger ongoing emotional state to keep up with the increasing demands of his daily responsibilities at work.

"Everything has been different since the day I decided to take care of my physical animal," he joked, years later.

If your life is perfect, then you get a pass. But if you need a boost, if you feel inadequate to meet your challenges, if you feel doubtful of your ability to endure life's trials, exercise is the cure to unlock your full powers.

"I go for a face sweat," said Steve Young, "as a minimum daily workout." If sweating doesn't appeal to you, then aim to exert yourself enough to cause deep breathing. At least go for a walk, or try daily yoga.

A peak state helps us thrive. "I believe that when the body is strong," Henry Rollins said, "the mind thinks strong thoughts." Cicero told us, "It is exercise alone that supports the spirits, and keeps the mind in vigor." With a sharp blade, every hour is better.

Beyond its obvious physical benefits, exercise provides clarity of mind, increased cognition, higher energy, quicker thinking, greater stress-handling capacity, more self-confidence, more poise, and steady composure in the face of interminable problems.

"A good sweat, with the blood pounding through my body, makes me feel alive, revitalized. I gain a sense of mastery and assurance. I feel good about myself," said Arthur Dobrin. "Sweat cleanses from the inside," said George A. Sheehan. "It comes from places a shower will never reach."

Of course, we don't absolutely need to exercise. We can swing an ax with a dull blade and still be productive. But if we choose to exercise, our days in the world will be better because we will be better in the world.

Buddha said, "To keep the body in good health is a duty—otherwise we shall not be able to keep our mind strong and clear." Exertion turns worry into confidence and fatigue into vitality.

No other remedy does more for the spirit.

THE LIFE LESSON: PEAK STATE

I learned to distrust my thinking under exhaustion,
And to build my strength to operate in my best state.

LESSON 4-7 · SELF-TRUST

Self-trust: Confidence in one's ability to achieve an objective.

An optimistic gardener is one who believes that
whatever goes down must come up.

LESLIE HALL

The Wealthy Gardener stood in front of the classroom at the reformatory for troubled teens. The power of self-trust is integral to wealth, he thought, because in life we get the poorest conditions we will tolerate.

"So as I mentioned in the last class," the Wealthy Gardener began, "upon your graduation, your lifestyle in this world depends on your legitimate means of earning a living. Can any of you right now imagine excessive wealth and prosperity?"

No hands went up, and the room was dead silent.

"And that's a problem, isn't it?" he said. "Without hope, the will to start is absent. And without self-trust, the will to endure is lost. My aim is to teach you the ways of wealth so that you can avoid futility. If you knew you could prosper legally, you would likely give it your best effort."

The Wealthy Gardener turned to the chalkboard and quickly wrote:

SELF-TRUST

Confidence dictates standards

1. What is the poorest condition you will tolerate?

2. Do you trust that you'll rise to every challenge?

3. Do you trust that you'll figure it out along the way?

When he'd finished writing, he strolled back to the podium and then turned around to study the board. "Rule number one is that you will not get the richest condition you want, but the poorest condition you will accept. At this moment, you may want a lot. But what will you tolerate and accept?"

"I want to be rich!" a kid shouted whimsically.

"But do you have the confidence to accept nothing less?"

The kid smirked without a response.

"Will you demand, require, and accept nothing less than riches, properly earned?" asked the Wealthy Gardener. He moved slowly between the rows of desks, hands clasped behind his back. "What will you accept as your lot in life?"

He scanned the classroom and sensed that the boys were not absorbing the essence of this critical message. He decided to try a new approach.

"Let me tell you the parable of the sculptor," he said, walking back to the podium where he paused a moment before he began.

"One day, a man climbed onto a boulder and hit it with a hammer and chisel. His dream was to sculpt a masterpiece. In the evenings that followed, after each day's work at his full-time job, the chiseling continued. The sculptor, fueled with a beginner's enthusiasm, carved away at the stone.

"Within a year, however, the newness of the work had faded. The exertion had produced little. The masterpiece was still a shapeless form. As fatigue set in, so did the sculptor's inevitable self-doubt. Was it really worth it? 'Am I really worthy to complete this task?' he asked himself. 'Am I capable of achieving my unique vision?'

"But within him was the defiant power of a human set upon a cherished goal. The sculptor had begun this crusade with a naive confidence that the dream could be actualized; he endured due to a growing trust that, with enough time, he would figure out a way to shape the rock into his imagined vision.

"Within five years, the rock had begun to take shape. He continued to chisel, fueled now by the emerging results. After another five years, the masterpiece was done. Satisfied at last, the sculptor examined the fruits of his labor.

"'How did you do it?' the townspeople asked in amazement.

"'By overcoming my doubts each day for years,' the sculptor said. 'Had I heeded my doubts, I would have never begun nor endured. But with trust, I gave my life to it. I possessed a knowing, a certainty of the future sculpture, and I accepted nothing less.'"

The Wealthy Gardener looked around the classroom. "In your lives, confidence is too vital to be left to chance. You must command your mind and set upon the building of your character. Like a sculptor with a rare vision, the seeker of wealth needs extraordinary resolve to achieve uncommon riches. You must always trust that you can achieve."

"What did he make out of the boulder?" a kid asked.

"The sculpture is a symbol representing your prosperity," said the Wealthy Gardener. "You are each sculptors of your own masterpiece. It will take years, and vision, and work, and resolve, to overcome all doubts. And you must cling to a self-trust beyond the capacity of most other people."

SELF-TRUST IS CONFIDENCE IN one's ability to achieve an objective. If we think we can live the life of our dreams, we'll usually try. Our self-trust determines the size of our goals, what we tolerate, and what we strive to attain. By contrast, self-doubt allows poorer conditions.

"Self-trust is the first secret of success," said Emerson. "Argue for your limitations, and sure enough they're yours," wrote Richard Bach. "Self-confidence is the first requisite to great undertakings," said Samuel Johnson. Virgil told us, "They are able because they think they are able." And Pierre-Claude-Victor Boiste reminded us, "He who has lost confidence can lose nothing more."

I was sitting in the bleachers watching my son, Mike, play a varsity basketball game. In our town, basketball is important. And in my family, while my son was growing up, basketball was a form of adversity training. Though this was our joke, there was a lot of truth in it—the sport of basketball was the crucible of many formative life lessons between father and son.

Mike was playing against a team that consisted of friends with whom he had gone to grade school. He was determined to give his best performance. I know he was emotionally charged up for the game. But then he scored a dismal two points.

When we talked after the game, he was despondent. We discussed his response to adversity, about burying it and not even giving it another thought, using it as fuel. But still, he was unusually quiet for a week.

I left him alone.

After the setback, he had had enough. Mike would no longer tolerate that condition in his life. In the next game, against a superior opponent, he scored thirty-two points. He later told me that he had visualized a thirty-point game.

I'll never forget the scene, the crowd chanting his name. I was overcome with emotion. I didn't care that he was being glorified, but I did care deeply about something more vital: He had found the confidence, the self-trust, the *power of knowing* that would serve him throughout his life.

His performance may seem like a trivial sports triumph, but I saw it as profound. It was a display of personal mastery and overcoming life adversity. It was that get-out-of-my-way-because-this-is-happening-today attitude. It was the defiant power of the human will in the quest for success. On that occasion, Mike didn't try to believe. He didn't hope or want. He experienced the *knowing* of self-trust.

Our lives' conditions are not determined by what we want, but by what we will accept and tolerate. If we *want* financial freedom but will *accept* financial stability—a good job that pays the bills—we will get the latter. If we want prosperity but will accept financial struggles in the middle class, we will live and retire in the middle class. If we want abundance but will accept mediocrity, it is certain that our fate will be one of mundane struggles.

Confidence determines what we dream, what we tolerate, and what we strive to attain. "It's not what you are that holds you back," said Denis Waitley, "it's what you think you are not."

Self-doubt is the weed in the garden.

"Low self-confidence isn't a life sentence," wrote Barrie Davenport. "Self-confidence can be learned, practiced, and mastered—just like any other skill. Once you master it, everything in your life will change for the better." Sir Edmund Hillary agreed: "It is not the mountain we conquer but ourselves."

How do we gain self-trust? Trammell Crow, one of the wealthiest real estate tycoons of his day—who was responsible for developing much of Dallas, along with the national Wyndham hotel chain—once said, "There must always be a burn in your heart to achieve. In the quiet of your solitude, close your eyes, bow your head, grit your teeth, clench your fists. Achieve in your heart, vow and dedicate yourself to achieve, to achieve."

With the confidence to achieve, we trust ourselves to pay any price, handle any adversity, overcome mistakes, and occasionally reroute to a new end destination. William James said, "The will to do springs from the knowledge that we *can* do." And the belief that you *can do* elevates your ambition to create your own masterpiece.

THE LIFE LESSON: SELF-TRUST

I saw that confidence conquers unwanted conditions,
And self-trust influenced what I would not accept.

LESSON 4-8 · CONVICTIONS

Conviction: A firmly held belief or opinion.

Weeds are pulled up by the roots to clear the fields
for the growing grain. Why should not mental weeds
be pulled up by the roots also, and the mind cleared
for growth?

HORACE FLETCHER

We are prisoners of our environment, mused the Wealthy Gardener, when we adopt the financial convictions of family and friends. It is thus wise to choose beliefs that empower wealth.

He was staring mindfully at his notebook on the desk when the door swung open and Jimmy, in a mild sweat from a midafternoon run, entered without knocking. They exchanged greetings, and Jimmy sat down for his weekly tutoring session.

"The problem with Santos's operation," Jimmy said, "is that he doesn't let anyone else think. He's opinionated and won't consider ideas to enhance production or trim expenses. I swear he'd rather be right than rich."

The Wealthy Gardener chuckled. "Santos is sixty years old and set in his ways," he said. "Opinions can grow into convictions that prevent wealth."

Jimmy sighed. "I'm not sure what you mean."

There was a long pause as the Wealthy Gardener leaned back, searching for the right words. How could he explain that we are ruled by our dominant beliefs?

"Santos is the best worker I've ever employed. But in his past, he gained trust in work alone. It's a responsible belief of full accountability but an unimaginative one that limits his potential."

"You're saying he doesn't think much?" Jimmy asked.

"He has a conviction to believe in what he sees and understands. He will think within those narrow limits. Santos rejects anything that seems unrealistic. He won't pause to listen to his inner wisdom. He will have an orderly operation in the end—but nothing more."

Jimmy nodded. "And so what are you telling me?"

"If you want to accumulate wealth, effort is vital, but it has its limits. We can only work so hard, and there are only so many hours in a day. It's wise to stay open to new strategies and possibilities. Adopt a belief that work is essential, but so, too, are Intangible Forces. Don't be intolerant to that which you don't yet comprehend. According to your faith, so shall it be done unto you."

"Believe in a mental rain dance." Jimmy said, raising an eyebrow.

"Yes, but beware," advised the Wealthy Gardener. "Some people pray for wealth to be given to them—a divine blessing of favor that requires little work or personal sacrifice."

"They believe in a wish-granting genie?"

"Unfortunately for them, yes. They pray for unearned rewards. They neglect their duty to work hard in their days. They sit in a state of earnest prayer while weeds overtake their gardens."

"And so they shirk their work," Jimmy said.

"If you want to accumulate wealth, the ritual of daily mental practices is valuable, but don't neglect your duties. Adopt the belief that you will concentrate on your desires and cultivate faith in your goals, but also give a sacred effort to uphold your part of the bargain."

The Wealthy Gardener looked out the window. "Most people will never be wealthy because of their convictions that too much work is misguided, that the aid of Universal Intelligence is a delusion, or that too much wealth is wrong or immoral. They won't realize their full wealth potential due to these limiting beliefs."

"Some people believe wealth is wrong?" Jimmy said.

"Who really knows?" the Wealthy Gardener asked. "I suspect that most people who say excess money is wrong really don't want to work too hard, sacrifice, or be inconvenienced to amass it. Of course, pious indignation sounds a lot better than admitting the bare truth—that they don't want to give up their comfort for it."

Jimmy laughed. "What convictions should they adopt?"

"If you want to accumulate wealth, adopt the conviction that present-day sacrifices are worth future rewards. And far from being evil, know that money, possessed by good people, is peace of mind, lifestyle satisfaction, family protection, financial security, and power."

A CONVICTION is a firmly held belief. During my Catholic education, I believed that meekness was a virtue. *Blessed are the meek, for they shall inherit the earth.* Since I wanted to own some of the earth while living on this planet, I chose to adopt more empowering beliefs, leading to plans and actions that produced wealth.

Many people believe the wealthy aren't happy. They state that they'd rather be happy than wealthy. They seem to believe that it's one or the other, but happiness can be had on both sides of the tracks. And it's easier to be happy when the mind is not consumed by worry.

At the age of thirty, I was on the side without savings. And one of the first convictions I adopted was that I could be happy and wealthy.

Growing up in the middle class, I saw that with hard work alone, I could have a good life. I could have a nice house, a good family, a nice yard, and a tail-wagging dog. But to enjoy prosperity to fulfill my richest dreams, I would need to adopt some uncommon convictions.

As explained already, I possess an empowering conviction that a mysterious Universal Intelligence exists and that we are all a part of it. I choose to believe in a real-life matrix governed not by machines but by this Universal Intelligence. I choose to believe this regulating force of the matrix is not oppressive but rather cooperative with our goals. And I choose to believe I can tap into this matrix force through daily concentration and applied faith.

Of course, this concept may be delusional, but what if it empowers me to believe in a cooperative energy? I wanted more than a normal life, so I chose to believe the world was conspiring to aid me. I adopted a conviction that hard work is critical, but it's not everything. I chose to adopt the useful conviction that spirituality works for me and no harm ever results from too much faith in prosperity and future wealth.

Another middle-class conviction I needed to confront was the ideal of a balanced life. I saw that a balanced life would lead to average results. Many with this type of conviction will say, "I have a family and don't want to give my life to my work."

I had a family, too, but I chose to believe that my sacrifices benefited them, and I was willing to trade my time for their welfare. I chose to believe that balance is the way to mediocrity, money worries, financial instability, and helplessness to withstand setbacks.

I also needed to drastically change my middle-class convictions about happiness and freedom. To amass wealth, I adopted the conviction that I am willing to trade all my current freedom for the ultimate freedom of time and money later. I chose to believe that financial freedom was for me, even though I knew no one else who had it.

I also had to fight an adventurous streak within me that didn't like to stay in one place too long. I realized that without years in one place, I could do everything right, but my efforts would not have the necessary time to take root. I could fail to achieve my goals due to impatience.

To accumulate wealth, I adopted the conviction that with an attitude of patience, I'll pay any price for as long as it takes so that my daily efforts have time to compound into meaningful and life-changing crusades.

Perhaps one of the greatest limiting beliefs I had to overcome in the middle class is the general idea that life is meant to be comfortable. The problem is that all worthy achievement requires sacrifice, inconveniences, and discomfort. I would need to change my beliefs and accept the price required for uncommon financial rewards.

To accumulate wealth, I adopted a conviction that if I wanted to prosper, I would have to devote as many hours in each passing day as I could to productivity. I would constantly pursue a goal that commands my spirit, and then I would pause to consult my inner wisdom in times of choice.

I also had to overcome middle-class tendencies about spending money. If I didn't control the outflow of money, then my life would be vulnerable to calamities. Trying to amass wealth without tightfisted spending is like trying to fill a bathtub without plugging the drain—it is the insanity of adult self-indulgence.

To accumulate wealth, I adopted the conviction that spending is the enemy of amassing a fortune and that it is a virtue to live below my means without an ostentatious display of wealth or extravagant luxuries. I chose to believe that the best things in life are the simplest pleasures.

The last conviction that empowered my financial fate is that life is about self-actualization. It was my duty to be all I could be, if not for myself, then for others. It was my assignment to use my full potential. It was necessary to set goals that commanded my energy, left me exhausted, and challenged me to the edge of my fullest capacities.

At the age of thirty, I didn't know how I would amass enough money to reach my financial dreams, but I chose to believe that I was destined for wealth, so I'd figure it out, and be aided by Universal Intelligence along the way when I concentrated on my goals with absolute faith. I chose to believe that I could influence my life by deliberately choosing my convictions. And wealth has unfolded—as I chose to believe.

Phineas Quimby said it all in four words: "Man is belief expressed."

THE LIFE LESSON: CONVICTIONS

I learned that my convictions defined my limits,
So I adopted beliefs to eliminate self-sabotage.

LESSON 4-9 · FULFILLING WORK

Fulfillment: A feeling that we have, or are progressing toward, what we want from life.

No two gardens are the same. No two days are the same in one garden.

HUGH JOHNSON

It is practical to choose fulfilling employment, mused the Wealthy Gardener, because wealth requires stamina over the course of many years. The price of financial success without intrinsic rewards is a heavy burden to carry to the finish line of achievement.

The Wealthy Gardener sat across from Santos, who was in his office to discuss the progress on the neighboring farm.

"I want to talk to you about Jimmy," said Santos. "I like the kid, but he's always coming up with crazy ideas. I swear he just sits around and thinks. Now he's reading books about happiness, passion, business, and getting rich. He even wrote down his personal goals—I saw them. And the kid actually wants to be a millionaire by thirty!"

The Wealthy Gardener grinned. "And what's the problem?"

Santos's mouth fell open. He was a worker, a man of action, and a believer in the supremacy of labor. If given a task, the operations manager would get it done. But he never thought too deeply, and he could not fathom why others cared about a sense of inner fulfillment.

"Well, he's building castles in the air," Santos said. "It's dangerous for a boy to chase wealth and have unrealistic expectations."

"I wouldn't worry about him," said the Wealthy Gardener. "Jimmy's exploring his options. Starting out with ambition doesn't sound like such a bad idea for a young man."

"He's setting himself up for a fall with those big goals."

The Wealthy Gardener shrugged. "Who are we to judge? Can we predict his future? Do we know his fullest potential?"

"I'll go out on a limb and say he won't be a millionaire," scoffed Santos. "And he won't be happy if he expects to love all of his work. I've seen kids who want passion at work, and you know what? They're never happy. Work is a sacrifice, and they need to suck it up."

The Wealthy Gardener gazed out the window. Would it be useful to explain that fulfillment is essential to fuel the stamina of long-term work? Should he say that intrinsic rewards are part of fitting labor?

"Let me ask you a question," said the Wealthy Gardener. "What happens when we transplant a young sapling on the farm?"

Santos paused. "It goes into shock for a few years."

"Indeed it does," agreed the Wealthy Gardener. "And after the tragedy of his youth, Jimmy is adjusting to being transplanted. I'm impressed by his eagerness. He's studying philosophy, strategy, finance, money, career options, mental practices—these are his current immersions. While other kids are wasting time, he's thinking and learning and calculating. He's using the days for good."

"And what then?" Santos asked. "What happens when he learns that work is hard, and we do it for the money? What happens then?"

"I don't think it will happen. I've been called a workaholic all my life by people who dislike work. But they didn't grasp that I was satisfied in my days as I progressed toward my goals. I trust that Jimmy will find the same joy in accomplishment that I did."

"That's easy for you to say, considering your success!" exclaimed Santos. "I don't want Jimmy expecting life to be easy. He needs to accept the pain and struggle of earning a living!"

"Okay, I get it. I believe in a strong work ethic as much as you do. But I have a confession for you: Do you know why I chose to expand our ventures with a vineyard and winery instead of just adding more acres of farmland?"

"It seemed logical to diversify your income."

"I wish it was so reasonable," said the Wealthy Gardener. "I chose that course because I was interested in winemaking. I realized that work consumed so much of my life that I needed to do what interested me in order to sustain my enthusiasm for decades. Suitable work is more sustainable."

Santos shook his head without a response.

"Take a lesson from Nature. The weeping willow thrives in the same wet soil that kills the hemlock. The dogwood prefers acidic soil, while the maple does best in alkaline soil. Where a tree is planted matters a lot for its future."

"Hogwash," Santos muttered. "We must bloom wherever we're planted."

"What we do for work matters, and it influences our work ethic. It's the content of our life. We find our fullest potential in tasks that are suited to our powers and interests. And Jimmy is deciding where he wants to thrive."

FULFILLING WORK empowers the long journey to gain financial prosperity. But what is fulfilling work? It's a subtle feeling of pleasure, well-being, or gratification from knowing that we are getting what we want from a job, or that we're at least heading in the right direction.

A sense of fulfillment indicates how closely we are aligned with our inner values, inclinations, knacks, ambitions, and inner voice. In other words, when we operate in an environment that is most fitted to our unique individuality, we feel intrinsically rewarded.

"Learn what you are and be such," Pindar wrote. "The destiny of a man," Herodotus told us, "is in his own soul." And Sydney J. Harris wrote, "Ninety percent of the world's woe comes from people not knowing themselves, their abilities, their frailties, and even their real virtues."

After working for thirty years in the middle class to win financial freedom, I can attest that the key to my stamina was aligning myself with activities that provided not only monetary excess but also deeper intrinsic rewards. I was frustrated—and fulfilled—during my journey to prosperity.

I learned that it's absurd to want to love every aspect of my work. Gainful employment will always have duties that are dreaded, or even hated. I loved some of it; I liked most of it; I hated some of it. I found that the work that led to wealth was, well, just a lot of hard work.

But in time I earned the right to do more of what I loved, less of what I dreaded, and almost none of what I hated. It is vital to know that every time new work is begun, there will be an adjustment phase. We always require several years of acclimation in new soil before we begin to thrive. Since a tree replanted too quickly never sprouts roots, it may take years to bloom in unfamiliar surroundings.

But still, in the end, work that is fitting contains intrinsic rewards. It is sustainable work. It is where we belong. It is where we can thrive.

"Be true to one's self, follow not every impulse, but find out who one is," advised Earl Nightingale. "Discover a combination of interests and powers, and find through experiment and thought the course of life to fulfill those interests and powers most completely."

Seek the work that provides a sense of fulfillment.

The most fulfilling work matches our varying values, inclinations, knacks, ambitions, and inner voice. These fascinating characteristics of our unique individuality—the subjects of the following five life lessons—are the legs on which our sense of fulfillment stands.

THE LIFE LESSON: FULFILLING WORK

I saw that upward mobility requires extraordinary work,
And greater stamina was found in work that suited me.

Inner value: Something we absolutely must have
in our lives or a part of us will die.

Can plants be happy? If they get what they need, they
thrive—that's what I know.

TERRI GUILLEMETS

We can find our best work by meeting our unique values, considered the
Wealthy Gardener, or we can ignore our values and a part of us will die.

Peering out his study window, the Wealthy Gardener spotted his
neighbor Fred taking a puppy for a walk. He called to Fred from the
window, and moments later they were strolling together on a gravel
walkway through the vineyard. They hadn't discussed Fred's retirement
struggles since playing cards a month ago.

"So who's the new fellow?" asked the Wealthy Gardener, patting the
puppy.

"His name is Buddy. He's my new best friend."

The Wealthy Gardener nodded without responding.

"Connie rescued him from the pound," Fred said, sighing. "She tells
me that Buddy was for her, but I think she brought him home to keep me
company."

As they walked without speaking, the Wealthy Gardener thought
deeply. Years ago, when Fred was trapped in a supervisory position at the
plant, he had found a better position elsewhere and turned in his resigna-
tion. In response, the company he worked for at the time upped the ante;
they matched the competing offer and gave Fred command of the floor.
In this new leadership role, Fred thrived for many years. He was fulfilled
until the day he retired.

"So how is it really going for you?" asked the Wealthy Gardener.

"Buddy's a good dog," Fred joked, "but not exactly what I needed."

"I wouldn't have thought so."

Fred smiled and turned to his friend. "I've heard my wife's opinion and my son's opinion, and so I might as well hear your opinion. As long as you don't buy me anything that eats or craps, I'm willing to listen to you."

"Fair enough," said the Wealthy Gardener as they strolled. "I knew a man who was unfulfilled in his midlife. He wasn't satisfied, but he didn't complain. He was dutiful in providing for his family. But one day he was promoted to a leadership role. It was where this man belonged, and you could see it in the way he stood and walked. He had major responsibilities, and his employees looked up to him."

Fred was nodding. "Would I happen to know this man?"

"Nothing really changed inside him," continued the Wealthy Gardener, "but the man retired, and his life changed a lot. The things that used to excite him were gone. Now he spent time alone. He had no responsibilities. He had no leadership role in his life, except maybe for a son who wouldn't listen to him. And so all the responsibilities that once made this fellow feel good no longer existed."

"And what is your wise council to such a man?" Fred asked soberly.

"I'm a simple guy," said the Wealthy Gardener, "so I would tell this fellow to remember who he is and not forget what fulfilled him in the past. The man I knew needed meaning. He needed people. He was a great leader, and he thrived when he had a purpose."

Fred's eyes misted as they walked.

INNER VALUES are unique needs within every individual, possibly gained through nurture, possibly fixed by nature. Clarifying our core inner values, and then meeting these individual needs, can lead to the type of work in which we thrive. We either meet our inner values in life or a part of us will die.

"The way you live your life provides clues, such as how you spend your time and money," writes Sidney B. Simon, author of the popular book *Values Clarification*. "Choice of aim is clearly a matter of clarification of values," said W. Edwards Deming, "especially on the choice between possible options."

I'll offer my own search for fulfillment over many years to magnify the practical relevance of discovering personal values. As I relayed in a previous chapter, for many years I split my days between two separate occupations: I was a chiropractor and a real estate guy.

As a chiropractor, I dressed well and worked in an enviable setting. I spent my time in my own clinic building. I had the respect of my peers and friends. I interacted with polite people seeking help in a professional environment. I had loyal employees. It was a pleasant life by every exterior measure. So why was I vaguely and inexplicably unfulfilled in this work?

My role in the real estate business was quite different. I dressed in dirty jeans, paint-speckled shirts, and old shoes. I was usually stressed out due to unexpected and costly repairs. I was pressured by deadlines. But these problems paled compared to the challenge of managing the laborers. I constantly hired and fired workers who drank on the job, lied to me, stole from me, and took shortcuts (if they believed they could get away with it). Then, as a landlord, my worst tenants trashed their units and screwed me by not paying their rent. So how could I be energized and bizarrely fulfilled by these unpleasant conditions?

If you understand my core values, maybe you'll understand why. My core work value is achievement and the ability to see tangible results. I need projects with beginnings and ends. I value big challenges with complexity (like writing this book). I value progress toward a goal and advancement up the economic ladder. I need freedom of choice. I require time to think. I value financial opportunities and calculated risks. I fulfill these values, or a part of me dies.

The chiropractic profession, for all its worthy advantages, didn't meet my core work values. Patients recovered, but then new patients replaced them. I experienced results, but not tangible ones with a finish line. A practice is a perpetual merry-go-round with a doctor as the operator. This service profession should have been satisfying, and I felt guilty for being unfulfilled in it.

Conversely, despite the overwhelming problems in real estate, this occupation met my innermost work values. There were big challenges with tangible results. Projects were completed—there would come a day when I took photos and planted a For Sale sign. There was progress toward a specific end goal. The job required planning and thinking. And I loved the steady calculated risks.

Our success is more assured when we build our goals, behaviors, and lifestyle around the core values we absolutely must fulfill to feel alive. Engaged in work that suited me best, I was naturally driven to be among the top performers in my occupation. I may have earned a living as a chiropractor, but I earned wealth by fulfilling my values.

If I could live my life over again, I would choose a career by studying these things called values that seem to be the must-haves—needs embedded in the code of our souls—that lead to inner satisfaction. I would learn all I could about values, and then I'd look within and try to decipher my own code.

These inner values have nothing to do with morality. I'm not referring to values like patience, honesty, or treating others as you want them to treat you. A value is not good or bad. It's more aptly who we are.

A value can be a need for achievement, influence, freedom, money, love, peace, or many other things. These inner values are traits of the intangible self, and they can be fulfilled through work and hobbies.

Books like *Values Clarification* and *StrengthsFinder* were useful to me in unearthing these unique values. I also explored my past for patterns that could suggest clues to my individuality—my core inner design.

I contemplated (1) peak moments in my life, which might unearth a value being fulfilled; (2) moments of frustration or anger, which could indicate a value being abused; (3) times of despair or demoralization, when it felt like a part of me was dying, which may suggest a value being ignored; (4) obsessive traits that others find atypical, but may indicate a strong value (i.e., an orderly person who is teased as obsessively compulsive). Clarifying values helped me to know myself.

"Success in the knowledge economy comes to those who know themselves," said Peter Drucker, "their strengths, their values, and how they best perform."

Values are the start of self-knowledge and fulfilling work. It's been said that "what gives our life meaning and relevance are our values." And in our choice of life work, we experience meaning and relevance to the degree we fulfill the values that are buried in the soul.

Do not ask, "What should I do with my life?" Ask, "What individual values must I fulfill in my life's pursuits?" This question leads to a more fulfilling journey toward prosperity.

THE LIFE LESSON: INNER VALUES
. . . .

At age twenty, I asked, "What career should I pursue in my life?"
At age fifty, I asked, "What values must I fulfill or a part of me will die?"

LESSON 4-11 · INCLINATIONS

Inclination: A natural tendency; a pull to regularly do something.

What is a weed? A plant whose virtues have not yet been discovered.

RALPH WALDO EMERSON

Countless are the plans that can lead to wealth, mused the Wealthy Gardener, and varied are the traits of the workers who can earn it.

Jimmy knocked on the door of the Wealthy Gardener's house and waited. After a minute with no response, he walked around to the rear yard to find his mentor reading in a chair. It was evening, and they had scheduled a late meeting.

"I'm very busy," joked the Wealthy Gardener. "This had better be good."

Jimmy laughed, sitting down beside him. "I'll get to the point. I've been thinking a lot about convictions since we talked. And I've been choosing bolder beliefs about accumulating wealth."

The Wealthy Gardener nodded. "So what's on your mind?"

Jimmy was hesitant. "I don't care about the stuff money buys, but I want the freedom of wealth. I want choices in life, and I'm willing to do whatever it takes to have those choices. The problem is that I'm not exactly sure how I'm going to get the money, and the uncertainty frustrates me."

The Wealthy Gardener smiled. "Most young people want wealth, but they don't know how to get it. If you can't see the way, you're just about running average. Cling to your goal in faith, and Universal Intelligence will hand over the plan. It never fails—it is a law of Nature."

Jimmy nodded, but his expression remained troubled.

The Wealthy Gardener studied him with compassion. He then looked at the gardening magazine in his lap and handed it to Jimmy.

"What's this for?" Jimmy asked.

"Does that magazine interest you?"

Jimmy glanced at the front cover and grinned. "Not one bit."

"But it interests me. Why is that?"

Jimmy stared blankly. "I don't know."

"And I don't know, either," he said, with a thoughtful gleam in his eye, "but in gardening, there is a feeling of suitability for me. I feel comfortable. I wouldn't call it a passion as much as a deep friendship. I enjoy spending many long hours with it."

Jimmy nodded. "So how do I figure out my life purpose?"

"I'll tell you what I think," said the Wealthy Gardener. "If you engage in a service that feels right, that's comfortable to you, that you can be friends with, and that only asks you to be yourself, then that is your path. Don't ask a vocation to be a passionate lover. Rather, consider it an enduring friendship that you want to spend time with daily."

Jimmy sighed. "Okay, but how do I find work that's a friend?"

"Seek a valuable service that interests you," said the Wealthy Gardener. "When I was a kid, I worked at many odd jobs. I was fascinated by the person in the business who controlled the money. I wanted to be in this exact role, and step by step, I grew into it. Our purpose in life unfolds slowly, I think, by following our inclinations."

Jimmy exhaled audibly, studied the gardening magazine, and recalled his own subscription to a fascinating magazine on real estate investment and entrepreneurship. Was this curious interest of real estate an inclination?

AN INCLINATION is a natural tendency, a pull to regularly do something. It is an interest, penchant, preference, tendency, proclivity, propensity, curiosity, fascination, or natural urge to act. It is an individual calling, an attraction that compels, a curious leaning.

"When you put your preferences on the altar of your life and say: THIS. THIS is what compels me. The real you emerges," said Danielle LaPorte. We are unique in our interests and fascinations.

"How can we explain such inclinations?" wrote Robert Greene. "They are *forces* within us . . . draw[ing] us to certain experiences and away from others. As these forces move us here or there, they influence the development of our minds in very particular ways . . . If you allow yourself to learn who you really are by paying attention to that voice and force within you, then you can become what you were fated to become—an individual, a Master."

We have a life task, suggests Greene, to express our uniqueness through our work. We are here to fulfill our values through the work that we are deeply inclined to pursue.

"There is a vast world of work out there in this country," said Richard Nelson Bolles, "where at least 111 million people are employed in this country alone—many of whom are bored out of their minds. All day long." Sadly, these people live for the weekends.

The obvious but challenging solution is to follow inclinations into much-needed services with viable incomes. "If passion drives, let reason hold the reins," advised Benjamin Franklin. If we want wealth, we must work where money is likely to exist in abundance.

It requires no more than a click on a computer or cell phone to determine the top-earning jobs, careers, and occupations. Within seconds, we can see what income each job, career, or occupation earns. Is it wrong to start with a search of top incomes and figure out which job we like the most, based, in part, on those search results?

My best friend from childhood is now the richest and most fulfilled friend in my adult inner circle. When choosing a career, he considered his options like we all did, except he used the "income down" approach. He was very close to becoming a pharmacist, but he thought the job had an unacceptable income ceiling, so he took another route to become an orthodontist.

The schooling was endless, and the sacrifice was steep. Despite graduating after the age of thirty, however, his annual income has quadrupled mine despite working only half the weekly hours as me. Deeply engaged and committed to excellence, his fulfillment is fueled by a devotion to work and an extraordinary income.

We should think of ourselves as explorers who travel the world looking for curiosities and fascinations. We can find interests by searching online, walking into bookstores, or sitting in a library. I was fascinated by the biographies of Trammell Crow and Harry Helmsley, and their stories fueled my inclination to pursue real estate.

Be reverent of the things you find fascinating and enthralling. Your unique fascinations expose the inclinations, tendencies, interests, and proclivities hidden deep in the substance of your intangible soul.

"You begin by choosing a field or position that roughly corresponds to your inclinations," wrote Robert Greene. "This initial position offers you room to maneuver and important skills to learn . . . You adjust and perhaps move to a related field, continuing to learn more about yourself, but always expanding off your skill base . . . Eventually, you will hit upon a particular field, niche, or opportunity that suits you perfectly. You will recognize it when you find it because it will spark that childlike sense of wonder and excitement; it will feel right."

The right pursuit is a friendship. It is satisfying to do things that interest us. But, maybe more important, we will be more apt to give our fullest effort to suitable work. As Charles Schwab said, "A man can succeed at almost anything for which he has unlimited enthusiasm."

THE LIFE LESSON: INCLINATIONS

I thought rugged determination was the way to wealth,
But learned to work hard within my unique set of interests.

LESSON 4-12 · KNACKS

Knack: An activity or subject that comes naturally
to one but is difficult for others.

Talent is like a flower, you have to fully tend to it if you
want something beautiful.

MARINELA REKA

What we must discover, thought the Wealthy Gardener, are the activities
that are peculiarly easy for us. One's full potential will never be realized
until one's gift is employed for productive work.

The Wealthy Gardener stood at the podium, while Jimmy sat in a
chair near the door. Over the course of the past month, he'd been lectur-
ing on vocational guidance at the reform school, hoping to prepare the
troubled teens for the uphill battle they would surely face in their working lives.

"While there are no limits to your imagination," he said, beginning
the lesson, "there are limits to your possibilities. And the reason is due to
your finite resources of time, energy, capacity, and talent."

The classroom grew still, the kids quieting as they began to pay attention. Jimmy watched the Wealthy Gardener scribble hurriedly on the
chalkboard.

"We've talked about success strategies," he said, finishing and turning
to the class, "and how, all else being equal, taking the right actions will
assure your fullest prosperity. But let's be honest now, shall we? All things
are rarely equal in this world. The fact is, we're all very dissimilar individuals."

He walked between a row of desks and stood at the back of the room.
He waited a minute to allow the boys time to consider the writing on the
chalkboard:

INDIVIDUALITY

1. Values

2. Inclinations

3. Knacks

4. Ambition

5. Inner Voice

"What makes you unlike anyone else on this planet," he said, "is the unique mix of your values, inclinations, knacks, ambition, and inner voice. Any effective wealth strategy begins with discovering your best qualities and then applying those assets to good work."

He eyed the chalkboard for effect.

"Life may be hard, but it gets less hard when you use your strengths to your advantage. The secret of your fullest wealth is using your individuality."

A kid raised a hand. "What if we ain't got special talent? How are we gonna get ours in the world by working for minimum wages?"

"I'll tell you a parable about talent," said the Wealthy Gardener, striding to the podium. "There was once an eagle raised by chickens on a farm. As the eagle grew up, she loved her chicken family despite not fitting in with them. The eagle wasn't good at scratching in the dirt for worms, and she struggled to perform what were everyday activities for the other chickens. Worse, it was evident that the eagle had no interest in these chicken activities. To say the least, life was difficult for the eagle trying to exist as a chicken.

"One day, another eagle flew overhead. The sight of it caused a stir in the chicken-eagle. The confused bird confided to several chickens that she felt drawn to fly like that mighty eagle. The chickens laughed, of course, and ridiculed the idea. As the story goes, the eagle was miserable. One fateful day, she finally spread her wings and rose into the air, while the chickens watched in shock. From heights of the heavens, the eagle could spot subtle movements on the ground below. And she could swoop down to grab her food with talons that were not made for scratching in the dirt for worms. You see, for her, it was easier to be a mighty eagle—the monarch of the sky—than to be a chicken. In being an eagle, she found her self-worth and fullest potential."

He looked around the room. "What's the moral of the story?"

"Don't hang out with chickens?" wisecracked a kid.

The Wealthy Gardener chuckled. "Your joke may not be as false as you think," he said. "But there are two morals: First, the eagle was never interested in activities for which she had no talent. And second, it was easier for the eagle to do greater tasks when the tasks were aligned with her strengths. Each of you will graduate as an eagle to fly in your own direction."

The class was quiet.

"You need to discover and follow your interests," he continued slowly, "and in those interests, notice the activities that are easiest for you. You're gifted for a few best activities. You can do a few things more naturally than the crowd, and you can learn some things more easily than others can. Look for the things that are difficult for others but not for you. A chicken will live in defeat trying to be an eagle, and an eagle will live in defeat trying to be a chicken."

"My dad makes minimum wage. Is that living in defeat?"

"I don't know his situation. But if you want to avoid his fate, you'll follow the strategy of discovering your talents and using them. Master a set of rare skills that are valued by others, and you'll have a different story to tell your kids. Disregard your talents, and success will be a constant struggle."

The kid rolled his eyes. "Are you saying my dad is a chicken?"

Jimmy stood up from his chair. "He's telling you to discover your talents and work your ass off during every waking hour to make them work for you. Or shut up and be like your dad!"

The kid was speechless. The class stared at Jimmy with expressions of curious respect, and the Wealthy Gardener sensed a very special moment.

A KNACK is an activity or subject that comes naturally to one but is difficult for others to pick up. A knack is an aptitude, a capacity, a gift for learning. It is not a skill, per se, but rather the natural ability to acquire a skill and master it more easily than others are able to. It is a potential competence or effectiveness, an inborn advantage.

A knack is an ally in the quest for wealth.

"Nature arms each man with some faculty which enables him to do easily some feat impossible to any other," Emerson stated. While we may not have a faculty unique to all others, we do have knacks that enable us to more easily perform some feats that seem impossible, or very difficult, for most other people.

"But I don't have unique talents" is the cry of the multitudes.

I am reminded of people who complain about not being able to find the right church. They haven't found a place where they fit in, but they have never visited new churches. Answers come to those who seek solutions. And we find our hidden knacks by taking the time to think, testing our aptitude and evaluating our past for curious moments.

At one time, I was tempted to look back on my unexceptional youth with the common opinion that no talents stood out. I was an average and ordinary kid. But with perseverance and steady patience, the search revealed times when I had been deeply immersed in a particular moment.

During those times in my life, I was so absorbed by my interests that I wasn't aware of the world around me. Knacks can usually be found within and around deep immersions like these.

As a Little League baseball player in fifth grade, the best players on the team were placed at the top of the batting lineup, while I batted at the bottom. I was annoyed. At nine years old, however, without instruction or guidance, I made a grid on a piece of paper and labeled the columns with headings representing statistics like those that are recorded for Major League Baseball players.

After each game, I loved to record my own statistics. I could then see how my numbers reflected my performance, good or bad, and I craved this clarity. Thinking back on this as an adult, this trivial act in my past provided a revealing insight into a knack of tracking my efficiency.

What is the take-home lesson from this story?

First, as you search for your knacks, don't worry about how they will be used. Find them the way you might search your kitchen shelves for available ingredients. Once you've gathered the ingredients, you can then decide on the meal. Once your knacks are known, you can then decide how best to apply them.

Second, look for times in your life when you found yourself in a state of deep immersion or mental absorption. These instances may reveal your learning knacks.

As a kid, I'd sit in my bedroom and stare at the columns of numbers I'd recorded, seeing my impact revealed in the statistics. I made the mistake of telling some friends I was doing this, and they laughed at me. It was abnormal to them, but I could not stop. It was just a subtle knack; it was by no means an amazing, trumpet-blaring sign of greatness. It was an odd peculiarity.

Third, search your values and interests to find your talents. We are equipped with the ability to thrive in the areas in which we are inclined to spend our time. A person gifted in math will be naturally inclined to work with numbers. Our knacks hang around our keenest interests.

Last, immerse yourself in resources like online aptitude testing, books on aptitude, and standard evaluations like *StrengthsFinder* or the Myers-Briggs Type Indicator, which, in my case, has been consistently accurate for decades.

A classic example of a knack is Warren Buffett counting the alphabetic letters in newspapers as a boy. How many *b*'s existed on page one?

How many *c*'s on page two? Either that boy had something wrong with him, or he had a peculiar genius that, if used for good, could lead to staggering results.

"A winner is someone who recognizes his God-given talents," said Larry Bird, "works his tail off to develop them into skills, and uses these skills to accomplish his goals." "If only every man would make proper use of his strength and do his utmost," said Cicero, "he need never regret his limited ability." When we discover our knacks, we find our strategic advantages.

"Skills vary with the man," said Pindar. "We must . . . strive by that which is born in us." In fifth grade, I was riveted by tracking my results. Along with my game statistics, I started tracking my weekly batting practices. In the end, I made the All-Star team. This odd aptitude has specific or general applications. Is it any wonder that I now use a chart on my wall to track my weekly hours of writing, real estate work, and exercise? Tracking efficiency is an inborn knack, one that is natural for me but may not be for other people.

We operate from a position of knacks or weaknesses.

"In my clinical experience, the greatest block to a person's development is his having to take on a way of life which is not rooted in his own powers," said Rollo May. Life may be hard, but it gets less hard when we use our strengths to full advantage.

THE LIFE LESSON: KNACKS

I learned that using my odd and peculiar traits,
Was a necessary advantage for uncommon prosperity.

*Ambition: A strong desire to achieve a goal, typically
requiring determination and hard work.*

Gardening is a kind of disease. It infects you, you cannot
escape it.

LEWIS GANNETT

Our ambitions are the call of our fullest potential, the Wealthy Gardener thought, for Nature wouldn't give us a desire if we weren't equipped with the ability to fulfill it.

On a May afternoon, the Wealthy Gardener was on his hands and knees in the garden. The tulips had exploded a week earlier, and it seemed every known weed was following suit. He heard a shout and looked up to see Jared leaning on the picket fence between the properties. They hadn't spoken since Jared had introduced him to his new girlfriend at the winery last winter.

"So where the heck have you been?" asked the Wealthy Gardener, walking over to greet him. "I haven't seen your truck lately."

"I moved in with my girlfriend a month ago."

The Wealthy Gardener froze. Just last fall, Jared had decided to swallow his pride, find temporary employment, and live with his parents to save every penny to regain a financial direction.

"The young lady I met at the winery?" asked the Wealthy Gardener.

"Yes, that's the one," Jared said. "We've been together for five months now. Things are really going great. I think maybe she's the one."

"Well then, I congratulate you. If I recall, she was giving you resistance about your job search in distant places. Have you resolved that yet?"

Jared grinned. "We signed a two-year lease on a rental house."

The Wealthy Gardener paused at this news. Jared seemed content in his everyday affairs. If he were truly ambitious, would he have signed a two-year lease to lock down his current position in life?

"I know what you're thinking," Jared said, interrupting the Wealthy Gardener's thoughts. "You think I'm giving up on my ambitions. But I still want more out of life."

"How am I to respond to that?" the Wealthy Gardener asked with a sigh. "I'm happy for you if you're happy. If she's really the one, then she's worth any sacrifice. But if she really is the one, wouldn't she also be willing to sacrifice for you?"

Jared looked at the ground for a moment.

"We can ignore a lot of things," he continued, "but we can't ignore our ambition. We are born with it, and we're stuck with it. When we deny our desires, ambition becomes agitation. It's best to go with it."

"So leave her for a job?" Jared asked. "Is that what you're saying?"

"I can't say what's best for you, Jared. But I can tell you that the difference between an ambition and a wish is sacrifice. When we give up our dreams, it may seem okay for a while. But it will eventually lead to resentments."

Jared was defiant. "So I won't be happy without accumulating money?"

"It depends on your ambitions."

"What does that mean?"

"Everyone has a destiny that needs to be actualized, and this future reality is driven by our ambition," said the Wealthy Gardener. "Do you recall the acorn on my desk, and how it always reminds me of the Universal Intelligence that governs every living thing?"

Jared rolled his eyes. "I remember it all too well."

"There's a potential within the acorn, an ambition, if you will, to become an immense oak tree. If one day I plant the acorn in soil, but then cover it with a plastic crate, the sun and rain and the soil's fertility will cause the acorn to take root. It will emerge into life, but the crate will confine its growth."

Jared glared at him.

"The acorn is naturally driven by an innate ambition to grow," said the Wealthy Gardener, "but a crate will limit its growth potential. In time it will feel trapped, frustrated, agitated, and constrained. The oak tree may try to adapt to the crate, but the fight will be in vain because, in the end, an oak is only satisfied when it's growing into a great tree and becoming all it can be."

"What are you saying, in plain terms?"

"Listen to me, Jared, and don't view this as a harsh judgment. Only you can decide what you want from life. You say you want to save money and get ahead financially, but your current choices and actions aren't aligned with those ambitions."

AMBITION FOR WEALTH is a natural tendency toward security and personal freedom. It is personal drive, desire, determination, and motivation. It is the will to work hard—sometimes even an inability to *not* work hard—for a personal dream or aspiration. Ambition is a stubborn resolve to strive against opposition and adversity. And it's an inborn beast that begs to be unleashed.

After I attained financial freedom, I met one of my favorite young friends, Josh. While taking college courses in criminal justice, Josh had followed his ambition and started his own business tinting car windows. In time the business thrived, and he postponed college. At age twenty-one, Josh employed a dozen of his high school friends. Within five years, he expanded his services and bought a warehouse for his business.

Josh possesses fiery ambition, and he submits to the sacrifices that differentiate true ambition from wishful thinking. On the day we met up, we talked about his aspiration for financial freedom. Josh asked me about my sacrifices. Was prosperity worth it?

"All I can tell you for sure," I said, "is that an ambitious life is not always the happiest life, but it's a satisfying life. And satisfaction, to me, is better than happiness. If you have true ambition, you're pretty much screwed anyway. You won't be happy doing nothing, sitting on a beach, or ignoring your ambition. You're driven, like it or not, to achieve something."

Josh laughed aloud, because my words confirmed what he sensed to be true. Of course, we all want happiness. But it tends to be an elusive emotion for those who seek it. Meanwhile, our satisfaction can be earned.

If we have ambition, we have no real choice—we either use it or fight against it. We must follow our ambition or feel trapped, frustrated, agitated, and constrained. If we pursue our prosperity, ethically and without hurting others, it is a driving force that assures a worthwhile contribution in our lives. We will realize that wealth is a reward that is reserved for those who add value to the common good.

"A man's worth is no greater than his ambitions," wrote Marcus Aurelius. "Not failure, but low aim, is crime," said Ernest Holmes. Walter H. Cottingham once said, "A man without ambition is a bird without wings."

One night when I was a teenager, my dad sat with me at the dinner table and talked about the power of his own ambition. "I am thankful to God for all the blessings in my life," he said. "But I am also thankful for the ambition I was given to earn these many blessings in my life." As a youngster, those words resonated with me.

Satisfaction and personal growth are the yield of ambition.

You can thank your inborn ambition when you feel frustrated by life conditions, trapped by circumstances, and unable to endure mediocrity. Your distress is the fuel you need to achieve your best life. You'll rise due to ambition.

In adulthood, I saw ambition as a beast that I needed to learn to ride, not suppress, if I was to ever have peace. Ambition simply gives us no choice; it will not be tamed or bottled up without unsettling distress.

Ambition is not something we try to have; it's something we cannot escape or ignore.

"People who are unable to motivate themselves must be content with mediocrity, no matter how impressive their other talents," said Andrew Carnegie. "The artist is nothing without the gift," said Émile Zola, "but the gift is nothing without work." The fruit of ambition is work satisfaction.

Like an acorn destined to be a great oak tree, we wouldn't be given ambition without the ability to fulfill it. Our ambition foreshadows our reaches. We can ignore ambition, but a crate over an acorn only frustrates the fullest potential of a mighty oak.

THE LIFE LESSON: AMBITION

I came to see my ambition as a beast of burden,
And rode it like a bull to reach my financial ends.

LESSON 4-14 · INNER VOICE

Inner voice: A sense beyond reason or evidence.

I have never had so many good ideas day after day as
when I worked in the garden.

JOHN ERSKINE

The persistent intuition that never recedes, believed the Wealthy Gardener, is the whisper of an inner voice that will not let us down. New worlds open naturally to those who listen and act.

It was an overcast Memorial Day weekend. Fred sat with the Wealthy Gardener on an iron bench beside a pond at the edge of the farm. Fred was fishing, while the Wealthy Gardener had come to escape the mobs at the winery. It was a secluded spot, a place of solitude appropriate for Mary's tombstone, which rested atop a nearby knoll.

Fred gazed at the still pond. "I've been thinking lately."

"That doesn't happen too much."

"Very funny," Fred snapped. "About our conversation last month. I believe you were right on the money. Since I retired, I've gotten away from the things that fulfilled me."

The Wealthy Gardener nodded without comment.

"Now this may sound crazy but hear me out," Fred said nervously. "I've never admitted this to anyone, but I've always had a secret dream. It isn't very reasonable, but I can't quite shake the idea of it. In fact, it's not even—"

"Fred, just spit it out already!"

"Okay, I'm trying. All my life I've wondered if I have what it takes to own a small business. And for thirty years, I've loved teaching Sunday school at the church," Fred said carefully. "I love working with the kids, and I want to try my hand in a venture. Now I'm thinking of starting a commercial day care center. It would challenge me, and I could serve hundreds of children."

The Wealthy Gardener's mouth opened, but he didn't speak.

"You think it's pretty stupid, huh?"

"I think it's genius!" said the Wealthy Gardener. "Absolutely perfect."

Fred scrutinized his friend. "To be honest, I was hoping you would try to talk me out of it. Why are you so quick to support it?"

"Well, because you have a dream, you can't quite shake the idea of it, and you want to serve others. That's the start of every successful business."

Fred stared at his friend. "I'm listening . . ."

"I think we each have a right path," said the Wealthy Gardener, "and we all have an inner voice. When a dream persists in the heart and has staying power over many years, I view the attraction with a sacred veneration. It's the guidance of a deeper inner wisdom."

"You think it's a personal calling of God?"

There was a sparkle in the Wealthy Gardener's eyes. "I cannot lie. I do like the idea of a divine assignment or duty. Where do aspirations originate? It seems that the inner voice resonates with something deep within the Universal Intelligence that governs this world."

"Well, let me play devil's advocate," Fred countered. "I'm old enough to appreciate the fact that ninety-five percent of businesses fail within the first five years."

"And I agree that it's wise to be cautious of impulses," said the Wealthy Gardener. "But still, I've found, over the years, that true callings have a stubborn kind of staying power. They're not passing whims or fantasies. Our authentic pull of the inner voice is a persistent aspiration that won't die. It lasts the test of time. And thirty years is a pretty conservative test of time, you old fool."

Fred grinned, reeled in his line, checked his bait, and cast back into the center of the pond. "I'll be honest with you," he said at last. "I'm okay with admitting that I'm afraid to flop. At my age, if I fail, I'll look like an idiot. It's going to cost twenty thousand dollars. And truly I don't have time to recoup any lost investment."

The Wealthy Gardener stared at the pond for a moment without speaking. "Why not ask yourself if you can live with the worst possible outcome?"

"I could survive it financially," Fred said, then laughed. "My ego is another matter."

"Well, you have a few options," said the Wealthy Gardener. "You can decide not to try. You can try and fail. Or you can try and succeed. The only question is, upon your final breath, how will you feel about yourself having not tried?"

INNER VOICE: A sense beyond reason or evidence. It describes our curious hunches, intuitions, promptings, or warnings. It is an instinctive sense, a deep subconscious perception; it exists as an inscrutable psychic phenomenon. It describes an acute sensitivity, unavailable to the conscious mind, that can be honed and trusted for guidance to avoid regrets.

The number one regret of the dying is failure to pursue an aspiration. The failure to act, stand up for a dream, or follow one's inner wisdom—this is regret *number one*. Our greatest regrets arise from missed opportunities to live an authentic life aligned with our individuality. And these regrets arise from ignoring the inner voice.

Listening to my inner voice led me into real estate, helped me to earn financial freedom, and eventually compelled me to write this book. My inner voice feels like either a silent pull toward or a strong repulsion away from a person, choice, or direction.

For example, I didn't simply want to write this book; rather, I couldn't *not* write this book. It felt like a persistent instinct that would not recede. The inner voice influences our direction before we can see the map. And the road always leads us into uncertainty.

After I achieved my lifelong goal of financial freedom, my life changed quickly. My brother died, and this brings up another story about the inner voice. He somehow sensed his demise as a premonition. In perfect health, at the age of fifty-two, he was struck by a car and died instantly. But later we learned that he had confided to friends during the preceding month that he knew he was going to die soon.

How can we explain intuitive knowledge?

My brother's inner voice foretold a future event, just like my inner voice told me it was my time to begin to write. After his passing, I felt an unshakable call to duty, and I started to talk with my son about these life lessons on prosperity. I drove into the unknown.

"Sometimes the heart sees what is invisible to the eye," said H. Jackson Brown Jr. And Wilhelm Reich advised, "First and foremost, think straight, trust the quiet inner voice that tells you what to do." It doesn't need to make sense, and it often leads us into new pastures.

The inner voice is waiting to guide us if only we ask good questions and stay attuned to our feelings during our days. What will you regret if you don't do it, see it, or try it? The answer, when it comes, and, most important, when it *stays*, is commonly the inner voice.

I once spoke with an attorney's wife who informed me that her husband was considering a campaign for county judge. It was an elected position, and he was on the fence about running. Just to compete, she told me, would require an outlay of $60,000, which would have to come from their personal savings. With four children, their family finances were tight. It was monetarily risky since a successful outcome was uncertain.

"He's been talking about this for ten years," she said, and sighed.

"For what it's worth, all I can tell you," I said, "is that I take very seriously any desire with that kind of staying power." I said nothing more, but I like to think that my words had something to do with his current role as our county judge.

"We all have an inner teacher," expressed Dean Ornish, "an inner guide, an inner voice that speaks very clearly but usually not very loudly.

That information can be drowned out by the chatter of the mind and the pressure of day-to-day events. But if we quiet down the mind, we can begin to hear what we're not paying attention to. We can find out what's right for us."

THE LIFE LESSON: INNER VOICE

....

I learned to notice the prodding of a Silent Voice,
That provided the directions before I could see the map.

*Courage: The ability to do something that frightens
us, but is likely to be of benefit.*

The mighty oak was once a little nut that stood its
ground.

UNKNOWN

Ambition without caution is a bus without brakes, considered the Wealthy
Gardener, but ambition without courage is a bus without keys. Wealth
favors the individual with courage and caution in the right measure.

The Wealthy Gardener sat in his gazebo with Connie, Fred's wife,
watching a sudden deluge flood the land. They'd been working in adjacent gardens when there was a rumble of thunder, followed by a rustle of
leaves and then a heavy rain. The Wealthy Gardener was now teasing
Connie about the dog she had recently given to Fred. She then admitted
that she was deeply worried about her husband.

"Fred's been sitting in the basement," she said, "depressed."

"I'm surprised," said the Wealthy Gardener. "A few weeks ago, Fred
and I were talking about his plans for a day care center. He was more
than enthusiastic about it. I imagined by now he'd be working out the
details."

Connie sighed, slumping in her chair without response. If she didn't
want to talk more about her husband, it was certainly her own preroga-
tive. They sat in silence for several minutes.

"Can we speak confidentially?" Connie finally asked.

"Of course, you're an intimate friend."

"Fred's done this before," she said carefully. "For years it's been the
same pattern with him. He comes so close to following his dream, and

then he falls into a pit of despair when he can't act on it. It's his lifelong torment."

The Wealthy Gardener nodded.

"Fred hides his insecurity," she continued. "He puts on a strong front for the world to see, just like we all do. I've never told anyone about it, but it's our secret. He gets close to acting on his dream, but he just won't do it."

"I'm sorry to hear about it, Connie. How long has this been going on?"

"It's not a constant topic in our life," she said, "but talk of a day care center has surfaced for at least the past twenty years. Every time it's come up, Fred has talked himself out of acting on it due to his work responsibilities. Now he can't fall back on that worn-out excuse."

"So now he's depressed in the basement."

"He is in the basement thinking up reasons not to do what he wants most to do," she said, then sighed. "He can never take the first step. He dwells on what he might lose and ignores the fact that he's not happy where he is."

The Wealthy Gardener nodded sadly. "Isn't it common?" he said. "We fear the consequences of action but ignore the costs of inaction."

"That's about it," Connie agreed. "And now he's depressed because his normal excuse is gone. But if I know Fred, he will figure out some other reason for inaction. He'll find a creative excuse."

The Wealthy Gardener offered no response.

"To be honest," Connie continued, "I wouldn't even mind if the business failed and we lost money. We've worked all our lives, and we have enough to lose. Fred needs to do this to know that he gave it a shot before it's too late. I think it's now or never."

"I told him the same thing," agreed the Wealthy Gardener.

"What am I supposed to do?" asked Connie.

"Fred's a big boy, and he's going to do what he wants. Just do us all one favor," he said with a wry smile. "Don't buy him another puppy, okay?"

. . .

COURAGE: THE ABILITY to do something that frightens us, but is likely to be of benefit. Wealth favors the person who uses a dose of courage and a dash of caution in the right proportions.

The story of outdoor adventurer Aron Ralston is an extreme example of smart courage. While Ralston was canyoneering all alone in a remote desert, a boulder dislodged and pinned his arm against a wall in a narrow crevice. Day turned into night, and night into day. For five and a half days, alone and with virtually no sleep, the twenty-seven-year-old was trapped and seemed likely to die.

We all know the ending: To survive, he cut off his arm.

It was a rational decision born of courage. Weighing the cost of action versus inaction, Ralston assessed the situation, pulled out a multitool with a dull two-inch blade, and did what was necessary to live. He decided that an amputation was preferable to death. It was reasonable courage. It's this kind of rational courage that empowers upward mobility.

Smart courage is the ability to walk into uncertainty when the upside is worth the risk. It is the bravery to act when fear is reasonable—and pain is likely to arise from our choice. It is action when there is something to lose, when known hardships are inescapable, but the desirable outcome offsets the dangers.

Accumulating wealth requires defining moments of weighing the consequences of action against the dangers of inaction. What would we do if we knew our future was in jeopardy? Could we face the fear of change and unfamiliarity to avoid the despair of regrets?

We all know the story of Jeff Bezos, who walked away from a lucrative finance job for his dream of Amazon. "I knew that if I failed I wouldn't regret that," he said, "but I knew the one thing I might regret is not trying." It's an iconic story, but, with all due respect, this extraordinary man had a fallback plan with a safety net.

More impressive to me is an ordinary example of the middle-class struggle for upward mobility. Kaylin was married with a toddler, and another baby on the way. She worked at a department store; her family income barely covered the monthly bills.

One day she spotted an opening for a manager position at a post office. It paid double her current salary. She applied, was granted an interview, and was chosen as one of six final candidates for the job. The hiring process involved all the finalists undergoing three weeks of training, and this presented Kaylin with a frightening dilemma.

After those three weeks, just one person would be hired. To attend the three-week training, however, Kaylin would need to quit her current job. And without her contribution to the family income, her family couldn't survive a month. It was a one-in-six chance to double her income at the expense of her current job and possibly her family's security.

It was a tremendous opportunity with obvious risks. But the easy choice is not always the safest choice. Sometimes bold actions can save our lives.

Kaylin quit her job and attended the three-week training. "Every day I prayed I was doing the right thing," she confided to me. "I was scared to death." She ended up getting the job at the post office, but even if she hadn't, she would have been okay with trying, failing, and figuring it out. Her story is the embodiment of personal nerve and smart courage.

She took a calculated risk for a reward.

"It is hard to fail," said Theodore Roosevelt, "but it is worse never to have tried to succeed." In real estate, it's been said that we don't go broke from a great deal that gets away—we only go broke from the bad deals that we do get. This reminds me to be cautious and bold.

THE LIFE LESSON: COURAGE

I learned that the secret of freedom was courage,
But financial freedom required both courage and caution.

*Unrealistic: An opinion of doubt; a thing
considered unlikely to be achieved.*

Gardening is a way of showing that you believe in
tomorrow.

UNKNOWN

Realistic goals are for common lives, mused the Wealthy Gardener, but
wealthy are they who trust themselves to rise to the heights of their
loftiest ambitions.

On a sweltering summer weekend, the Wealthy Gardener stopped by
the neighboring farm for a final inspection. During the past year, Santos
and his family had worked hard to turn the abandoned farm into a potential business. It was almost time to honor the deal and transfer the
deed. Hoping to surprise Santos, the Wealthy Gardener walked into the
farm's office.

Jimmy, seated at the front desk, looked up. "How's it going, old timer?"

"Better than good and better than most," he said, beaming. "Are you
alone?"

"Santos has some unfinished business at your vineyards," Jimmy said.
"He'll be back here by noon, if you need him."

"I'll catch up with him later." The Wealthy Gardener sat in a chair
beside the desk. "How's it looking here—financially, I mean. Are you
okay?"

"Good, if nothing breaks, the weather's perfect, and everyone works
for free!" Jimmy laughed. "In truth, we'll barely turn a profit."

"Well, that's not bad for the first year. But now I'd like to hear about
your plans. If I recall, you made it very clear that you're done after a year."

Jimmy clasped his hands on the desk. "I wish I could just leave," he said slowly, "but I can't. Not just yet, anyway. We're doing well, but there's no money for someone to take my place. I'll stay here for a while longer, but I'll be working on my own plans during my free time."

"That's mighty big of you. I'm sure you'll never regret it."

"Thanks. I owe these folks that much. But here's my dilemma. At my age, what can a person do to start building wealth? I'm working for minimum wage, I have no savings, and I have no help financially."

"I agree that's a tough pickle."

"I've decided one thing," Jimmy said. "I'm not going to sit around every evening wishing life was different. I've contemplated my goals, and I've studied my options. I may have no money, but I have time after work. And so I'm starting to see a plan coming together."

The Wealthy Gardener grinned, immensely enjoying the suspense.

"When the possibilities are as limited as mine, the choices are easier. I don't have the world to choose from, not like the rich kids with privilege and advantages. With no money, I have few options. And so I'm going to be a real estate agent. At least, that's where I'll start, and I can get my training online."

"A real estate agent," said the Wealthy Gardener. "Why did you choose that?"

"Why choose that?" Jimmy repeated. "My number one reason is because I can. It doesn't cost much. I can get accredited after work in the evenings. I can be licensed with a criminal record. And I find real estate to be interesting. I already passed a basic exam online, and the national test is in three weeks. And that means once I pass it, I plan to be organized and in business within a few months."

The Wealthy Gardener was impressed. "What I see in front of me is a man with a plan—the inevitable fruit of a mind that's focused on a clear goal. But tell me, what's your boss think?"

"Santos says it's an unrealistic idea. He reminded me that I'm not a salesperson, and that I can't compete with the full-time agents. He thinks it's a risky business, and that I'll never survive on commissions."

"And what do you say about it?"

"I say it's realistic because I will do anything." Jimmy laughed. "I'll learn what I need to learn. I'll grow as I need to grow. I'll work as much as I need to work. It's realistic because I can't afford to lose. And so I will win."

The Wealthy Gardener laughed in delight. "And how will you pay for it?"

"You will loan me the money," Jimmy shot back. "I'll repay you and double your investment with my first commission check. You'll make a killing."

THE TERM *UNREALISTIC* can be used to describe high aims, uncommon purposes, or ambitious pursuits that seem implausible for ordinary people. It describes inspired hopes and aspirations far above the average of a group or family. It refers to an objective not easily attained by ordinary effort and thus not reasonable for the masses.

But unrealistic is just an opinion.

Being unrealistic means believing in something big when you haven't yet figured out the way to attain it, when you know what you want, but not how to get it. "Once the 'what' is decided," said Pearl S. Buck, "the 'how' always follows. We must not make the 'how' an excuse for not facing and accepting the 'what.'"

Big goals need faith before we know the way. "The way to see by faith, is to shut the Eye of Reason," said Benjamin Franklin.

Before entering college I sat down with my parents and discussed how I might proceed with my life. "Here's the deal," I said, with all the nerve I could muster. "You seem to be willing to pay my living expenses while I'm in college. My end is to take out loans for tuition. But I have another option. I might like to go into real estate. How about if you just give me the money that you would spend for my years in college, and I'll head into real estate? It's no different on your end, and it will give me a head start in this career."

My parents considered the proposition unrealistic at the time, and I can't blame them. But it made sense to me, and while my audacity has been the butt of family jokes, the same "unrealistic" thinking has served me in later years.

Decades later, when I was a real estate investor, a block of six individual duplexes came on the market as part of an estate sale. Other investors made lowball offers, trying to snatch the best deal for a single duplex—they were thinking small. The estate's sellers, who lived overseas, would not agree to individual lowball offers. It was the dead of winter, and the tenants were uncooperative and even belligerent with potential buyers.

I could sense the upside potential of buying all six units, but it was unrealistic for me to even consider due to several formidable obstacles. First, these duplexes were in the best location in town, near the park and the library, and their prime location meant it was unrealistic to expect the sellers to accept a low price. For me, the units had to be purchased cheaply in order for me to afford the necessary renovations. But from a seller's perspective, it was highly likely that rentals in this great location would command full market value.

Second, buying the duplexes was unrealistic for me because I had no spare time. I was overextended, working full time, managing forty rentals, and overseeing three flip projects that were currently stalled. While the duplexes had great potential, remodeling them would require a year of steady work.

Third, it was unrealistic for me because I had recently fired all my workers and contractors. I was an army of one, in over my head, facing a massive undertaking. Considering this project without a team was scary.

Finally, and perhaps the primary reason this deal was unrealistic for me, I simply had no money. All my cash and credit lines were tied up in the flips that were now sitting vacant and unfinished, waiting for me to hire new workers.

It was practical to conclude that investing in this block of duplexes was unrealistic—if not impossible—for me at the time. I could have backed away and focused on my obligations, choosing the more sensible path.

I was at a curious juncture of life, the importance of which is only visible looking back. I gathered all my nerve and made an unrealistic offer, half the asking price for all six units. To entice the sellers, I waived inspections and offered to close in a month. For me, it was a worthwhile gamble; for the sellers, I hoped it would solve their ongoing problems with their tenants.

To the surprise of all the real estate agents, experts, and other investors interested in the duplexes, the sellers accepted my offer. I was elated and terrified—I instantly needed to find money, workers, and time. I had none of these, but the *how* always follows the *what*. I had committed myself without knowing the *how*, so I needed to figure it out.

While this example may seem like an isolated real estate deal, the common opinion of *unrealistic* exists in all areas of life, including careers, personal freedoms, vacations, investments, and wealth.

What is unrealistic for us?

Our answer defines our dreams.

I bought the duplexes, got the work done, and somehow pulled it all off. The results surpassed my wildest expectations. I figured out a way, and that is the critical lesson. We always seem to figure out the *how* after we commit to the *what*. Our capacity always rises to match the size of our most pressing demands. I had to scramble for cash, sure, but the *how* followed the commitment. I succeeded because I had no choice *but* to succeed.

This one deal was a big part of a larger design that led to my financial freedom. And that's how success happens: one step at a time. We get crowned with uncommon rewards only after we stretch beyond our realistic expectations.

The tragedy of being realistic is that, despite the term implying wisdom and practicality, we will never attempt the impossible. A realistic opinion is an argument for excuses that limit our goals and validate mediocre efforts.

"Faith that the thing can be done is essential to any great achievement," said Thomas N. Carruthers. "I have learned to use the word 'impossible,'" Wernher von Braun said, "with the greatest caution."

Unrealistic is just an opinion.

Never diminish your dreams due to lack of know-how or practicality. You must start with the dream, maintain it in your mind, dwell on it, and let the *how* catch up to it. And then be forever cynical of realistic expectations. "Being realistic," Will Smith once said, "is the most commonly traveled road to mediocrity."

THE LIFE LESSON: BE UNREALISTIC

I discovered that "unrealistic" was just an opinion,
And my capacity always grew to match the size of my goals.

*Fortitude: The strength to endure suffering and
sacrifice without self-pity or complaint.*

Farming looks mighty easy when your plow is a pencil,
and you're a thousand miles from the cornfield.

DWIGHT D. EISENHOWER

Ambition is wasted on the irresolute, mused the Wealthy Gardener, since achievement demands endurance long after inspiration has fled. Fortitude is the character to finish what we start without self-pity.

The Wealthy Gardener sat on a shaded bench under a mature oak tree with Santos, whose work ethic during the past year had been extraordinary. Santos's labor had gone beyond the capacity of two ordinary men, thought the Wealthy Gardener, and the man never complained.

"I want to thank you again," said Santos.

"It is your just reward, my good friend. But you're welcome."

A week earlier, the Wealthy Gardener had signed over the deed for the neighboring farm to Santos at a private ceremony at the winery. Santos had choked up as his extended family applauded.

"I've been watching you this year," said the Wealthy Gardener. "From dawn to dusk, you worked at my farm every day, and then you went to work on your own project every night. I even saw you there early on Saturdays and Sundays. Tell me, how did you maintain your strenuous discipline?"

"I wanted change. You once told me there's never a certainty of future rewards," said Santos, "but we go for it anyway or we keep what we've got. I've never forgot that lesson. And I used my free hours to better my life."

"Many people want change, but they don't work like you."

"I was afraid to miss my opportunity a second time. And I thought of my family and what our own business would mean to us. I carried these thoughts with me during the longest days of the past year."

"Most interesting," said the Wealthy Gardener. "You stayed mindful of why the work was important, and this helped you finish it."

"Without a doubt."

"But still, sixteen-hour days and weekends surely must have tested your strength," said the Wealthy Gardener. "We all have limits to our energy."

"What is work, really?" asked Santos. "I wasn't digging ditches all day. I was just moving, ordering supplies, planning, using power tools, sitting in a chair, and following a checklist. In the end, is our daily work so hard?"

"It is only filling our hours with purpose."

"That's all there is to it. And let's be honest," Santos said with a playful grin, "the work that paid my living expenses required no willpower from me at all—this labor fed me and my family. I had no choice. It was only the use of my free hours that required any resolve."

"That's a keen insight," agreed the Wealthy Gardener. "Our sacrifice is found in our free time. The workday is the price we all pay to stay alive. But our free hours are the price we pay for our dreams."

"I used my free time this year to better my life," Santos said simply. "And I realized that my best life had previously been lost in the empty hours. It's a shame how many years have passed without progress."

This was Santos's way of saying that in wasting his time, he had wasted his potential. The Wealthy Gardener was pleased with his friend. Previously, the operations manager had always been a man of solid action—an employee on the payroll who got things done—but now he was growing wiser.

"What have you learned over the past year?"

There was a thoughtful pause. "I learned to pray for the strength to handle my demands. I learned to focus on why I was doing the work, and not on the burden of it. And I learned that sacrifice is temporary, but self-respect and the pride of effort are permanent."

FORTITUDE IS THE STRENGTH to weather storms and work through adversity when ambition, courage, and willpower have waned. It's the resolve to soldier on, stay the course, and plod forward into obstacles long after inspiration has fled. Fortitude is the ability to indefinitely endure struggles, workloads, sacrifices, and rejections for our dreams.

In the previous life lesson, I described a personal story about purchasing six duplexes at a time when this action was "unrealistic" because I had no liquid cash, no workers for renovations, and no free time. While this example may seem to be a trivial event in an ordinary life, it is wise to consider that every life, great or small, is built on decisions and actions. When we go after the unrealistic, we must endure the consequences and overcome great odds.

I was ready for the challenge not only due to my previous decades of experience in real estate, but, more important, because I had developed fortitude. I had the ability to endure sixteen-hour workdays, seven days a week, without regard for my comfort, health, or pleasure.

I could endure the workload of unrealistic goals.

During the year after I purchased the duplexes, I hired strangers. I helped tenants move. I worked in each unit. I fired workers. I doubled rents. I evicted tenants. I managed forty other rentals. I lined streets with trees. I slept sparingly. I showered at a nearby YMCA to save time. I worked as a full-time chiropractor. I drank a lot of coffee. I essentially gave the undertaking a year of my life.

The key to enduring our hardest work is to focus on meaning. I focused on why I was in this project. I had willingly signed up for this trouble despite my other obligations. And I never forgot that I was engaged in this undertaking to win my financial freedom. I focused not on the drudgery, but on the hope that my family would benefit from my labor, struggle, fatigue, and sacrifice. When self-pity descended on me, I focused on my *why*. During that year, almost every day, I repeated a mantra from a favorite literary verse:

For Life is a just employer,
He gives you what you ask,
But once you have set the wages,
Why, you must bear the task.

People called me a workaholic. I was told, in no uncertain terms, that my life was imbalanced. By the end of that year, I looked gaunt. One friend asked me if I had cancer. I was told to ease up. Rash judgments were cast by others who were golfing, skiing, watching television, drinking on weekends, and enjoying comfortable lives. I was engaging my free time in the pursuit of my personal freedom.

It required fortitude to survive that year, but while the time passed, the rewards have stayed with me. We must make it across the finish line of our unrealistic pursuits. Starters are common, but finishers are rare.

"Genius begins great works; labor alone finished them," said Joseph Joubert. It's fun to dream, but achievement is built on hours.

Sooner or later, we either give up on amassing wealth and prosperity, or we gradually come to accept its price. Uncommon rewards are available to those who can pass the test of sacrifice and persistence.

"You will never succeed beyond the purpose to which you are willing to surrender," said Albert E. N. Gray. "And your surrender will not be complete until you have formed the habit of doing the things that failures don't like to do."

THE LIFE LESSON: FORTITUDE

....

I learned that wealth follows draining journeys,
And the quest must endure after inspiration has fled.

LESSON 4-18 · INNER CIRCLE

Inner circle: A small, intimate group of people who usually have influence over one's mind-set and ideas.

Friends are the flowers in the garden of life.

MARY ENGELBREIT

A band of brothers becomes one another, mused the Wealthy Gardener, since we rarely outperform our inner circle. Wise is the one who is choosy with associates, for a friendship with a fool can be a costly affair.

He stood at the podium in the class for troubled teens while Jimmy sat in his usual chair. "We talked about the story of the chicken-eagle," the Wealthy Gardener said, "and today we're going to talk about the problem of hanging out with chickens."

The class laughed politely.

"Chickens aren't necessarily bad people," he continued, "but they don't want you to be unlike them. They try to influence you. They question your ambition. They tell you to aim for balance. They advise you to be happy with an ordinary life. They ask why you need more, and if you think you're better than them. Who do you think you are? Does anyone in this class know a chicken?"

The boys all laughed, indicating they understood chickens all too well.

The Wealthy Gardener waited for the room to quiet. "Guarding your mind against the negative influence of others is a skill you must acquire to become wealthy," he said. "The negativity of others has stolen many a fortune."

The classroom atmosphere quickly sobered.

"I have a close friend," he continued, "who is facing a defining moment. He's retired and has a dream to start his own business. But day after day, he spends time in crippling worry. And every morning he drives to McDonald's for coffee with his other retired friends. His friends are good people, but now that they're retired, they're done striving in their lives. The problem isn't that they're lazy. It's that they're coasting, while my friend has a dream. He's not done living yet, but he hangs out with old guys who love leisure. And due to his own fears, combined with the company he keeps, he may die with the regrets of a chicken." He paused to emphasize this last point to the class. "A band of brothers becomes one another."

"You think he'd be better off not seeing his friends?" asked one kid.

"That is a very fine question," said the Wealthy Gardener, "and one that few people have the courage to ask. Let me ask you another question," he said, pausing for a long moment to build suspense. "How tall should a tree grow?"

The kid shrugged wordlessly, and the other kids laughed at him.

"As tall as it can," said the Wealthy Gardener. "In nature we see that a tree grows to its full height, and whatever impedes its growth is a problem."

"So his coffee buddies are a problem?"

"True friends help you become all that you can be," said the Wealthy Gardener, "and they delight in your growth. Those who will help you become your best, who want you to reach your potential, are fit for your inner circle."

"So stay away from old chickens," the boy joked, causing more laughter.

"I have another friend who is younger," said the Wealthy Gardener, "and he's unhappy because he has no savings and no financial traction. But now he's wrapped up with a girlfriend who has influence over him. And he's hanging out with a partying crowd on weekends. They're all fun people, but he's becoming like them. He's aimless, without goals. In a few years, if he doesn't change, he'll be plagued by many regrets. He'll wake up one day with no power over his life, and then he'll exist in a trap without hope."

AN INNER CIRCLE consists of people who occupy our time, influence our minds, and normalize our behaviors. Wealth requires a selective inner circle with a guard at the door to prevent the negative influence of others. A friendship with a fool can be a costly affair.

"He that walketh with wise men shall be wise," states Proverbs 13:20. Euripides said, "Every man is like the company he is wont to keep." And Confucius advised: "Have no friends not equal to yourself."

In my thirties, I started to guard my mind against negative influences. I became more protective of my aspirations. I didn't reject my close friends and family, but I erected a barrier to prevent any of their negative suggestions from affecting me.

It was challenging being surrounded by well-intentioned people who wanted "the best" for me. And their advice was steady: "Life is short, so live for the day. Why are you killing yourself? You need balance. Everybody works until they're old, so why should you be any different? It's normal to worry about bills. We're happy, why aren't you? Who do you think you are?"

Our inner circle is those people we take into our confidence. We can be surrounded by good people without letting them inside our walls. We can coexist with others without giving them the key to the door of our mind.

The sanctity of my mind became so important to me that when I spent a year learning about real estate, I told nobody, except for my wife, about this undertaking. When I bought my first rental unit, nobody knew what I had done. In fact, to avoid negative influences, I operated under the radar until I owned and operated twenty units. After I had a proven track record in real estate, few people could offer unsolicited advice. But I was still told, "Everybody ends up selling their rentals, and you will, too." Of course, this statement came from a family member who had sold all his rentals.

Many a fortune is lost from susceptibility to negative influences.

It may seem lonely to guard your aspirations from negative attacks. In fact, during the years I was acquiring my first twenty units, I was surrounded at my clinic by masses of people. I was in the chaotic activity of multiple house renovations. I was dealing with renters in the growing landlording business. And yet, in many ways, I was on my own. Into my inner circle, I allowed just one person.

I spent those years with Earl Nightingale.

These days, we see young people looking for mentors to guide them in the ways of success. For me, Earl Nightingale was that mentor. His voice was constantly in my ears, although he died decades before I'd ever heard of him. After I had found him, however, he coached me and imbued me with his philosophy through audio recordings while I drove my car, exercised, and performed mundane tasks that required little concentration.

My mentor taught me that ambition is good. I learned the value of using constructive discontentment to improve my life condition. I was assured that work-life balance is okay, but only if one *chooses* balance. Life is about being useful, and we are happiest when we are on the road to something we want very much. Success is the progressive realization of a worthy ideal. And money comes from giving value and service to others. My inner circle expanded to include other teachers, but Nightingale was the godfather at the head of the long table.

Through the years, we may find people who support us and want us to reach our fullest heights. They are fitting members of our innermost circle.

I cannot leave this subject without mentioning that I spent many evenings with the "eminent dead," a term used by Charlie Munger to refer to the greats of the past. I gave my free hours to intimately get to know these exemplary figures by reading their biographies.

In fact, in a private room in my house, I have a wall of framed pictures of people from the past whose lives I admire; on each picture is a small phrase that represents my "takeaway lesson" from that person's biography. The following is not a comprehensive list of the characters on my wall, but rather a sampler of the people who have become my own inner circle:

- **Jesus Christ:** As you believe
- **Earl Nightingale:** A purpose and faith
- **John D. Rockefeller:** One percent of one hundred men's efforts
- **Steve Jobs:** Reality distortions
- **Napoleon Hill:** Read goals with emotion
- **Andrew Carnegie:** Definite chief aim
- **W. Clement Stone:** Creative think time
- **Wayne Dyer:** Imagine wishes fulfilled
- **Walt Disney:** Plus it
- **Benjamin Franklin:** Personal development
- **Ray Kroc:** Always think evergreen
- **Jim Rohn:** Choose discipline or regret
- **Abraham Lincoln:** Forbearance

Reading the biographies of the "eminent dead" has been an ongoing course of study in human greatness and worthy achievements, and it has provided insights for living. For example, when struggling with the decision to write this book, I revealed my uncertainties to my son.

"Nobody in my world will understand why I wrote this book," I told him. Mike thought about it. "That's probably true," he replied coolly, "but ask yourself this question: What would those guys on your basement wall think about you writing the book?"

My inner circle—the exemplary figures on that wall—were uncommon characters who would judge my fear of criticism far more harshly than my taking a bold action. Why not try to do something unusual in my time? What is the alternative to pursuing a worthy goal?

And so I wrote the book due to the influence of my inner circle. It is no different than recalling a deceased parent or friend and wondering what that person would say. But during the years I was writing this book, I told no one of the project. I didn't need any negative suggestions.

"Be courteous to all, but intimate with few," said George Washington, "and let those few be well tried before you give them your confidence."

If you desire riches, guard your mind against the susceptibility to negative influences. And focus on your most coveted goal.

THE LIFE LESSON: INNER CIRCLE

I found that my inner circle had to change to achieve wealth,
But what was lost in quantity was offset by rare quality.

LESSON 4-19 · DECISION

Decision: A resolution defined by its action.

> What I've always found interesting in gardens is looking
> at what people choose to plant there. What they put
> in. What they leave out. One small choice and then
> another, and soon there is a mood, an atmosphere, a
> series of limitations, a world.
>
> HELEN HUMPHREYS

A decision without action is a delusion, mused the Wealthy Gardener. Wealth favors the one whose decisions are influenced by clear goals and are visible in execution.

After speaking at the reformatory, the Wealthy Gardener had a restless night's sleep, worrying about his neighbor Fred. When they had last spoken, it had seemed as though Fred had decided to start the day care center, but he still spent most of his time doing a whole lot of nothing.

Upon waking in the morning, he resolved to speak with his neighbor one more time. And now they strolled through the vineyard with coffees in hand, following Buddy, who trotted ahead without a leash.

"I haven't taken action yet," Fred admitted. "I'm still thinking about it."

They walked for a minute before the Wealthy Gardener spoke up. "Last night I dreamed about you," he finally admitted. "To be perfectly honest, it was more of a nightmare, really—"

"You had a nightmare about *me*?"

"Well, yes . . . but not exactly," he stammered. "I saw you at the end of your life. You were a frail, pathetic old man. You were defeated and gaunt. You were the picture of desolation, and after that dream, I couldn't sleep a wink."

"Well, son of a gun," Fred quipped. "Now *I* won't sleep!"

"Better you than me," offered the Wealthy Gardener. "And besides, a little restless sleep might just do you some good."

"What do you mean by that?"

"I mean this decision in your life must be faced," said the Wealthy Gardener. "Our defining moments don't arrive with a trumpet blast to get our attention. When we don't decide, we erase all future possibilities."

Fred walked in silence for a moment. "By God, I know you're right," he said at last. "I sometimes don't know what's wrong with me. What the heck keeps me from doing it? At times I think I should just follow my heart. But the next day, I'm inclined to use my rational mind and play it safe. I'm never too sure, and so I end up not deciding at all. You're right about my indecision, and I admit it."

The Wealthy Gardener smiled. "Stand up for your dream, Fred."

Fred smiled, nodding. "It's now or never, isn't it?"

"I think maybe it is," said the Wealthy Gardener. "In our lives, we are what we are, we have what we have, and we do what we do because of our past decisions. We have nobody but ourselves to blame."

A DECISION is a resolution defined by its action. Our conditions today can be traced to our past choices and actions. "We are all self-made," said Earl Nightingale, "but only the successful will admit it."

As I was building my financial freedom, I had lunch with another chiropractor and shared with him that I had begun a real estate business on the side. We were longtime friends, but he looked down at this idea of running a side business. He wasn't alone. To most people, it seemed that I must be in financial trouble if I was willing to spend my free time dealing with renters, contractors, and dirty houses to earn extra money.

"How's the rental thing going?" he would ask on subsequent meetings. But I sensed contempt in his attitude, as if I'd crossed over the tracks and entered the blue-collar land of get-rich-quick desperadoes.

"So why are you doing it?" he point-blank asked me one day.

"As a small business owner, I don't have a pension. This is my retirement income," I told him. He nodded but said nothing. It seemed that maybe I'd touched a nerve.

It was clear that we were in the exact same situation. We were solo practitioners facing the same headwinds of shrinking insurance reimbursement. All the facts pointed to nothing but trouble in the years ahead. With an uncertain future, my goal was to build an income independent from my chiropractic clinic.

A decade later, he called on me. Now *he* needed to do something for extra income. Times were tough. "Could we sit down and talk about real estate?" he asked. We talked, but it was too late.

The cost of complacency is lost opportunity; our indecision erases many future possibilities. We all have windows of opportunity, and we all have intuitive senses. Mindful of my clear goals, I could always sense financial opportunity as well as the danger of inaction.

"It is in your moments of decision that your destiny is shaped," said Tony Robbins. In our decisions, we have power over the future. We hold the reins of our fate. We are in charge, at least before our choices and conditions gain the upper hand and then control us.

Clarity of goals is at the heart of making better decisions. The presence of a target, a financial objective, provides the essential criteria by which we can judge the consequences of our many decisions.

Should we buy the luxury car? *What are our savings goals?* Should we accept the new job or go back to school? *What are our income goals?* Should we exercise or relax? *What are our health goals?* Should we save for retirement? *What kind of life do we want to live when we're older?*

It is in our moments of decision that our destiny is shaped.

THE LIFE LESSON: DECISION

I learned that my decisions were moments of power,
And saw that indecision erased future possibilities.

LESSON 4-20 · SACRED EFFORT

Sacred effort: An ultimate exertion at the edge of capacity.

Gardening is the work of a lifetime: you never finish.

OSCAR DE LA RENTA

What matters most in a purposeful life, thought the Wealthy Gardener, is giving one's fullest strength to one's cause. Great efforts assure satisfaction, while common efforts can lead to regrets.

Jimmy bounded around the Wealthy Gardener's house and found him lounging on the patio with a new gardening magazine and a bowl of ice cream. It was eight o'clock on a Friday evening, and the sun had set.

"Well, look who finally surfaced!" exclaimed the Wealthy Gardener. "The guy who borrowed two thousand dollars from me several weeks ago and I haven't heard from since! I figured you took an exotic vacation!"

"Lucky for you, it never occurred to me."

The Wealthy Gardener chuckled. "What have you been up to?"

"I've been putting in ten-hour days with Santos," Jimmy said, "and every evening I've been taking my pre-licensing courses online. It's been a three-week blitz, but tomorrow's the test, so we'll see how it goes."

"Are you ready?"

"All I know for sure is that I couldn't have studied more to prepare for it. Whatever happens tomorrow, I'll know that I did my best."

The Wealthy Gardener leaned back and gazed off into the distance. "You know, Jimmy, what you just said—those are words to live by. You're young, and you have the world ahead of you. And all you can ever offer is your best."

Jimmy laughed. "If I fail the test, it won't be from lack of trying. I can accept being stupid, but I can't live with being lazy."

The Wealthy Gardener looked thoughtful. "I don't doubt you, but isn't it interesting that everybody claims to give their best effort?"

"What do you mean?"

"I bet everyone who takes the test will claim they gave their best," said the Wealthy Gardener, "but not everyone studied the same number of hours. And those hours weren't spent studying with equal intensity. It's the same thing you'll encounter at your work. Everybody is busy. But the best people not only put in more hours, they put in *better* hours. Our best effort is both the quality and quantity of the hours we give to our goals."

"I could have done no more," Jimmy said, "but now I have to pass this one test. If I don't clear this first hurdle, nothing else matters."

"You'll do just fine."

"Well, it's out of my hands," Jimmy said, shrugging. "At this point, it is what it is. I've done my best, and that's all I can do. It's time for the test."

"I admire your mind-set," said the Wealthy Gardener. "What you feel right now, always make that a part of your life. Find that sacred effort again and again—that work in which you give your soul and know that you could have done no more. You'll then know an inner satisfaction that transcends any subsequent outcome."

A SACRED EFFORT is an ultimate exertion at the edge of one's capacity. It's our fullest potential expressed through deep exertion. Uncommon efforts assure satisfaction, while common efforts lead to regrets.

When Abraham Lincoln finished writing his second inaugural address, he believed the speech was possibly his best one ever, topping even the Gettysburg Address. He expected it to "wear as well as—perhaps better than—anything" he had produced. In the crowd the day Lincoln delivered the address was a man named Frederick Douglass, a former slave. Douglass had been invited into the White House after the speech. A black man in a sea of white faces, he described the scene:

As I approached [Lincoln] he reached out his hand, gave me a cordial shake, and said: "Douglass, I saw you in the crowd today listening to my inaugural address. There is no man's opinion that I value more than yours: what do you think of it?" I said: "Mr. Lincoln, I cannot stop here to talk with you, as there are thousands waiting to shake you by the hand"; but he said again: "What did you think of it?" I said: "Mr. Lincoln, it was a *sacred effort* [italics added]," and then I walked off. "I am glad you liked it," he said. That was the last time I saw him to speak with him.

We all know a time when we wanted something so dearly that we put our souls into the struggle for it. We might even say that we gave our life for it. A sacred effort is the ultimate exertion of one's fullest potential.

We see it in a medical student who works to exhaustion, an athlete who strains in the off-season, a manager who meets an impossible deadline, or parents who selflessly give their lives to their children for decades. The result of these sacred efforts is always the same: calm reassurance that nothing more could have been done. This assurance is the measure, and the reward, of striving to our full capacities.

"Satisfaction lies in the effort, not in the attainment. Full effort is full victory," stated Mahatma Gandhi. "I am seeking, I am striving, I am in it with all my heart," said Vincent van Gogh. Andrew Carnegie advised, "Do not look for approval except for the consciousness of doing your best."

This approval comes from the inner wisdom.

Sacred effort involves deep immersion and absorption, work that is challenging and at the edge of our capacity—we almost aren't smart enough, we almost aren't strong enough. It requires disciplined intensity, the exertion of many long hours. It rewards each day with the knowledge that it was a full day, and it often requires fortitude to endure the strain and stretch ourselves.

Our everyday best efforts may contain a sprinkling of these ingredients, but if we were told to "try harder" with a gun to our temple, we could reach deeper and give more. If the same demand was posed during a sacred effort, we would be powerless to improve. We'd take the bullet. We'd have no choice.

A sacred effort is notable when we can say, "I've done my part, and I could have done no more, and now it's in the hands of Fate." We may never like flunking a test. We won't enjoy missing out on a promotion. We're never going to like seeing our work criticized and disparaged. But somehow these shortcomings are more palatable when we have given a sacred effort. Only after we've offered it all to the work, without holding anything back, can we accept disappointment with dignity, grace, and calm acquiescence. I believe in a sacred effort formula:

Impact = right actions (work) × right intensity (effort) + right quantity (hours)

In other words, it's doing the right things in the hours, trying hard in the hours, and giving a whole lot of hours. A sacred effort causes the soul to bleed. What mattered most to me was looking back at my years with satisfaction, knowing that I had nothing left in me to offer to my dreams—I had given it all. I wanted to be proud of my body of work. I wanted it to please me. And now I'm thankful it does.

"To have striven, to have made an effort, to have been true to certain ideals—this alone is worth the struggle," expressed William Osler. We can only give a sacred effort in the time we're given. "It is by spending oneself that one becomes rich," said Sarah Bernhardt. It is only our common efforts that lead to our future regrets.

THE LIFE LESSON: SACRED EFFORT

I found that my best effort assured satisfaction,
And anything less left me vulnerable to regrets.

LESSON 4-21 · MONEY GOALS

Money goal: A clear aim for earned income, savings,
possessions, and/or passive income.

We learn from our gardens to deal with the most urgent
question of the time: How much is enough?

WENDELL BERRY

The average person with clear goals, the Wealthy Gardener believed,
can outperform the most gifted person with no definite chief aim. We
leave our wealth to chance by failing to set financial goals.

Jimmy sat with his mentor on a bench under a mature oak tree. It was
two days after the exam, and the Wealthy Gardener had noted a brooding attitude in his young friend. Jimmy had passed the exam, but seemed
unenthused about the achievement.

"The way I see it," Jimmy said, "all I achieved is the opportunity to
prove myself in the world. I passed the test, but now I see that my income
relies on chance. It seems like rookie agents just sit in the office waiting
for the phone to ring with a new lead."

So that was what the brooding was all about. The Wealthy Gardener
thought about this. Jimmy was trying to figure out every step of his success in advance. He was stuck on the obstacles in the way of making
money. He wasn't trusting the magical power of goals.

"Let me ask you a question," said the Wealthy Gardener. "I'd wager
my recent loan that you now see real estate signs in yards, on cars, on
billboards, and on buildings. I bet you see signs everywhere."

Jimmy looked startled. "How did you know?"

"It's our nature to see what we're thinking about," he explained.
"Those signs were there all along, of course, but they were invisible to
you. It's the same when you buy a car. You then see the same make and

model everywhere. And the same principle applies to money," he continued. "If you hold in your mind an amount of wealth, you'll begin to see opportunities that were there all along. It may take months or even years, but you will find the means to get it. Ideas and plans will always materialize due to your goals."

"But I have real obstacles," Jimmy snapped. "I'll begin as a part-time real estate agent, and I'll be competing against full-time pros. And I'll be working on a commission of about one percent of every sale."

"It's plain to see that you're trying to figure out the *how*, when your top priority should be building your faith," said the Wealthy Gardener. "Goals are to be trusted, not questioned."

"Is it wrong to formulate a plan?"

"It's not wrong," said the Wealthy Gardener. "But you're trusting the obstacles—not the possibilities. How's that working out for you?"

Jimmy raised an eyebrow. "Not so good yet."

"You are not appreciating the true power of goals," the Wealthy Gardener continued calmly. "Goals are not for the ordinary challenges of life; we only need a checklist for those things. Goals are for extraordinary dreams we can't achieve from our current position. Goals invoke an inner wisdom we will never fully comprehend. Goals open doors to unreasonable possibilities."

"Are you talking about the law of attraction?"

"Call it what you want, but what good is an archer without a target?" asked the Wealthy Gardener. "Goals clarify life, and they illuminate opportunities that are otherwise invisible—like those signs you see everywhere. They also provide criteria for your many decisions. And most important of all, goals can even cause coincidences to show up according to your faith."

Jimmy sighed. "So what do you want me to do?"

"The only way to leave your income to chance," the Wealthy Gardener said, "is by failing to set a goal for it. Decide exactly how much money you desire and why you want it, and focus on that daily. If you can imagine this money with absolute faith that you will have it, and if you can maintain this mind-set for as long as it takes, then everything else will work out. You'll be guided by your inner wisdom."

A MONEY GOAL is a clear aim for earned income, savings, possessions, and/or passive income. We leave wealth to chance when we fail to set goals. Why is it so hard to live with a definite goal for money?

"Money is better than poverty," joked Woody Allen, "if only for financial reasons."

At the age of thirty, I set specific financial goals with completion dates for their attainment. My ambitious goal was financial freedom, which was quite audacious at a time when my net worth was zero.

I even wrote out a fantasy check with a multi-six-figure number on it, representing the passive income I planned to have one day. I stuck it on a vision board with other images of my goals for the future. I didn't dwell on this fantasy check. But I'd see it in passing, and it surely entered my subconscious thoughts.

What happened after I committed myself to my goals? Nothing, for a long while. Just as it takes a ship at sea a long time to change its course, so, too, does it take time to change our direction in life. It requires persistence to develop faith in our financial goals.

And we don't always need to be perfect about reviewing our goals.

In my thirties, I struggled continually to establish the habit of reviewing my financial goals. There were times when, without consciously quitting, I just mindlessly stopped doing it for no good reason. But there was a string of years when I got it right, when I stayed focused daily, and that is when I saw the magic of goals.

"The victory of success is half won when one gains the habit of setting goals and achieving them," said Og Mandino. Once a goal takes root in the mind and we gain faith surrounding its attainment, the world slowly changes—and coincidences show up.

As the weeks turned into years, my daily review of financial goals crystallized into a habit. And finally a day came when I sat in a chair, facing that vision board, and I realized the awesome power of having goals.

I had met with my accountant that day to reconcile my business finances for tax purposes. I sat in a chair and my eyes drifted to the fantasy check on my vision board, the one I had written decades earlier to represent my passive income goal.

When I was dead broke, I had written a multi-six-figure number on the check.

Now my actual income was within a hundred dollars of that number!

I could only stare in awe. What were the statistical odds? Was it a miracle? Or was it the outcome of a natural law, an Unseen Force that works if only we master deep concentration and faith?

We leave our finances to fate if we fail to set money goals. Our definite chief aim is the mental clarity that precedes all strategic plans, key decisions, and subsequent actions. It is the start of directing the inner wisdom that's available to those who will pause to listen.

Goals are not for the ordinary challenges of life; we only need a checklist for those things. Goals are for extraordinary dreams we can't achieve from our current position. Goals invoke an inner wisdom we will never fully comprehend. Goals open doors to unreasonable possibilities.

"An average person with average talent, ambition and education can outstrip the most brilliant genius in our society, if that person has clear, focused goals," said Brian Tracy. My story is proof of this truth. For me, goals led to good decisions. They led to clarity. They led to best actions and concentrated efforts. And goals backed by faith led to the illumination of opportunities that were previously unnoticed.

THE LIFE LESSON: MONEY GOALS

I learned that a daily review of money goals was magical,
And attuned me to opportunities that were previously unseen.

LESSON 4-22 · SCHEDULE

Schedule: A plan for our hours.

A day is Eternity's seed, and we are its Gardeners.

ERIKA HARRIS

If time is the stuff of life, considered the Wealthy Gardener, then life is determined by our schedules. Both prosperity and scarcity grow from the seeds of the passing hours.

Jared's dark hair was disheveled, his complexion ashen, and his brain foggy when the Wealthy Gardener arrived in the morning to pick him up from jail. He had been arrested on a DUI charge the night before. They rode in silence, and Jared sheepishly got out of the truck when they stopped in front of his rented duplex.

The Wealthy Gardener sighed as he drove away, deep in thought.

Jared had claimed he wanted more out of life, the Wealthy Gardener reminisced, but his actions told another story. He lived with his new girlfriend, drank at the bars, and was growing comfortable with the ordinary routines of life. He wasn't choosing to lose—he just wasn't choosing *anything*. Sometimes we can't save people from themselves.

By noon, the Wealthy Gardener was in his backyard on his hands and knees, pulling weeds. Jared approached from the other side of the fence.

"Can we talk?"

"Of course," said the Wealthy Gardener, slowly standing up. They walked to a pair of chairs and sat down together. "Would you like a strong cocktail?"

"Very funny. I want to thank you for picking me up."

The Wealthy Gardener sighed. "Don't thank me. Your parents are out of town, and I only picked you up as a favor to them."

"You think I'm a screw-up, don't you?"

"I've known you since you were a child, Jared, and I've always believed in you. But I fear that you are off track. Your potential is being
wasted due to how you spend your time. One day you may wake up with
nothing to show for the years."

"According to you," Jared said, "each tree grows at its own pace."

"That may be so," said the Wealthy Gardener, "but a tree grows naturally without having to make any decisions. You, on the other hand, have
free will. Your potential depends on how you engage your time. And your
time, it seems, suggests that you have no clear purpose other than paying
your bills."

"Why would you say that?"

"Your actions reveal you. Show me your weekly schedule, and I'll tell
you what you care about most in life. With just a glance at your schedule,
I can predict your future. The hours of today are a forecast of tomorrow."

Jared's head was whirling from the hangover, and he couldn't think of
a cogent response to defend his recent aimlessness. He couldn't deny
that he was trapped by his conditions. And his living expenses rendered
him powerless.

"I'm doing the best I can," he said at last. "I know what I want, but I
don't have the time at this moment to get ahead. My days are filled to the
max."

"Your days may be filled, but you still have no direction," the Wealthy
Gardener countered. "You're like a farmer who works to eat for just one
week. A wise farmer schedules his days so full that his actions lead to an
abundant fall harvest."

Jared shook his head. "My problem is my lack of time!"

"Well, you are plain out of luck," said the Wealthy Gardener. "We all
have the same hours. If you can't control your schedule, you can't control
your life. And if you can't make time, you need to surrender your hopes."

"Now you think I'm hopeless?"

"This I know for sure," said the Wealthy Gardener. "If you can't control your time, you'll never control your conditions. And worse, you'll waste your potential. Hours are the building blocks of life, and unremarkable lives are built on unremarkable hours. It's just that simple."

A SCHEDULE is a plan for our hours. Prosperity grows from the seeds of scheduled hours. Financial distress grows from unscheduled hours. If change is wanted, we must change our weekly schedule.

Once, when I was in my forties, I was staying at a friend's house on vacation. I had finished swimming and was sitting on a stone patio overlooking the lap pool, immersed in my phone. The owner of the house asked what I was doing.

"I'm figuring out my life," I answered. By that, I meant I was shuffling around the hours in my weekly schedule. Readjusting my schedule—my work hours and my free hours—was my perpetual attempt to regain control over my life. It seemed my upward climb required constant change.

"Let me know how that goes!" he said, laughing as he walked away.

Wasting time with nothing to do is not the challenge ambitious people face in adult life. Rather, the challenge comes from doing so many mindless things that there is no time left for important things. It's the constant whirlwind of life that occupies all hours. We fail our potential if we can't focus our efforts with a schedule.

"The highest value in life is found in the stewardship of time," said Robert M. Fine. Emerson told us, "To live the greatest number of good hours is wisdom." And Robert R. Shannon said, "Wasted time means wasted lives."

In the book *Grit*, Angela Duckworth introduced a novel formula for achievement:

Talent × effort = skill
Skill × effort = achievement

She advises readers to notice that in this formula, to get from talent to achievement, our effort factors in twice. As Duckworth writes: "Our potential is one thing. What we do with it is quite another."

What we do with our potential is directed by our daily schedule.

A plan of action is where the rubber meets the road in amassing wealth. We don't always get what we want in life. We don't achieve financial dreams because we have special abilities, charm, or brilliance. We don't gain prosperity because we have clarity of goals. We get only what we earn in our days. We reap what we sow.

It takes time to become a success, but time is mostly what it takes.

As a landlord, I see hundreds of tenants waging their middle-class financial struggles to get ahead. Though I have strict minimum income and credit score standards for renters, there is a wide disparity in financial directions among my top renters. Some tenants rent forever, while others eventually buy their own homes. Income level, more than any other factor, determines upward mobility. Some jobs are more valuable to the marketplace, and therefore two people working the same number of hours can find themselves in dissimilar financial situations.

I can predict which renters will be "moving up in life" by how they use their free time. I once rented a unit in a duplex to a young husband and wife who were both working minimum-wage jobs. But they were also attending classes at a local community college. They were eager toward life, and they sacrificed many "normal" activities to make time for their ambitions. Of course, within a few years, they had earned degrees that qualified them for higher wages. After five years, their combined family income had increased from $30,000 to $84,000.

A middle-aged couple with combined salaries of $45,000 lived in the same duplex. For extra money, the woman worked overtime hours while the man ran a part-time lawn care business. From their extra efforts, they earned $15,000 more per year, for a combined total of $60,000. They spent all of it to make ends meet. After five years, this couple was no better off financially, despite their sacrifices and efforts. They thought life was unfair because they worked just as hard as higher earners, but their lifestyle never improved.

Study these examples and discover the key to upward mobility.

"Lack of direction, not lack of time, is the problem," said Zig Ziglar. "We all have twenty-four hours a day." Charles Darwin told us, "A man who dares to waste one hour of time has not discovered the value of life."

It takes time to become a success, but time is mostly what it takes. Our daily schedule determines who we become, what we earn, and how much wealth we can amass in our lifetimes. The hours of today are the forecast of tomorrow.

THE LIFE LESSON: SCHEDULE

I learned that success or failure grew from a schedule,
And I gained direction when my hours were more valuable.

Big why: A purpose that drives sacrifice;
a cause that fuels persistence.

Gardening is a matter of your enthusiasm holding up
until your back gets used to it.

ANONYMOUS

A fast start is nothing without a strong finish. And the accumulation of money, thought the Wealthy Gardener, is the fruition of a strong purpose that endures despite the obstacles.

Jimmy scheduled a meeting to discuss his problem. "The only way you really leave your income to chance," the Wealthy Gardener had said the previous week, "is by failing to set a goal for it. Decide exactly how much money you desire and why you want it, and focus on that daily."

"Why does my reason for wealth matter?" Jimmy now asked.

The Wealthy Gardener leaned back in his chair behind his desk, a merry twinkle in his eye. As always, Jimmy was asking the right questions for his future.

"In your life, you will encounter inevitable adversities and obstacles—the storms of life—in your achievement cycle. Having a *big why* during these times," he said, "allows you to withstand the storms. Your compelling reason for wealth is like the roots of a tree that keep it anchored and ensure its survival despite the weather."

"So having a big reason is about not quitting?"

The Wealthy Gardener chuckled. "The accumulation of paper is nothing. What the paper will do and how it will serve us—that is what sustains the fight. People need a reason to choose wealth over ease. We all wage a daily struggle against resistance. Without a big why, people naturally procrastinate, make excuses, avoid sacrifices, and don't follow through with their plans."

"And so a *big why* assures a strong finish?" Jimmy asked.

The Wealthy Gardener smiled at this. "A *big why* will be the cause of your persistence. A compelling purpose for wealth provides the drive you need to overcome the odds."

"So aim for something more than a big house and a fancy car?"

"It's up to each of us to choose how we spend our justly earned money," he countered. "While I have simpler tastes, if I was motivated to have cars and houses, then I'd surely own them. Who can say what's the wrong use for the earnings of another? Just keep in mind that your reason is your root. Find the deepest root, the one that anchors your work."

"I'd sacrifice anything to earn financial freedom," Jimmy said, "But I don't want to wait until I'm seventy to be financially free. I want it while I'm young."

"And so you've found your root," the Wealthy Gardener said seriously. "What you seek in eight years will require all your waking hours. It will test your courage to risk wisely and repeatedly. And it will demand steady discipline to save money while others spend to gratify their desires. You'll be energized as your bank account grows, but the world won't see it. And you'll be tested with discomforts that sane people would never tolerate. For all these reasons, you must dwell on your *why* to ensure your persistence if you really want wealth."

Jimmy chuckled. "It doesn't sound like too much fun."

"If it's fun you're after, a goal of wealth isn't for you. But if it's freedom you need, the sacrifice is worth it. That's exactly my point: Your fortune is either worth it or not, depending on why you want it."

A BIG WHY is a deep purpose that drives sacrifice, a cause that fuels persistence. Our willpower is fueled by our *why* power. Our reasons for wealth ensure our persistence. Do we work extra hours to pay the bills this month? Or do we work extra hours to build our fortune?

With compelling reasons, we are willing to trade what we want *now* for what we want *most*. The deeper our motives for action, the harder we will work to overcome resistance, avoid excuses, choose sacrifice, build sound plans, and follow through on those plans.

"Great minds have purposes, others have wishes," said Washington Irving. "The more I want to get something done," said Richard Bach, "the less I call it work." Persistence is the expression of a compelling cause—a big why.

"Continuity of purpose is one of the most essential ingredients of happiness in the long run," said Bertrand Russell, "and for most men this comes chiefly through their work."

Great work endures due to great causes.

One of the greatest feats of human endurance were the exploits of Ernest Shackleton and his crew. In 1914 they embarked on the British Imperial Trans-Antarctic Expedition. The expedition intended to cross the Antarctic continent, but when Shackleton's ship *Endurance* became trapped in sea ice, the adventure became a story of survival. The Antarctic ice eventually crushed the ship, leaving its crew to struggle to survive in perilous conditions until they were finally rescued, twenty-one months after the *Endurance* first set sail.

When we closely consider this story, however, we come to see the greatest *why* of all—life or death. These lost explorers could either persist through the hardships or perish in them. Incidentally, not a single member of Shackleton's crew died during the failed expedition.

A deep why sustains mighty actions.

"Nothing can resist a will which will stake even existence on its fulfillment," said Benjamin Disraeli. "If you really want to do something, you'll find a way. If you don't, you'll find an excuse," Jim Rohn told us. "Always bear in mind," said Abraham Lincoln, "that your own resolution to succeed is more important than any other one thing."

But what fuels one's resolution?

After my worst professional adversity, I was resolved to attain financial freedom. I'll detail the story in a later lesson, but for now it is enough to know that I was reduced to the recipient of a decision that could alter my financial condition for life. I faced a nightmare known as a *post-payment audit review* that seemed destined to bankrupt me. Time would vindicate my practice, but the threat to my ability to provide for my family changed me.

During that nasty experience, I gained a huge *why* for amassing money. I vowed to myself that I would never again face such vulnerability, and I learned to give a fuller effort in my quest toward financial independence.

Before this life trial, I had believed I was giving a sacred effort. But after the storm passed, I learned how much deeper I could dig. I learned to give *all* my hours, focus, thoughts, and actions. I vowed to never again be that defenseless. Where people saw persistence, I saw a *very big why*.

I found that wealth requires either willpower or *why* power, and the latter is often the real source of the former. A *big why* pushes us, regardless of our mood, energy, state of mind, or even attitude. A *big why* may be the welfare of a family, paid college education, or freedom from debt. It may be the fear of losing a job, an escape from wage slavery, or the end of financial insecurity.

For me, the storm passed and I earned my freedom. During many long years of persistent effort, I was motivated by a very big why: I wanted to be the decider of my fate, never the one whose fate was decided by others.

This reason was my root. When we lose our why, we often lose our way. "He who has a *why* to live," said Friedrich Nietzsche, "can bear almost any how." A big why will be the fuel of our uncommon persistence.

THE LIFE LESSON: A BIG WHY

* *

I learned that prosperity required uncommon persistence,
But my willpower was assured by my why power.

LESSON 4-24 · GRATITUDE

Gratitude: An intense feeling of appreciation.

In all things of Nature there is something of the
marvelous.

ARISTOTLE

A burning gratitude for future triumph, mused the Wealthy Gardener, is
the silent command that awakens a Sleeping Giant. With gratitude, we
trigger Universal Intelligence to help our cause.

Jimmy sat at a cramped desk assigned to rookies at the real estate firm.
The other agents were gone this evening, and the workplace was vacant
except for a receptionist at the quiet front desk. The phone rang occasionally, but none of the calls were forwarded to him.

To fill the empty hours, he contemplated his financial goals. He had
pondered why he wanted money and had decided he wanted enough to
not have to think about it. Just get the money problem out of life, he
figured, and move on to more important things. His first big step would
be to repay the Wealthy Gardener's generous loan.

In his cubicle, Jimmy closed his eyes and concentrated. He focused on
the emotion of gratitude. He felt himself repaying the loan to his investor. He steeled his mind on this image. More than having money, he
wanted to repay that loan. It was a moment he craved, and he felt it now.
For thirty minutes, he stayed in this state of gratitude while imagining
the experience.

When he opened his eyes, he felt more empowered, assured, and
calm.

He stood and walked past the receptionist on his way to the restroom.
Just then, a young couple walked in the front door. Jimmy had been
warned that it was office policy to stay away from the clients unless

they'd been assigned to him. The receptionist was supposed to dole them out fairly and evenly to all agents.

Jimmy felt an inner wisdom in that moment. On impulse, he turned and held out his hand to the couple. "May I help you?"

"Ah, sure, we're here to start looking for a house—"

"What a coincidence," Jimmy said, smiling. "I happen to show houses."

They laughed, and Jimmy winked at the receptionist behind the counter. She glowered in response, and he led the young couple to his little desk. Surely it was not due to gratitude, he thought as they walked along. But he had been forewarned that he'd feel doubtful when it worked. No, surely this was luck. It was an odd coincidence, he reasoned in a surreal state.

He picked up the phone and paged the receptionist. "Why don't you bring us three coffees?"

He heard a loud clang as the phone slammed down at the front desk.

GRATITUDE: AN INTENSE FEELING of appreciation. With gratitude, we speak the language of Universal Intelligence and ask for an assist—even if our purpose is material wealth.

When things aren't going our way, worrying about money is dangerous. When all seems lost and there's no hope, we must focus with burning gratitude on a successful outcome.

I was trying to obtain the most coveted commercial real estate in the local area where I had my chiropractic practice. It was prime property on the busiest road, and it had previously been under contract four times. In each instance, medical doctors had wanted the building for their private practices. Due to a lack of ample parking in the front, however, the sale of the property always fell through.

The unsolvable problem stemmed from the property being a residential house, zoned commercial, with a front lawn of green grass. The township supervisors required a *green strip*—a twenty-foot barrier of grass along the main road—as curb appeal for passing traffic. But with a new parking lot, a green strip would be impossible, since the property sat too close to the road. Without parking, of course, the building was useless. With ample parking and signage, it was a treasure.

I made an offer with a contingency clause of getting a variance for a parking lot on the green strip. If the city wouldn't budge, I was out of the deal.

By that stage of life, I was devoted to the power of mental disciplines. I wasn't going to try gratitude in the hope that it would work. I was going to use gratitude in full expectation of results, because I'd seen it work in my life—it wasn't a theory. And I would use every advantage, including the power of my mind, to get an optimal result.

I engaged in mental practices in a state of gratitude for this perfect clinic falling into my possession. "Prayers not felt by us are seldom heard by God," said Philip Henry. "We give thanks for unknown blessings already on their way," is a sacred chant of ancient rituals.

Gratitude is an emotion that empowers our prayers.

It's the vibration of thought that seems to influence people, places, and events. Gratitude is an Intangible Force. Things get arranged, it seems, in unfathomable ways. We call it synchronicity or serendipity when life curiously unfolds in harmony with our thoughts of gratitude.

When we are grateful in advance, we take our foot off the brake and move into a dimension of allowing good things to happen. It feels like success is the natural order of things—and it is. We begin to sense that we can attain a plane of higher spiritual consciousness.

And so every day, I cultivated a sense of gratitude for the parking variance and the perfect clinic. The process took several months.

During the long wait, I would go to my sauna daily—my private sanctuary far removed from the physical world—and lose myself in the invisible dimension of thought. I was faithful in feeling confident and imagining the perfect outcome. I'd close my eyes and sense the deepest and richest gratitude for a favorable decision.

One by one, the dominoes began to fall my way. The township supervisors were remarkably friendly people, not a bunch of irrational idiots as I'd been forewarned. Was my gratitude paving the road ahead, turning their minds to favor me? Or was I more intuitively in touch with them due to my daily mental practices? What I knew for sure was that we got along remarkably well. We clicked.

And then a "lucky break" saved my cause.

There was one senior board member who seemed obstinately opposed to my variance request. He was an immovable obstacle. No matter how much I tried to gain his support, he just didn't warm to me.

Months passed, and the rest of the board seemed reluctant to oppose him.

Finally, the evening arrived when the city planners were set to meet and decide on the variance. It was winter, and the snowfall was intense. With my headlights on, I could barely see ten feet ahead of me as I drove to the meeting. The side of the road was indiscernible. I inched along in this unexpected blizzard, arriving fifteen minutes late for the fateful meeting.

Unbeknownst to me, my adversary, the oldest member on the board at the ripe old age of seventy-four, was also straining to see the road as he drove to the meeting. Before making it to the meeting, he understandably decided that it was unsafe for him to drive any farther that night. And so he turned around and went home to the safety of his house.

It's beyond my power to explain serendipity. I can only attest to the fact that coincidences happen at a frequency so consistent that it makes me believe in a causal relationship when I do my part to discipline my mind in gratitude.

You can call it luck, and the weather was indeed fortuitous. You can call it a coincidence or a remarkable fluke. You can say it had nothing to do with feeling gratitude in advance, and you're entitled to your opinion. I've struggled with these same questions myself.

On the one hand, I am certain that I'm not important enough for the universe to whip up a blizzard to help my cause. On the other hand, the timely weather change was a factor in the subsequent outcome.

I can only bear witness to similar "uncanny coincidences" in my life and leave them for study. At this crucial meeting, one seat at the table in the front of the room was empty. The board asked me relevant questions. I answered them with ease. And when the meeting ended, the supervisors voted unanimously in favor of my variance.

What I know for sure is that a deep faith feels like gratitude. Jesus gave us his thoughts on the matter: "Whatever things you desire, when you pray, believe that you receive them, and you shall have them."

THE LIFE LESSON: GRATITUDE

I learned that a burning gratitude for wishes fulfilled,
Awoke a Sleeping Giant that scared me with amazing results.

LESSON 4-25 · CERTITUDE

*Certitude: Absolute faith; a level of confidence that
gives power and magnetism to our goals.*

A garden is a grand teacher. It teaches patience and
careful watchfulness; it teaches industry and thrift;
above all it teaches entire trust.

GERTRUDE JEKYLL

If gratitude opens the door of opportunity, the Wealthy Gardener believed, then certitude kicks it down. If gratitude is the state of mind that works in prayer, then certitude is the state of mind that works in war.

The Wealthy Gardener stood at the lectern with Jimmy sitting behind him, both facing the class at the reform school.

"So the most important mental act for success is . . . ?"

"Set a goal," someone said, "and review it daily."

"Why would a goal in life matter?" asked the Wealthy Gardener.

"To clarify a top purpose," another voice called out.

"To make better decisions," another said.

"To help to prioritize our best actions!"

The Wealthy Gardener beamed. "But once we have the clarity of purpose that isolates our best activities, what do we do about it?"

"Rearrange our schedule," a kid said.

"And why would you do that?"

"To make a plan of actions," the kid replied, "that earn the goals."

"Because goals don't work unless we work," added another boy.

The Wealthy Gardener considered how this classroom now had a vigor that had been nonexistent just a year ago. Only a few rough characters remained among the group. Even Jimmy, who was usually serious and reflective in class, was smiling.

"So after scheduling the hours to earn our big goals," the Wealthy Gardener continued, "what's the next practical step for us to undertake?"

"We put work in those hours and faith in our goals," a boy replied.

"Okay, but how do we build faith in a goal?"

"With burning gratitude," another kid said, "like we already own it."

"That's very good," said the Wealthy Gardener. "And what comes next?"

"Certitude?" asked a boy from the middle of the pack. The classroom laughed, since the word was written on the chalkboard in plain sight:

GOAL: *clarity of intention*
SCHEDULE: *the hours we'll pay*
GRATITUDE: *build your belief*
CERTITUDE: *absolute faith*

"Nice guess," replied the Wealthy Gardener, laughing. "Certitude is the winning mind-set of the day, the first test of your backbone. The first three steps are relatively easy, but not certitude."

"What's so hard about it?" called a crude character from the back of the class. "Just be confident and move people out of your way!"

The Wealthy Gardener was about to respond, but then Jimmy eased up from his chair and walked forward. "I'll take this one," he said steadily.

"Anyone can set and review goals," he said, "but when life starts to slap you—"

"How would you know anything?" the kid interrupted.

"I know because I once sat where you're sitting," Jimmy said flatly, "but I'm now on the outside of these prison walls. Trust me—it's hard to have faith when you carry the demons of your past, and everything you see around you is unlike every dream you have inside you. It's hard to have no doubt when it seems like nothing happens as fast as you want it to, and your impatience leads to frustration. And it's difficult to be confident when you're fighting a voice inside that says, 'You can't do this. You're just a fuckup from a reformatory. You don't deserve success. Go home, your critics were right.' Absolute faith is knowing, in the face of all this, and against a world that opposes you, that you absolutely will not fail!"

As Jimmy finished and returned to his chair, the Wealthy Gardener was speechless.

CERTITUDE IS ABSOLUTE FAITH, a level of confidence that empowers and magnetizes a goal. If gratitude is the state of mind that works in prayer, then certitude is the state of mind that works in battle. Gratitude is faith during peace; certitude is faith during war. Both are mind-sets of the Higher Self.

What exactly is a state of certitude?

Certitude is *knowing*, not believing. It is undiluted faith, a supreme form of consciousness that transcends reality and, at its height of empowerment, imposes its authority. In this state, the odds don't matter. Certitude is an angry stubbornness that won't be denied; it is a certainty, an inevitability of outcome, no matter what. It is a nonnegotiable idea, a foregone conclusion in the mind.

When I first considered buying the commercial property I described in the previous lesson, the events were triggered by an inauspicious start. I was a tenant in an office building that had just been sold; the new owner planned to double the rent, and in desperation, I went scrambling to find any new office space in town.

I used gratitude in my private moments, alone in my sauna and away from the world. I used gratitude in advance for the perfect building, for sellers who'd be open to creative financing, and for all the details working out perfectly. Our gratitude sets events in motion, but our certitude wins the battles during the days.

The odds of obtaining that property were against me.

I met daunting sellers who were agitated by my owner-financing offer. Worse, I faced the threat of a competing bid—an all-cash offer at the full asking price. I endured pesky interactions with city planners, and a fight against a tax reassessment. I also faced skyrocketing expenses that doubled my cost estimates. I saw my cash reserves dwindle. I had key employees quit. In the face of these dire events, my duty was to maintain my certitude that this building was already mine and that everything would be just fine.

An attitude of certitude—tenacious mindfulness that influences people, places, and events—is a common trait of goal achievers.

"Goals are like magnets," said Tony Robbins. "They'll attract the things that make them come true." If goals are magnets, then certitude is the magnetism. It's the invisible force surrounding the goal we hold in mind that attracts the coincidences, cooperation, and lucky breaks.

In the end I asked the seller why she had opted for me instead of choosing the cash offer. "It just seemed like the place was meant for you," she replied.

I thanked the city planners and asked why they had approved the variance for me when they'd denied the same request made by the medical doctors. "It just seemed like you were the right fit for the place," they said curiously.

In the quest to reach our fullest achievements, we become masters of our minds. We grow to be unruffled by adversity, poised under pressure, and steady in the face of doubt. Goal setting is easy, but goal *getting* requires strength. A goal may be claimed by our gratitude, but it's earned by our daily certitude.

Certitude is typified in the words of General Creighton Abrams Jr., who, in the heat of battle, shouted, "They've got us surrounded again, the poor bastards!"

THE LIFE LESSON: CERTITUDE

....

I found that faith required daily vigilance of thought,
And faith was the magnetic force surrounding my goals.

LESSON 4-26 · INTENTION

Intention: One's supreme focus or central purpose.

Your mind is a garden. Your thoughts are the seeds. You
can grow flowers or you can grow weeds.

ANONYMOUS

We control little more than our daily intentions, meditated the Wealthy
Gardener, but intention is the conductor of our wealth affairs. Scarcity
cannot long survive in a mind of rich thoughts.

In his study alone one night, the Wealthy Gardener focused his attention on a binder labeled "Unfinished Business." The private binder contained an assorted collection of his lifelong intentions: the thoughts,
dreams, goals, pursuits, conditions, and experiences he desired in his remaining years.

Using his imagination, he created images to give shape and form to
thoughts and ideas. And then he gave attention to these images as a re-
petitive mental practice. He trusted the power of concentration.

He told every class that attention and intention are the cure of hopelessness. Energy flows where attention goes. We become what we think
about. Hold a goal within you, and everything else will take care of itself.
Within the mind lay the solutions to overcome the worst economic
hardships. Plans emerge from goals wrapped in faith.

He now focused his eyes on one page. In the center, there was a scribbled, hand-drawn etching of a building (the reform school). From the
building, arrows fanned out in every direction. At the end of the arrows
were stick figures (the graduating boys). Each stick figure carried a small
briefcase (their employment). He believed that his mental imagery practices focused his daily intention. And this time alone centered his inner
wisdom on what he wanted most in life.

His eyes returned to the binder, to the drawing of the building with the arrows and the stick figures with their briefcases. The drawing was just a tool to give shape, form, and substance to his thoughts. It represented the young men, like Jimmy, who, despite their tragic pasts, emerged from the school to acclimate successfully to society.

The boys needed economic success to live their fullest lives. They needed to earn money to overcome their disadvantages. He trusted the power of intention to help him find a way to ensure their futures, because this same force had always helped him to realize his dreams in the past.

Long ago, he'd envisioned a hundred-acre farm, and then a 2,000-acre farm. He'd envisioned a winery with vineyards, and these past intentions, held tenaciously, eventually grew into present facts.

His eyes returned to the drawing of the building with the arrows and the stick figures. Every man-made creation we see today, he contemplated, was once a vision held in someone's imagination. Could this drawing be actualized in the real world?

INTENTION: ONE'S SUPREME FOCUS or central purpose. Our daily intention—the longings that dominate our waking hours—is the conductor of wealth affairs. And an inner wisdom emerges from inner vision.

In my forties, I finished three house renovations, but each one lost money, resulting in the worst stretch of my investing career. After nine months of sacrificing my free time and risking great sums of money, I didn't even break even. I was tempted to feel pity as the victim of misfortune due to setbacks that devoured my profits.

To make matters worse, the next project was a house that my crew had dubbed "the *Titanic*," a label that arose from its condition—we would have to raise this one off the bottom. I'd bought it for a pittance while working on other houses, but now the time had arrived to face it. After the defeat of the previous three projects, I sat in that house alone, and mental despair overwhelmed me.

There are times when we face hardship and know that the only way out of our misery is through our problems. We just can't retreat. This house was a dilapidated combination of everything I had encountered in all my previous years of renovating fixer-uppers. It would test not only my accumulated knowledge but also my strength of mind.

In solitude, facing this intimidating rehab job after three unsuccessful projects, I focused on the one thing under my control—my daily power of intention. I opened a notebook and wrote a description of the finished house:

Three-bedroom ranch, three ceramic tile showers, amazing new kitchen and island with granite countertop, Jacuzzi, new roof with skylights, new hardwood floors, new plumbing and electrical, new furnace and gas fireplaces, outdoor whirlpool, new stone patio, new windows—all new EVERYTHING!

I created this written description to shape future reality.

"Vision is the art of seeing things invisible," said Jonathan Swift. And somehow our attention on things invisible leads to their future realization.

The description went into a notebook beside pictures of the most extraordinary bathrooms, kitchens, and home layouts I could find. I aimed to turn this dilapidated mess into a luxury house. I was using the power of intention to overcome this unprecedented challenge.

"All things are created twice," said Stephen R. Covey. "There's a mental or first creation, and a physical or second creation, to all things." Robin Sharma echoes this: "Everything is created twice, first in the mind and then in reality."

The power of intention is directing the energy of a human mind on things yet unseen in the physical world. "You can only see one thing clearly, and that is your goal," says Kathleen Norris. "Form a mental vision of that and cling to it through thick and thin."

During the *Titanic* renovation project, the obstacles felt insurmountable. Alone in that house at night, I shed private tears of frustration and exhaustion.

At times I knew that I was in over my head. I was not equal to this one. But every night, I refocused my attention back on the notebook containing my intention. I returned to the vision of my dreams.

Before bed, the collage of pictures and images sustained me, maintained me, fueled me, and drove me. I learned that during our most soul-crushing hardships, a vision inspires the work and energy needed to overcome great odds. Due to my intention, an inner wisdom emerged that prodded me to press on and finish strong.

After six months, the immense project was finished, but had come in overbudget. It went on the market, and I asked for the highest end of the price range. Nothing happened. Two weeks went by, and then a month. Still nothing. But then I remembered the most basic lesson of so many of my past successes: When I felt gratitude for future results, lucky breaks showed up.

I took home one of my promotional flyers for the house and pinned it to the sauna wall. With a bold red marker, I wrote *S-O-L-D* on the flyer. And then I gave my daily attention to this final intention to attract the perfect buyer. Within two weeks, I had multiple offers on the house. In the end it sold for a $50,000 profit, which had been my exact profit goal.

Focus on the end, cling to your ideal outcome through thick and thin, and concentrate your attention. James Allen had it right when he said, "Dream lofty dreams, and as you dream, so shall you become. Your vision is the promise of what you shall . . . at last unveil."

THE LIFE LESSON: INTENTION

I found that I controlled little more than daily intention,
But discovered that intention was the conductor of wealth.

LESSON 4-27 · MEDITATION

Meditation: Deep awareness in solitude.

There is always Music amongst the trees in the Garden,
but our hearts must be very quiet to hear it.

MINNIE AUMONIER

Meditation is most needed by those lacking time, thought the Wealthy Gardener, for a demanding life requires daily renewal. In the stillness, we regain our center and our strength.

For two months, Fred had avoided his unfulfilled dream by staying overly busy. And tonight the two old friends were once again playing cards together. The Wealthy Gardener had resolved to stop pressing Fred about his lifelong dream. We each choose, or neglect to choose, our own destiny.

"So the new youth pastor," Fred said candidly, picking up a card, "is teaching our kids about prayer. And at the end of the class, the pastor told them to sit in the presence of God. The kids were dead silent for maybe fifteen minutes. To be honest, it's difficult for me to sit quietly that long," he said. "I feel like jumping out of my skin!"

They both laughed as Fred discarded onto the pile.

"I know what you mean," said the Wealthy Gardener, staring at his cards. "When Mary died, I was a bit screwed up inside. And I used to dread being alone. I had to have noise, motion, always something going on. Stillness was unbearable to me."

Fred rearranged his cards. "But now you can handle it?"

"I'll tell you what I learned, Fred," said the Wealthy Gardener. "The more I hated the silence, the more I needed it. The more I dreaded stillness, the more I needed to stop moving. I was evading my problems by staying in motion and in the noise. I finally took up meditation to regain my peace."

Fred raised an eyebrow. "I never knew you meditated."

"I started after Mary's death. But then I saw how it benefited me in other ways. Before I practiced meditation, my life was successful," admitted the Wealthy Gardener, "but I'm more effective with it. I don't claim to know why, but my days are better after meditation. It does something, and now I welcome the silence. There's guidance for our actions in the stillness."

"By sitting still and thinking of nothing?"

The Wealthy Gardener laid a card on the pile. "Your youth pastor may call it sitting in the presence of God, but my personal meditation is not quite the same. I direct my mind, and I sit in the presence of my intentions. At times I also sit in the presence of my frustrations," he admitted. "And I can meditate on walks, too. For me, it's a daily practice of gratitude. If nothing else, it gets me in sync with the day."

"I try to quiet my mind," Fred said, "and I feel restless as hell."

"I felt that way, too, and that's when I needed it most. I was a mess inside, but meditation was my medicine. In the silence I confronted my worries, stresses, emotions, and problems. And I can tell you, it wasn't always fun."

"No wonder I run from silence," Fred said, laughing.

The Wealthy Gardener only grinned as he studied his friend. What he wanted to say, but couldn't, was that meditation was exactly what Fred needed. It would remove him from the distraction of motion, introduce him to his own inner wisdom, and maybe help him get unstuck.

MEDITATION IS THE PRACTICE of deep awareness. I took up meditation to restore my depleted batteries. The daily pace of work was unsustainable. I'd been consistently working sixteen-hour days.

"Your phone has a charger, right?" asks Jerry Seinfeld. "It's like having a charger for your whole body and mind. That's what [transcendental] meditation is!"

You may argue that during this stretch of sixteen-hour workdays, I needed to work less, but my intention was financial freedom, a reward that is not earned by working less. I didn't need advice to stop burning the candle at both ends; I needed more wax. I was running multiple small businesses and the daily stress was beating me down.

In the past I had tried meditation without committing to it. I'd never made it a daily ritual because I had no extra time to waste. To do nothing seemed to be a luxury for the rich. And truth be told, meditation led to uneasiness. Why should a striving individual want to be still?

I was about to find out.

"Prayer does not change God, but it changes him who prays," said Søren Kierkegaard. "Meditation is a mental discipline that enables us to do one thing at a time," said Max Picard. And Russell Simmons said, "When you focus on repeating that mantra over and over again, soon the noise will die down and all you will hear is your inner voice."

I learned that in silence, we sense our inner wisdom.

When I meditated daily, I became sensitive to business issues that had been calling for my attention. I needed to change key employees. I needed to rearrange my schedule to give more time to one business versus another. I needed to communicate better to gain the support of my family and employees. I needed to slow down and focus. I needed to consider my instincts, intuition, and silent pulls. I needed to maintain my poise under pressure. These imbalances caused my inner voice to scream with discomfort in the quiet stillness.

Within a year, due to a new sense of awareness, I fixed these imbalances. I changed the conditions that caused my restless mind. When a mind is directed, all sorts of marvels are possible. And my life became a match of my chosen intentions. I didn't ignore the stress of everyday life, but used meditation as a tool to navigate through it.

I also experienced greater awareness after meditation. It seems we all fight a *monkey mind*—a Buddhist term referring to a state of restlessness and confusion—that resists deeper awareness, but with mastery, we can find inner guidance. We'll feel equanimity and deeper insights.

"If you just sit and observe, you will see how restless your mind is," said Steve Jobs. "If you try to calm it, it only makes it worse, but over time it does calm, and when it does, there's room to hear more subtle things—that's when your intuition starts to blossom and you start to see things more clearly and be in the present more." Jobs continued, "Your mind just slows down, and you see a tremendous expanse in the moment. You see so much more than you could see before." His favorite book was a mystical one: *Autobiography of a Yogi*.

Ray Dalio once said:

> I think meditation has been the single biggest reason for whatever success I've had . . . I can be stressed, or tired, and I can go into meditation and it all just flows out of me. I'll come out refreshed and centered . . . Meditation helps you stay in a calm, clear-headed state so that when challenges come at you, you can deal with them like a ninja—in a calm thoughtful way. When you're centered, your emotions are not hijacking you.

Meditation kept me sane during stressful times. Now when time is moving too fast, I increase meditation to slow down the clock. Time shouldn't fly—if it does, that's a sign of lazy mindlessness.

As Deepak Chopra explains, "Meditation is not a way of making your mind quiet. It is a way of entering into the quiet that is already there—buried under the fifty thousand thoughts the average person thinks every day."

THE LIFE LESSON: MEDITATION

I started meditation as a way to recharge my batteries,
But found equanimity and wisdom lurking in the silence.

LESSON 4-28 · MINDFULNESS

Mindfulness: Attention on the present; keen awareness on the here and now.

In order to live off a garden, you practically have to live in it.

KIN HUBBARD

Mindfulness aids the striver due to concentration of thought and energy, mused the Wealthy Gardener. Little good comes from prayers at night if we can't control our thoughts during the day.

It was harvest season, the time at a farm when the rewards of the year's efforts are gathered, measured, weighed, sold, and shipped. In so many ways, the fall harvest is the product of the human spirit devoted to an outcome, working in harmony with the Universal Intelligence that operates behind the scenes to make the crops grow. Since the spring, a farmer's every act is done with mindfulness of the harvest.

The Wealthy Gardener pondered this idea as he strolled to the neighboring farm to check up on his old friend Santos. He thought Santos's farm was in fine shape, but the man appeared to be working himself into the ground every day from sunup until sundown.

"How are you holding up?" asked the Wealthy Gardener, taking a seat in the farm's tiny office before the start of another workday.

"Never felt better," Santos answered. "Why do you ask?"

"I once worried if you could handle this farm," admitted the Wealthy Gardener. "I see now that your dedication is extraordinary, and it will ensure your continued prosperity. How in the world do you do it at your age?"

"Am I supposed to relax at my age?" Santos laughed. "I've never felt more alive in my life, and I have no plans of slowing down now!"

The Wealthy Gardener smiled in response. This man slaved day and night doing work that few others would find desirable, and yet he seemed energized as he spoke of it. And then, conversely, there was Fred, stuck in a rut of dull lassitude due to his chronic indecision.

"You do seem happy," commented the Wealthy Gardener.

"I don't even think about it," countered Santos. "Show me a person whose chief aim is happiness, and I'll show you an unhappy person getting nothing done! But show me a person who gets things done, and I'll show you a person who knows satisfaction. We're happier when we're busy and focused on getting something we want out of our days."

"Then how do you explain so many unhappy hard workers?"

"I'll tell you what I think is true," Santos said. "It's because they have no purpose. Work can be heaven or hell based on why we think we're doing it. I sweat under the smoldering sun, but I don't suffer when I think of the harvest and what it means for my family."

"That's a mighty big idea," replied the Wealthy Gardener. "So it's the focus during the plowing that determines the day's suffering."

"We all choose how we view work," Santos agreed. "I see kids start at the farm without any work experience. What do they do? They dwell on the drudgery of work. They suffer from self-pity, and it causes exhaustion in their bones."

"What do you advise them to do?"

Santos chuckled. "I tell them to suck it up and grow a set!"

"And when that doesn't do the trick?"

"I tell them to focus on one task at a time," Santos said, "and if they ever get tired, then focus on why they're doing the work in front of them. With more focus, they can do their best work, and they also forget to be miserable. And I tell them to be grateful for the day."

MINDFULNESS IS ATTENTION on the present, awareness on the here and now. I was drawn to mindfulness to focus on one task at a time. In addition, I wanted to maintain a state of wealth consciousness—a feeling of calm gratitude for, and assurance of, my impending prosperity.

Mindfulness was integral to the peak years of my work activity. At the clinic, the daily appointment book was full; a ten-hour blitz was the standard day. Once the day began, there was no time for breaks. This schedule was my six-days-a-week routine for years without interruption. During this era of my life, I learned, and relied upon, the power of mindfulness to maintain my output with a positive attitude every day.

Mindfulness helped my daily productivity.

In the morning I would often ask the staff and massage therapists at the clinic if they knew how many patients we would be seeing that day. They would answer with a number of scheduled appointments but then realize, by my expression, that they had fallen for a trick question.

"No, you're wrong," I'd correct them. "Today we are seeing just *one*." Of course, they knew I meant we would be seeing one patient at a time. We survived hectic and endless workdays by being present and focusing on one patient, one task, and one moment at a time.

This deep concentration on one task at a time was critical to daily productivity, but mindfulness also proved to be a useful tool to maintain wealth consciousness and to connect me with my inner wisdom.

A state of wealth consciousness is a feeling of success with certainty of prosperity. Riches grow from rich thoughts. "A man's life is what his thoughts make of it," said Marcus Aurelius.

Wealth consciousness is being in a state of wealth. "A man is literally what he thinks," said James Allen. "A man is what he thinks about all day long," Emerson agreed. I tried to be in a state of wealth.

And ultimately a state of mindfulness connects us to the inner wisdom available at odd moments in every chaotic day. Instead of reacting, we can pause for wisdom. Instead of replying quickly, we can pause for insight. Instead of choosing quickly, we can pause for guidance. If we are mindful to pause for a few seconds, we can consult an inner wisdom that is available to those who seek it.

"Mindfulness isn't difficult," Sharon Salzberg said, "we just need to remember to do it." Wealth consciousness is the first step; it is disciplined self-regulation. Some have used the phrase "act as if" to describe this state of being. The second step of mindfulness is remembering to consult the inner voice that can improve our choices.

Fortunately, life has subtle ways of reminding us when we're being mindless; we lose our keys, we can't remember things, we speak and regret our words, time seems to pass quickly, and we get easily distracted. Signs of mindlessness remind us to focus on now.

Mindfulness of one task at a time—one thought, one action, one breath—is a form of absorption that tends to transcend suffering and generate our most sacred efforts. We are at our best when we are dialed in, turned on, focused deeply, lost in each passing moment.

"If you want to hit a bird on the wing," said Oliver Wendell Holmes Jr., "you must have all your will in focus, you must not be thinking about yourself and, equally, you must not be thinking about your neighbor: you must be living *in your eye on that bird* [italics added]. Every achievement is a bird on the wing."

When we are mindful, our eye is on the bird. And then miracles happen through inspirations due to immersed concentration.

Make wealth your dominant thought and then listen.

THE LIFE LESSON: MINDFULNESS

* *

I learned to regulate my daily consciousness,
And to live each moment with gratitude for wealth.

LESSON 4-29 · RETREAT

Retreat: A period of seclusion, especially for contemplation;
a temporary withdrawal from the demands of life.

My spirit was lifted and my soul nourished by my time
in the garden. It gave me a calm connection with all of
life, and an awareness that remains with me now, long
after leaving the garden.

NANCY ROSS HUGO

The best plans unfold in uncompressed times, thought the Wealthy Gardener. The inner wisdom found on retreats occurs when the mind can expand, revitalize, and regain a detached perspective.

The twenty boys were gathered around a campfire at the edge of the farm's property for the annual Eagle's Club retreat. Tents and sleeping bags had been set up during the day, and now the kids were relaxed and in high spirits. Two security guards from the school served as supervisors.

The boys from the reformatory saw this weekend as a temporary jailbreak, but the Wealthy Gardener viewed it as an opportunity to teach these kids how to really dream about what they wanted in their lives. Every year, this weekend was crammed full of learning, and it always culminated with a Sunday gathering when former students of the reformatory returned to speak about their lives and goals.

"And when these two days are over," said the Wealthy Gardener, looking around at the faces lit by the flickering flames, "my hope is that we've used this time to think. By this I mean that we've reflected deeply on what we want most in our lives, and why we want it. We'll use our time here to dream."

There was a moment of silence as the fire sparked and the kids seemed to ponder his words. "We are all gardeners," he said, "just trying to shape the land we're given."

"I have a question," said one of the boys. "There's a rumor that after this weekend, you usually disappear for a few weeks. I was told a while ago that you go away every year, but nobody knows what you do."

The Wealthy Gardener chuckled and shook his head. "When this weekend is over, I will leave on a vacation. I go away every year to be by myself."

Jimmy watched the faces of the boys as they studied the older man. He, too, was intrigued by these vacations, yet had never wanted to violate the Wealthy Gardener's privacy.

"What do you do there?" another boy asked.

"I seek uncompressed time," said the Wealthy Gardener, "to get in tune with my inner wisdom, and to reevaluate my direction. I reflect on what I want most in life, and why I want it. When I like my direction, I think about how to improve my effectiveness."

"Why don't you just think at home?"

"Well, I *do* think at home," said the Wealthy Gardener. "I practice thinking alone daily. But there's just something about getting out of the whirlwind that allows the mind to relax, expand, and soar. I think best on a retreat."

Jimmy thought about his own life and how his days were packed full. He made time now for mental practices, but it was getting harder.

"It's said that we often can't see the picture when we're in the frame. We can't see the forest for the trees. These old sayings remind us that it's wise to periodically remove ourselves from the hustle to ponder the bigger picture."

There was a long pause. "So you sit like Yoda by a lake?" a boy asked.

All the kids laughed, and even Jimmy cracked a smile.

"I think about what I want," the Wealthy Gardener said quietly, "and what I don't want. I make lists of places to see, aspirations to fulfill, curiosities to explore. And I also consider my impact on others. Sometimes when I vacation alone, I return energized with a new life direction. But there are times when I spend days just thinking about and solving problems. I'm now trying to figure out how to better help you boys succeed in life. I feel a calling, at this stage of my life, to help you, and I am seeking ways to assist your financial prosperity."

The campfire crackled, and the teens were silent.

A RETREAT is a period of seclusion, especially for contemplation. For three months during the summer between my freshman and sophomore years of college, I worked as a groundskeeper at a lake resort in the mountains. Done at four o'clock each day, I returned to the lonely, isolated cabin I was staying in. I had no friends, no television, no distractions, and many hours. I often sat in front of a campfire beside the lake, all alone.

During that summer, at the age of twenty, I experienced my first retreat. It was a period of serious contemplation, not to be confused with a fun vacation. And it was the best thing that ever happened to me.

A retreat strips away the mundane distractions of life. It removes us from the whirlwind and provides uncompressed time to contemplate life's bigger picture. We see our direction more clearly; there's no hiding behind the frivolous, vapid, superficial engagements that keep us all too busy. On a retreat, we can question life. What do we want? What don't we want? Is our life going in the best direction? What would we change if we could? How can we adjust our course?

A retreat is not always a pleasant escape.

During that summer, I was uncomfortable in my skin and had no clear direction in my life. In moments of solitude beside the lake, life gradually became more authentic and real. I felt desolation in stillness, and I didn't like it. But silence can awaken the soul. When I returned to school that fall, I switched my major and changed my direction with renewed discipline.

"To do much clear thinking," Thomas Edison said, "a person must arrange for regular periods of solitude when they can concentrate and indulge the imagination without distraction." We need time alone to solve the problems that plague our days and, sometimes, to simply ponder the direction of life.

A friend of mine, Tom, was a factory worker whose uncommon habits had always fascinated me. He and his wife would take several vacations each year, just long weekends, to Amish bed-and-breakfast retreats in Ohio. On these getaways, they had no television, radio, or cell phone service.

"What do you do there?" I once asked.

He shrugged. "I sit around and think."

And because Tom thought, he chose his conditions.

Tom saved and amassed his money, and in his free hours, he started a small business. He bought used Camaros, tore them to pieces, and sold the parts for profit. He was captivated by the business, like a kid in a candy store, and eventually retired to do it full time. He envisioned this life on his solitary retreats.

"Most people spend their whole lives climbing the ladder of success," Stephen R. Covey reminds us, "only to realize when they get to the top, the ladder was leaning against the wrong wall." Retreats are times to take a closer look at the ladder and reevaluate the wall.

When I was fifty, my wife and I went on a vacation. On the last day of the trip, we sat on beach chairs, the expansive ocean in front of us, and I watched several picturesque sailboats drift lazily on the horizon. I was deep in thought, contemplating my life and dreading the return to the insane work schedule that awaited me back home.

"What are you thinking at this second?" my wife asked, evidently noticing my reflective disposition.

"I'm wondering," I replied slowly, "what it is about my life that makes me dread returning tomorrow. I don't believe in a life that I want to escape." As I watched the sailboats drifting at sea, she assured me that it was normal to not want to return to the "real world" after a vacation. "Well then," I said quietly, "I don't want *normal*."

This broad-stroke, big-picture, macro-view thinking is most possible in the uncompressed time of periodic retreats. It can be just a weekend spent reviewing goals or an entire week getting away from it all. We need to periodically get out of the whirlwind to think about the whirlwind. We must get out of the frame to repaint the picture.

On that beach, I realized that I no longer wanted to chase a dollar during my remaining years. I had earned my freedom, and I now wanted to use it. I had to begin working on my bucket list. And before the next year was over, I had changed my schedule to allow me forty hours a week to write this book. This is the power of a retreat.

THE LIFE LESSON: RETREAT

I saw that the best plans unfolded in uncompressed times,
And so I went on retreats to contemplate my life.

LESSON 4-30 · SIXTH SENSE

*Sixth sense: A feeling of resonance or discord
after weighing the known facts.*

Let us give Nature a chance; she knows her business
better than we do.

MICHEL DE MONTAIGNE

Best to avoid financial setbacks, pondered the Wealthy Gardener, and
run when something doesn't feel right. Warnings exist in feelings of discord for those who pause and listen to their intuition.

They jogged along a path within the vineyards, but soon the Wealthy
Gardener was breathing hoarsely and moving with slower strides. At the
one-mile mark, he eased to a walk. Jimmy slowed beside him.

"What's wrong with you today?"

The Wealthy Gardener was panting. "I don't feel so good."

As they walked back to the Wealthy Gardener's house, Jimmy recounted his initial months as a real estate agent. He had developed a
system to win the competitive market of expired listings, the houses that
had not sold after a year on the market. After three months, he now had
as many listings as the top agent in the firm. In addition, he had trained
a worker to replace him at Santos's farm, which would allow him to leave
and pursue real estate full time.

"So I have a dilemma," Jimmy said slowly. "I work for a great broker.
He's supportive and encouraging, and seems to like me. But my early
success has attracted better deals from other brokers. One made an offer
to double my commissions if I'd switch to his brokerage firm. My current boss claims he can't match the same terms because it would demor-
alize the others who have been working at his agency for many years."

The Wealthy Gardener was quiet a moment as he sipped his tea. "It's your moment of choice," he said with a curious expression. "What are you going to do?"

"I don't know for sure."

"What's your gut telling you to do?"

Jimmy sighed. "On one hand, I get a bad vibe about leaving. The broker making the offer is arrogant, and I don't like him. On the other hand, I'm not looking for an intimate friendship. I will be doing the same duties, but I'll be paid twice the commissions. I'll also be the top agent getting all the new leads on the phone. I can't ignore the upside of this deal. What do you think?"

The Wealthy Gardener looked upward, drawn by the sound of geese flying south for the winter. "Why do you suppose those birds are flying south?"

Jimmy looked at them. "Instinct?"

"I suppose they can't help themselves. But if you could somehow turn them around to fly north at this time of year, they would feel a sense of discord and agitation, that something isn't quite right. They would feel unsettled if they were made to fly in the wrong direction."

"And this relates to my decision how?"

"You asked for advice, so I'll give it," said the Wealthy Gardener. "Be wary of this lucrative offer. Only a fool ignores their intuition. When you sense a bad feeling about a direction, don't dismiss it as a trivial detail. I've never seen good things happen when one ignores a troubled sixth sense."

Jimmy was surprised. "But the money is double."

"When you consider a path that doesn't feel right in your soul, you proceed at your own peril," said the Wealthy Gardener. "You'll be a goose flying north in hopes of warm weather."

A SIXTH SENSE is a feeling of resonance or discord after weighing the known facts. Our sixth sense can warn us of impending dangers and help us avoid future financial setbacks.

After uprooting my family and moving five hundred miles away from Chicago, I searched for a temporary position in an existing chiropractic practice. I made inquiries, sent out letters, and explored options. An extremely lucrative offer stood out from all the others.

The offer came from a busy clinic that saw a hundred patients every day. I interviewed and was offered the job. The doctor seemed charismatic, was respected in the community, and, on the surface, seemed impressive. People had told me stories of how this man had made house calls to patients in the middle of the night. His offer amounted to twice the salary other clinics were offering, and I was asked to work only three days a week. It was too perfect.

Why did it not feel right?

Over the years, I have learned to consult my inner wisdom for an internal "red light" or "green light." It's the subtle feeling of resonance with a decision—a mild discord or an inner peace surrounding a choice. It's a gut hunch, a deep instinct, a sense that something feels right or wrong.

In this case, the facts were so good that I ignored my warning signs. I failed to pause and heed my inner wisdom. I disregarded the acute sensitivity that something didn't feel "right." This was a big mistake. We all have instincts that can guide us if only we pay attention to them.

During my first month of work, I received a phone call from the chiropractor's wife on a Sunday morning. She told me my new boss was in jail, and she proposed an emergency meeting.

It turns out he'd walked into a pharmacy with a fake prescription for drugs. Two undercover agents had arrested him on the spot. He had been using multiple pharmacies to buy drugs illegally for years, and the federal agents had finally caught up with him. His face was on the local papers' front pages that morning, and I wished I had followed my gut hunch.

I was stuck keeping the clinic afloat, when my original goal had been to be there for less than a year before opening my own practice.

"Trust your hunches," said Dr. Joyce Brothers. "They're usually based on facts filed away just below the conscious level." "Every time I've done something that doesn't feel right, it's ended up not being right," said Mario Cuomo.

In the silence, we sense the warning of future dangers. These warnings are the "red lights" of a troubled sixth sense.

Socrates was always mindful of red lights. He spoke of an "Attendant Force" that he claimed served him throughout life. It didn't always tell him what to do, he said, but it always instructed him what not to do. He saw a sense of discord and disharmony as a warning signal that danger awaited on the path ahead. He felt that a neutral feeling was a sign to proceed without any threat of future danger.

Later in life I faced a real estate investment with intense pressure to buy. The facts suggested a lucrative investment, and the selling agent offered me an exclusive chance to obtain it. Since I'd rejected several of his recent deals, our relationship was shaky.

But something felt wrong. I was not congruent with this obviously profitable deal. For unknown reasons, I didn't resonate with it.

"If it doesn't feel right, don't do it. That is the lesson," advised Oprah Winfrey, "and that lesson alone will save you a lot of grief."

In my life, I'd learned the hard way to pause, think, calculate, and feel my intuition on decisions. "To make the right choices in life, you have to get in touch with your soul," says Deepak Chopra. "To do this, you need to experience solitude . . . because in the silence you hear the truth and know the solutions."

I heeded my inner voice and backed out of the real estate deal. It turned out that the property had previously been home to a gas station. Due to environmental regulations, to resell this house, the underground fuel tanks would need to be removed at an exorbitant cost. And this hidden fact meant I would have lost a ton of money had I gone through with the deal.

We can sense future calamity if we simply pause during our hectic days and listen to our intuition. When we use both our reason and our intuition, it's possible to avoid all financial disasters.

"When something feels off, it is," said Abraham Hicks. Bryant McGill said, "You have permission to walk away from anything that doesn't feel right. Trust your instincts and listen to your inner voice—it's trying to protect you."

THE LIFE LESSON: SIXTH SENSE

I made better choices for upward mobility
By paying attention when something felt wrong.

LESSON 4-31 · DISCONTENTMENT

Discontentment: Frustration with conditions or affairs.

Without hard work, nothing grows but weeds.

GORDON B. HINCKLEY

Unfortunate conditions can break the spirit of many people, mused the Wealthy Gardener, but the winners of prosperity use their aggravations to fuel their advancements.

Jimmy set aside New Year's Day to think expansively about his life direction. Another year had passed, and what did he have to show for it? Did the recent year move him toward his goals? Or did he feel unfulfilled with his progress? How could he improve his condition in the following year? These questions were whirling in his mind.

Looking back, the past year had been dramatic.

He had started the year with an apprenticeship at Santos's farm operation and was now a real estate agent with a track record of success. He was the top listing agent in the area and was even featured in an industry journal as a newcomer to watch. But those listings were not sales, and only house sales pay real estate commissions.

Worse still, upon accepting the lucrative offer at the new agency, his life had become a struggle. The listings from his initial success had stayed in the possession of the previous brokerage due to a clause in the fine print of his contract. When he left, he had to start from scratch to build a new business.

Despite his achievements, he felt discontented with the results. Money was in short supply; his success had translated into scant economic rewards. He wanted financial freedom, but felt only frustration, since this goal seemed out of reach. Amassing wealth felt impossible from his current position.

Jimmy thought of his mentor and how they had not talked in the past two months. He picked up the phone. Thirty minutes later, they were eating ice cream at the Wealthy Gardener's family room table, and he felt the warmth of a crackling log fire.

"So you're unhappy with your life?"

"The top real estate agents in the nation sell about one hundred fifty listings each year," Jimmy said. "Maybe I'll be more satisfied when I reach that level, and maybe I won't. All I know for sure is that right now, I am nowhere near it."

"Why is that number important to you?"

"I want financial freedom," Jimmy answered. "I also believe that I have a potential to fulfill, and I want to see what I can accomplish in my life. If I am going to be working, why not aim to be the best?"

"Why not, indeed?" agreed the Wealthy Gardener. "You are young and blessed with ambition. It's good to be unsettled at your age."

Jimmy laughed. "Most people tell me to just be happy."

"And most people are living far below their potential," scoffed the Wealthy Gardener. "They'll never know the joys of accomplishment. Your discontentment is good and beneficial. It keeps you stirred up so that you use your time. And it can fuel you to do great things."

"Well then," Jimmy said, grinning. "I should be all set for next year. I'm now working for an arrogant jerk who cusses out the other agents. He uses me as an example to show them how worthless they are, and that doesn't help team morale. It's a toxic environment. Plus, our private agency has a huge disadvantage compared to the franchised agencies with name recognition."

"Why not return to your previous agency?"

"I considered it." Jimmy sighed, rubbing his forehead. "But I sense it would be a mistake. I'll struggle where I am, but I'll keep all my options open."

"You'll be fine," said the Wealthy Gardener. "The main thing is that you are now following your inner voice. And your discontentment is good—it will fuel the actions that lead to your success."

. . .

DISCONTENTMENT IS A STATE of frustration or dissatisfaction. I was sitting at an outdoor party beside a recent college graduate who was about to embark on her first job. She was well-spoken on many subjects, and we had an interesting conversation. But she was too firm in her views of work, I silently judged, before having been tested by the rigors of steady employment in the real world.

The conversation turned to my son. "He graduates next year, and he's pretty ambitious," I said. "He has a position waiting at one of the big banks. I suspect he'll have a successful life, and he'll pursue ambitious goals that stretch him."

She chuckled smugly. "So he will never be satisfied."

I chose to remain silent. She wasn't looking for my opinion. What I was thinking but didn't say was, "I sure hope you are right. I hope he's *never* satisfied. I hope he continually knows the thrill of achievement, the elation of pursuit, and the commitment it requires to become successful in this world. I sure hope my son stays fully engaged in his days, choosing and pursuing whatever is most important to him, knowing the pull of ambition and the deep fulfillment of self-actualization. I hope he never settles for less than his potential, and feels the pride of effort that is never known by those who compromise due to complacency. I sure hope he's never satisfied, not until the day—at last—when he has no more strength to offer."

Many other people in my life have echoed the notion that one's chief aim in life should be happiness. "When will you ever be satisfied?" they ask. "Will it ever be enough for you? Why not take it easier? Why work so much? Are you planning to take your money with you? Do you really want to be the richest man in the cemetery?"

For years I blundered through inept responses to defend my ambition for financial freedom. I finally stopped explaining it. I didn't need to make others understand. When I had thirty-two rentals, I wasn't content. I wanted to double that number. When I had $2 million, I wanted $3 million.

Of course, I never disclosed these figures. But it was my ambition, and nobody had to understand me. I was being true to my dream.

And then one day, when someone asked me why I wanted to run three businesses, I heard myself say, "I'm just working to fulfill my potential in life. I think I can do more. I want to see what I can handle."

The questioner seemed oddly placated by this response, and after decades of giving clumsy answers that led to blank stares, I felt understood. The next time I was asked a similar question, I gave the same response. And once more, the person was satisfied.

The drive to succeed and to overcome circumstances is about living at the edge of our fullest capacities. I was using my full potential to actualize a life of freedom.

"We're at our best and our happiest when we're fully engaged, climbing, thinking, planning, working," said Earl Nightingale, "when we're on the road to something we want very much." When we are fulfilling our potential.

And only by getting rid of the silly notion that doing less in our days leads to a better life, or that happiness and pleasure are the chief aims of living, can we come close to a useful existence that makes an impact for the common good during our brief time.

"From the discontent of man," Ella Wheeler Wilcox told us, "the world's best progress springs." Edison agreed: "Restlessness is discontent, and discontent is the first necessity of progress." And Emerson said, "People wish to be settled; only as far as they are unsettled is there any hope for them."

THE LIFE LESSON: DISCONTENTMENT

I accepted economic frustration as an unpleasant ally,
And used it as motivation to earn financial freedom.

LESSON 4-32 · FINANCIAL FEAR

Fear: An emotional response to a real or imaginary
danger, threat, or unwelcome outcome.

One of the worst mistakes you can make as a gardener is
to think you're in charge.

JANET GILLESPIE

Fear of financial calamity can be the greatest motivator, thought the
Wealthy Gardener, and should be used for all it is worth. And sometimes,
it can be worth millions.

Jimmy strolled between the desks at the reformatory for troubled
teens. This was his lecture day, and the Wealthy Gardener now reclined
in a chair, watching the show. Jimmy had a knack for reaching these kids,
perhaps because of his own past mistakes.

"So on the day you get out of here," he said, "you should be scared out
of your minds, if you're smart. You'll need to earn a living, and you'll
need to save money. And fear can help you do it best."

"I want money," joked one of the kids, "without much work."

"I don't blame you," Jimmy said, laughing, "and that's what will put
you in jail. It's best to accept that work is easier than worry or prison."

"What do I have to fear when I get out?"

"You should fear the future. Statistics show that sixty-eight percent of
reformatory kids will commit a crime, and get caught, within five years
of being turned loose in society. Two-thirds of you in this room will be
behind bars in five short years. Imagine the horrors in that future—and
I mean really picture it. Get in touch with your fears, and then use those
fears as motivation."

The kid who had spoken up was now quiet, and the room was dead
silent.

"And don't think you're unique," Jimmy said. "The statistics show that an average person will have more than one financial crisis in their life. We all have things to fear, but only the smart will use their fears."

"What was it like when you got out?" asked a kid.

"I was honestly surprised to find out that I was just like everyone else," Jimmy said. "But I have a felony, and that's an economic disadvantage. And so I use my fears to outwork others. I use the demons of my past. Because of my mistakes, I feel the need to prove myself to the world. And so I tap into my darker side to fuel my drive."

One of the brighter kids raised his hand. "I thought we were supposed to set big goals, maintain faith, and live with certitude and gratitude for success?"

Jimmy shrugged. "I'm a real estate agent and so I make money by selling houses. What I've found is that people aren't as hungry as me because they don't fear survival. They don't fear living just above broke. They don't fear having no savings. And so they won't work as hard as me."

"You think being scared is an advantage?"

"I think it is a daily advantage for me," Jimmy said. "I want a life above money worry. And that drive comes, I think, from my fear of poverty. My goals and fears both motivate me, and so I do the work that average Realtors won't do. That is my advantage. I'll do whatever it takes, as long as it takes, and I will accept the most unpleasant tasks. It's easier for me to work for money than to worry about it."

THE FEAR of financial calamity is a great motivator, and it should be used for all it's worth. I once had a patient named Brian, a good guy in his thirties with a family and a steady job. He earned a middle-class income as an engineer at a mammoth corporation. During his twelve-year career with the company, Brian had survived three waves of layoffs. He was devoutly religious, and he once told me that God not only provides but also shelters us from harm.

"Do you ever think about other job options?" I once asked delicately. From my detached viewpoint, his financial situation looked scary. Layoffs seemed to be the perpetual reality of employment at his job.

"I like what I do," he replied, "and it's close to home. I love my schedule, and I like my boss."

Okay, I thought, I'll leave it alone.

It was a solid job with benefits, and professional jobs in the local area were scarce—at least jobs within a convenient driving distance from his home. With each wave of layoffs, however, Brian accepted a pay cut to retain his position with the company.

He went to work early but left at four o'clock each day. His wife stayed home with the kids. They were responsible people. It was a comfortable life. They were a positive family leading respectable middle-class lives.

In success philosophy, it has been said that FEAR is an acronym for "False Evidence Appearing Real." It reminds us that many things that cause our anxieties are not true threats, just imaginary ones. We must conquer our limiting fears to undertake bolder challenges. Maybe it was fear that kept Brian at his job, or maybe he wasn't fearful enough.

Finally the day of reckoning arrived—Brian was fired in the next wave of layoffs. Although the company offered temporary severance pay to ease the transition, he was stunned by the job loss, and felt an overwhelming fear for his survival.

"The day after the layoffs was the worst day of my life," he confided. "On the first day, it seemed surreal. But then I missed a night of sleep. And on the second day I realized the situation. We had no savings and no income."

Six months later, the severance package ran out. He was unemployed. It took him three years to find an engineering job, for which he now had to commute into the city. During the interim, he worked odd jobs as a local handyman. I never asked him what he learned from this experience, but his actions told me.

Whereas he once pursued a comfortable life, Brian now spends his free time pursuing financial security. He loves his family, but now he sacrifices many of his free hours for them. He maintains a second job as a handyman and saves $1,000 a month from this side work. He is also paying down his credit card debts.

"Fear is a good thing," said Tamora Pierce. "It means you're paying attention." The fear of consequences makes us think clearer, feel urgency, and persevere through adversity. Without fear, we are only half-awake.

In the struggling middle class, it's been said that FEAR is an acronym for two other phrases, both differing from the one previously mentioned: Forget Everything And Run, or Face Everything And Rise. Without the fear of calamity, people tend to procrastinate and make a lot of excuses.

A motivating fear is the most useful tool to ensure action. Fear makes us accept the inconveniences for our best efforts. It compels our daily sacrifices and sustained discomforts. Fear pushes us when we feel small in the face of our obstacles. Fear leads to spending less for luxuries and accumulating for security. Fear motivates.

"Feeling fear is a good sign that your survival instincts are intact. You need to appreciate the dangers to stay safe," says Zoe Bell. We all have something to fear, but only the strongest will choose to face everything and rise.

THE LIFE LESSON: FINANCIAL FEAR

I learned that the things I fear may come to pass,
But only if I don't face those fears and use them.

LESSON 4-33 · STRAIGHT EDGE

Straight edge: The advantage of no alcohol and no drugs.

Gardening is a kind of disease . . . You interrupt the
serious cocktail drinking because of an irresistible
impulse to get up and pull a weed.

LEWIS GANNETT

A discontented mind is a powerful advantage, mused the Wealthy Gardener, but only for those who refuse to numb it. Whatever takes the edge off also takes away our fullest powers.

"Why don't you drink socially?" Jimmy asked the Wealthy Gardener, point-blank. "You do own a vineyard and winery."

"We all choose our ways," said the Wealthy Gardener, "and to me, alcohol is a mistress who tempts with fleeting pleasures. But her pleasures are costly since they come at the loss of my sharpest awareness."

Sitting on a sofa in front of the fire, Jimmy was silent as he considered the regret of his youth, and how one mistake had plagued him through life. His time in the reformatory was proof of the evils of overindulgence. On the other hand, however, what was wrong with one social drink to take the edge off?

"I'm only talking about responsible social drinking," Jimmy continued. "I don't think a drink alters much, but something always keeps me from doing it."

The Wealthy Gardener leaned back. "Have I ever told you the parable of stupefied smiles?"

Jimmy laughed out loud. "Nope."

"There once was a king who ruled an oppressed population," said the Wealthy Gardener. "The king stayed in power not by force, but through an economic system that kept the people under his control.

"The plan was simple. To survive in this oppressive system, the people had to stay productive during their waking hours so they could afford food, shelter, and other life essentials. And the king, eager to prevent a public uprising against this system of wage slavery, made sure there was a flow of cheap wine through the kingdom to keep them subdued in their free hours."

Jimmy sat in silence, listening to the story.

"The temporary escape through alcohol," continued the Wealthy Gardener, "kept his subjects tolerant of their intolerable conditions. They performed mindless work, accepted low wages, and put up with hard lives without rebelling. But they found pleasure in a medicine that induced many stupefied smiles."

Jimmy sighed and rubbed his forehead. "And the moral is to never use alcohol?"

"The clever king knew that whatever takes the edge off also diminishes the will to revolt," responded the Wealthy Gardener. "The moral of the story is to face your problems and use your fullest potential to stage a rebellion. Be the exception in an oppressed population by creating a lifestyle of prosperity for which there is no need to escape."

Jimmy sighed again. "But what about a social drink at a party?"

"It's not a question of right or wrong. Drinking may be okay for people who are settled with their life conditions," said the Wealthy Gardener, "but it's a poor strategy for those who are striving to shape their conditions. We want our edge for better or worse."

"So it's about choosing power over pleasure?"

"I can only speak for myself, and I am all for pleasure in life," said the Wealthy Gardener. "But I am against drugged pleasure. I want my fullest senses, and I want authentic pleasure. And I want my edge, especially when I'm unhappy with my circumstances."

Jimmy considered his next words. "Okay, but some heavy drinkers can be extremely wealthy. And alcohol doesn't seem to hurt them financially."

"And it is a testimony to the things they do right in their days, not to the things they do wrong in their free time," said the Wealthy Gardener. "What stressor does a wealthy person drink to escape? And why aren't they content without a drug? Alcohol is never the answer to any problem. It only makes us forget the questions."

THE STRAIGHT EDGE is the advantage of no alcohol and no drugs. I was sitting on the sofa with my small kids on either side of me, watching Disney's *Aladdin*. It was a Friday movie night at our home. It had been a stressful week of work, and I was glad to relax. My daughter asked me, "What's in the glass?"

"It's wine," I said.

"Can I have wine?" she asked.

"Wine isn't for kids."

"Why not?" she asked.

"Because wine isn't good for you," I said impatiently.

"Then how come you drink it?"

I don't recall my exact answer, but I remember that moment. It was the day when drinking no longer felt right to me. I didn't want my kids to know that Daddy was having a drink because he was stressed out and needed to take the edge off. I didn't want to say that alcohol was my medication for tension, but it's okay since other people use it, too. I didn't want to say that the world felt better in an altered state of consciousness, when Daddy felt less connected to his daily problems. I was suddenly ashamed of using a glass of wine to escape stress.

Of course, I have been on both sides of the drinking fence.

In college I was the social coordinator of my fraternity. This position was the highest level on the hierarchy of college popularity. I was the guy who planned our fraternity parties with sororities. During these lost years of my life, I would look forward to the endless kegs. Inebriation would not just happen; rather, it was the goal of our parties. I was a functional alcohol abuser, a fact hidden by the reality that my drinking was the cultural norm.

Many years later, however, I could barely recall the fraternity days. I had a wife and kids, a responsible job, and all the pressures of an adult lifestyle. What was the harm in taking the edge off with a glass of wine? Who cared if a responsible adult had a drink? Did it really matter if I had a cocktail?

Well, for me, it mattered a lot. And the following is my testimony.

My son was diagnosed with juvenile diabetes at the age of eight. At that moment, our family's habits had to change. We could no longer eat high-carb foods and then tell my son to eat differently. We were in this together. He would learn by example. I also knew that drinking alcohol was a serious danger for diabetics. I couldn't instruct my son to avoid alcohol when I indulged in alcohol myself. He needed to see me, his father, interact socially without drinking. I needed to lead my son by example.

And I never touched a drop again. What did I learn from abstinence?

I found that without alcohol, my inner voice grew more intense. "Your life isn't okay," it said. "Stand up for yourself. You are better than this. Change your unwanted circumstances. Don't put up with it. Fight harder for yourself and your ambitions. Shape your environment. Don't settle for less than your dreams."

Without alcohol, my urge to self-actualize grew more intense.

I also discovered an extra effort within me, and it made all the difference. Prior to this decisive moment, I *almost* gave a sacred effort. I *almost* listened to my inner voice. I *almost* focused on goals with absolute faith. I *almost* formed clarity about what I wanted and, more important, what I wouldn't accept, during this one life. I *almost* went all in spiritually, and I *almost* partnered with an Unseen Force that I sensed in the stillness. I *almost* exercised daily to raise my emotional state, and I *almost* signed up for a triathlon. I *almost* participated wholly in my life. I *almost* gave my absolute best.

But there's just something magical when an ambitious person has no escape from daily stress. When we don't take the edge off, the edge becomes an asset for change. The pressure builds up inside, and it finds an outlet of expression.

The results of abstinence were staggering.

Within seven years, I achieved the financial security that had eluded me during the previous twenty-three years. It turned out that I had needed my fullest capacities. My daily performance improved by small percentages, which, in total, made all the difference. I gained a slight advantage, and I started to steadily amass savings.

But being a nondrinker means being an outlier in a drinking culture.

Larry Ellison, cofounder and CEO of Oracle, is such an outlier. "I can't stand anything that clouds my mind," he said. "I have no problem with people drinking; I have no problem with other people smoking dope. If that's what they want to do, God bless them, that's their business. But I can't do those things."

Thomas Edison had logical reasons for abstinence: "I have better use for my brain than to poison it with alcohol," he said. "To put alcohol in a human brain is like putting sand in the bearings of an engine."

Wall Street is infamous for its drinking and clubbing culture. And yet Warren Buffett, the Sage of Omaha, is an alcohol outlier. "The two biggest weak links in my experience," he said, are "liquor and leverage." His observation echoes Pythagoras, who said, "Sobriety is the strength of the soul, for it preserves its reason unclouded by passion."

When big souls refuse alcohol, the world sees the rare burning star of an Abraham Lincoln, Theodore Roosevelt, Henry Ford, John D. Rockefeller, Thomas Edison, Steve Jobs, Mahatma Gandhi, Muhammad Ali, Warren Buffett, Nelson Mandela, Malcolm X, Friedrich Nietzsche, Bruce Lee, George Bernard Shaw, Henry David Thoreau, or countless world-class athletes, as well as Hollywood celebrities far too numerous to mention.

After my self-imposed exile into abstinence, I imagined my little girl asking, "Daddy, why don't you drink?" After many years of living with the straight edge, free of alcohol's effects, my answer to this innocent question is now easy: "Well, honey, your dad wants to approach life with his full senses. If there is a problem, and there always is, your dad will be strong enough to face it with total clarity."

I want her to know that her dad never runs or hides from life; rather, he fights to change the things that cause him stress. Dad wants to show by example that life is good if you make good choices, and that peace is found in self-mastery, not self-medication.

"And ultimately," I would tell her, "your dad wants an authentic life, for better or worse, without momentary delusions."

"I made a commitment to completely cut out drinking and anything that might hamper me from getting my mind and body together," said Denzel Washington, another alcohol outlier. "And the floodgates of goodness have opened upon me—spiritually and financially."

THE LIFE LESSON: STRAIGHT EDGE

I learned to avoid an alcoholic drink after a stressful day,
And instead use my full resources to alter the causes of my stress.

Discomfort: Uneasiness caused by risk of criticism
or failure, unfamiliarity, or uncertainty.

Why not go out on a limb? Isn't that where the fruit is?

FRANK SCULLY

The prosperous life, reflected the Wealthy Gardener, is a brave life. All worthy achievements require a walk into likely discomforts.

It was cards night, and Fred was sipping a glass of merlot. The Wealthy Gardener had a club soda, as usual, and had nearly lost all his quarters.

"I need to let you in on a secret," said the Wealthy Gardener. "I just got some unexpected news that I haven't told anyone. And it's not good news."

"You can trust me in full confidence," Fred assured him.

"To make a long story short, I went to the hospital last month after feeling exhausted from a jog. They ran some tests, and they found a rare form of lymphoma. They think I have stage three cancer, and so next week I'm getting a PET scan."

Fred was speechless for a long moment. "You told nobody about this?"

"Not until this moment," said the Wealthy Gardener. "But to be honest, I'm not surprised by the diagnosis. I could sense that something wasn't right inside me. And I'm strangely at peace with it."

"You're at peace with your cancer?" Fred asked.

"I'm at peace with my fate, whatever it is. I've felt a premonition lately, as if I had better take care of any unfinished business. I've walked into discomforts all my life. I can handle this, too."

Fred took a long sip of wine and then set his glass on the table. "I don't know what to say," he muttered. "Of course, if there's anything I can do for you—"

"There is one thing, actually," interrupted the Wealthy Gardener. They stared at one another across the table. "Tell me about your day care center. At this stage of our lives, for what it's worth, my sense is that we need to be open with one another."

Fred looked at his hands for a full minute before he spoke.

"It would be a faith-based day care center that would teach the kids love, honesty, truth, compassion, forgiveness—all the virtues—plus the many preschool skills. It would nurture their young minds and hearts. We could have a real impact if we taught those kids all week long. Sunday school class introduces them to values, but a faith-based day care center would change their lives."

The Wealthy Gardener was nodding. "I promised myself to get off your back about it, but my current predicament gives me a new perspective."

Fred nodded. "But my fragile ego always stands in my way."

"I'll politely disagree with that," countered the Wealthy Gardener. "It's not your ego that's preventing action. It's your anxiety about stepping into the unknown. It's the uncertainty of unfamiliar territory."

"Maybe you're right," Fred said at last. "It's a lot easier to stick to familiar routines than to face uncertainty at my age."

"You should consider all the things you're missing."

"What do you mean by that now?"

"You once told me to find a cause outside of myself and then lean into it," said the Wealthy Gardener. "You told me that every great purpose requires a cross of discomfort and someone willing to carry it. Maybe now it's your turn to carry that cross for others in your life."

Fred slumped in his chair. "I suppose it was easier for me to dish out this advice than it is to take a spoonful of it myself."

The Wealthy Gardener didn't respond as he watched his friend think. He saw a glimmer of sadness, a man struggling mightily with his private insecurities.

"Maybe you're right," Fred said. "I need to get out of my comfort zone. I am surely past my prime, but I still have enough life in me to do something."

"And the world would get a great crusade," said the Wealthy Gardener, "that could live on even after you're gone. But we will be deprived of your unique contribution if you won't disrupt your comfortable daily routine."

"So how do I get past my paralysis?"

"You take one step at a time. There's no freedom unless we can walk into the unknown," said the Wealthy Gardener. "To me, discomfort is the bridge between where we are and where we want to be. We either cross this bridge and accept all of its uneasiness, discomfort, and fear, or we shrink from our aspirations and stay where we are."

"I always hated bridges," Fred said, smirking. "But what about you? Your cancer doesn't equate to a death sentence. What are you doing with your own life?"

"I do have one last dream," admitted the Wealthy Gardener. "Unlike the kids you teach, mine at the reformatory have no bible of their own, no reference manual for life after they graduate. I may try to write an instruction manual for success, a bible, if you will, so the boys will have a guidebook for their financial affairs."

Fred looked inspired. "It would be a great purpose."

DISCOMFORT IS UNEASINESS caused by risk of criticism or failure, unfamiliarity, or uncertainty. The prosperous life requires a walk into discomforts and temporary inconveniences. Ray Dalio described these *discomfort bridges* as passing trials to attain our fullest prosperity.

"Imagine that in order to have a great life you have to cross a dangerous jungle," he wrote. "You can stay safe where you are and have an ordinary life, or you can risk crossing the jungle to have a terrific life. How would you approach that choice? Take a moment to think about it because it is the sort of choice that, in one form or another, we all have to make."

Self-actualization, and the accumulation of riches, is a reward unavailable for comfort seekers. The way to our best life involves bridges of discomfort. And every bridge is only a temporary passageway that leads to the other side.

When I invested in my first rental unit decades ago, I repeated the math for hours in the morning before signing the contract. It may seem like a trivial deal today, but my unfamiliarity with real-estate deals caused enormous discomfort.

In the end, I bought the rental as my sweaty hands shook. My heart raced, I felt scared, and I prayed to God that I wasn't making a foolish, naive mistake. It was an isolated moment of facing discomfort when I had the option to run.

"The quality of your life is directly related to how much uncertainty you can comfortably handle," said Tony Robbins. "What you are afraid to do is a clear indication of the next thing you need to do," Emerson said. "He has not learned the lesson of life who does not every day surmount a fear."

That first real estate deal was my initial step onto a discomfort bridge which lasted for roughly a year, until I got used to the new business. And this is a critical point to always bear in mind when anxiety is looming: Discomfort bridges are not permanent.

Our discomfort bridges pass, but change remains. We must cross a dangerous jungle to get to the other side. We must walk on the rickety bridge above the deepest canyon to get to a terrific life.

How did it work out with my very first rental? I completed the rehab under budget, rented the apartment to the very first caller and ended up with a drug addict who trashed the unit. After a year, I'd lost $4,000 due to my stupidity.

This setback didn't kill me, and I continued learning while my discomfort slowly faded. We expand our comfort zones by enduring discomfort until it eases.

"If we are not a little bit uncomfortable every day," Jack Canfield reminds us, "we're not growing. All the good stuff is outside our comfort zone."

Freedom in life requires stepping onto bridges of discomfort.

Those who aspire to gain wealth must accept uncertainty and vulnerability. We must forever choose ambition over comfort, effort over ease, exertions over excuses, and contribution over complacency.

"Nobody ever died of discomfort, yet living in the name of comfort," said T. Harv Eker, "has killed more ideas, more opportunities, more actions, and more growth than everything else combined. Comfort kills!"

The imposition of crossing a *lengthy* bridge to get a better life is perhaps the most common reason we fail to reach our fullest potential. The many years it takes to complete a worthy achievement, attain financial security, or amass enough money for a comfortable retirement can prevent the will to even attempt to start the quest.

"Don't let the fear of the time it will take to accomplish something stand in the way of your doing it," advised Earl Nightingale. "The time will pass anyway; we might just as well put that passing time to the best possible use."

"You will either step forward into growth," said Abraham Maslow, "or you will step back into safety." Discomfort is the bridge between where we are and where we want to be. We either cross this bridge—accept the uneasiness, discomfort, and fear—or we stay where we are.

THE LIFE LESSON: DISCOMFORT BRIDGES

I found that wealth required walking into discomfort,
And so I crossed bridges of discomfort to get a better life.

LESSON 4-35 · PROBLEMS

Problem: A matter or situation regarded as unwelcome or harmful that needs to be dealt with and overcome.

Every garden presents innumerable fascinating problems.

WINSTON CHURCHILL

Only those who solve big problems, the Wealthy Gardener believed, are fit to harvest wealth. A life of small problems produces a small income.

Late one evening, three people sat around a table in a coffeehouse. The Wealthy Gardener had organized this secret meeting with Fred's wife and son to talk about the day care center. Connie was eager to help her husband, while Jared—now working fifty hours a week and attending alcohol abuse classes, part of his sentence for his DUI—was reluctant to commit the time. It was rumored that Jared's girlfriend was pregnant and he was unraveling.

"Fred's got a problem," said the Wealthy Gardener, "and he needs a push. He really needs to do this day care center. So how can we help him?"

"I've tried to help," Connie said, "and he always seems to resist change. He withdraws, mopes around the house, and spends his time in the basement."

The Wealthy Gardener nodded. "So let's talk about a plan."

Jared rolled his eyes. "Have you considered that he doesn't really want it at the age of seventy?"

"We spoke about it last week," said the Wealthy Gardener, "and he wants it. I think he even needs it. He's had this dream for decades, and any dream that won't die is the call of the inner voice."

Jared chuckled. "Well, you can believe that if you want. But he needs to take a crap or get off the pot, and it's really up to him. If he won't do this thing, then he doesn't really want it."

There was a momentary silence.

"You know, Jared, in one sense you're right," said the Wealthy Gardener, eyeing him sharply. "But in another sense, you're wrong. There are times when people need help to overcome their inertia. Your dad needs this challenge and all the headaches that come with it. So how can we help?"

"I love my dad," Jared said, "but I have a shitload of my own problems. I'm maxed out with work, I don't have a minute to myself, and now I have a baby on the way. The reason I'm here tonight is to let you know I can't help."

The Wealthy Gardener fixed his gaze across the table. "I'll tell you what your problem is, Jared," he said. They glared at one another. "You're thoughtless. You react to life. You let things happen, and then you make excuses. Everyone is busy, everyone has problems, and that's just part of living. Life is one problem after another, and you need to accept it and grow up. We all have frustrations. And life will be a lot easier when you stop thinking you're unique. Accept your problems like the rest of us!"

"No offense," Jared sneered, "but I'm not here for a lecture."

"And I didn't come to lecture you," said the Wealthy Gardener, "but if you let this moment pass, you'll one day regret your self-absorption. Your life may be hard, but your dad needs your help now. You could help him find office space, or even start a website. If you cared enough, you'd find—"

"Are you freaking deaf?" Jared shouted, standing up. "I don't have time!"

"And you believe it," replied the Wealthy Gardener. "If you were smarter, you would figure out how to create the time to help your dad. You wouldn't focus on your lack of time. You would focus your mind on solutions."

Jared kicked his chair and stormed out of the coffee shop.

. . .

PROBLEMS ARE UNWELCOME SITUATIONS to be dealt with and overcome. Only those who handle problems are fit to harvest wealth.

A thirty-year-old man with two small kids and a stay-at-home wife
wanted to attain financial freedom. His income was ordinary, and it had
a ceiling that maxed out to a plumber's average salary. He worked six
days a week and had no free time due to his family duties. At the end of
every month, living frugally, he saved less than $1,000.

How can this man attain financial freedom in twenty years?

As you may have guessed, the man in the riddle was once me. When I
began my quest for financial freedom, I would write my specific goal at
the top of a page and then write *How can I . . . ?* below it. Then I would
stare at the blank page and wait for ideas, allowing my mind to imagine
the possibilities. My daily goal was to record five new ideas on the blank
page.

Through this process, we become inventors of solutions. We become
creative strategists who dig for practical plans. We must become more
resourceful thinkers. The method of thinking *How can I . . . ?* forced me
to write solutions.

"You must never, even for a second, let yourself think that you can
fail," said Henry Ford. "Thinking is the hardest work there is, which is
the probable reason why so few engage in it."

Ford wanted to invent the V8 motor, so he hired men to create it.
Months after they went to work, no progress had been made. "It can't be
done," his engineers told him.

"Keep working on it," said Ford. "I want it, and I'll have it."

Of course, a solution was found for the Ford V8 engine. We always
get what we think about, but we get it more assuredly if we demand solutions and maintain goals backed by faith. We can come up with the most
creative solutions by asking *How can I . . . ?*

Problem-solving and resourcefulness are critical in life and work.

When we are entrusted to handle big problems at work, we become targeted for promotion.

Over the course of his career, my father slowly gained a reputation as someone who could handle problems and responsibilities. His boss fell into the habit of delegating problems to him without following up. But my dad felt a duty to report back to the boss to give assurance that everything was fine.

One day my dad walked into his boss's office to provide feedback about an urgent problem facing the business. The boss was at his desk, immersed in his own frustrating problems of the day. Before my dad uttered a word, his boss raised one hand in the air. "I don't need you to tell me anything," he said dismissively. "I told you to handle it, and I trust that you did."

My dad exited the office, not feeling insulted but secure. He sensed that the CEO valued him. This gesture assured his continued employment and his rise to the top of the company.

When we handle problems, we are valuable to a business.

Expecting daily problems doesn't deprive life of joy; rather, it protects and maintains our best disposition during work. A ready mind is a steady mind. Success comes to those who consistently handle problems.

Malcolm Forbes said, "If you have a job without aggravations, you don't have a job." A life of small problems produces little income. "Life is not a continuum of pleasant choices," an Indian proverb reminds us, "but of inevitable problems that call for strength, determination, and hard work."

THE LIFE LESSON: PROBLEMS

I learned there is no success without aggravations,
And riches gravitate to those who solve the big problems.

LESSON 4-36 · THINK WALKS

Think walk: A ritual of brisk walking for creative thinking.

Half the interest of a garden is the constant exercise of
the imagination.

MARIA THERESA EARLE

Upward mobility demands accurate thinking, mused the Wealthy Gardener, and his best thinking happened on mindful walks. A body in motion gets the mind in motion—and out of the commotion.

The Wealthy Gardener strolled slowly, his head down and his hands clasped behind him, along the snow-covered path looping around his vast property. His mind was focused on a single problem, and he barely noticed the frigid wind jostling the branches of the stoic oak trees. He was on a think walk. He didn't know if walking helped his brain or just created time that allowed him to think.

A long walk allowed him to ponder a subject, contemplate possibilities, and formulate ideas and strategies to solve problems. One loop around his property was six miles, which gave him two hours to think; he never finished a loop without new ideas and fresh insights.

For several minutes, he walked and concentrated on the problem: *If I am now dying, how should I use my time?* Nothing came to mind except the recurring idea of a manual for the troubled teens.

He traipsed in the snow for five minutes. If he was to die, what was the unfinished business of his life? He could think of no vital purpose for his remaining days except the boys. They needed ongoing guidance. The troubled teens came from a harsh world with cultural disadvantages. The poor stay poor for many reasons, but the factor most under control is their daily behaviors and thinking. If the boys couldn't break the chains of their pasts, they'd never escape poverty.

He sighed with fatigue, then coughed into the brisk wind. He was out of breath, and he felt his health in decline. But this think walk was beneficial, and he followed the trail to find ideas. "How can I best impact their lives?" he asked himself. It was the centering question.

The snow-covered path led up a hill, and as he climbed his breathing became raspy. How could he best impact the lives of these young men? What could he alone do to help those boys, and how might his impact be measured? It seemed that many of his ideas were useless, but there were always a few gems. What was his capacity to help?

Trudging through the snow, he sensed his mind come alive with a flow of ideas, hunches, thoughts, and inspirations. Open-ended questions triggered a deep inner wisdom, and walking gave his senses the time to respond in silence.

From a distance, one could see a solitary figure shuffling along in the barren fields, stopping intermittently, then resuming his walk. When ideas flashed into his mind, he would capture them by speaking into an audio recorder. Sometimes he carried a notebook. He finally returned home, sat by the fire, and reviewed the harvest of thoughts.

Among the new ideas, he always returned to the practical syllabus for financial success. He would ponder it on tomorrow's walk. When he stayed with a problem long enough, giving it time in his days, leaning into the issue with focused contemplation, the solution always came to mind. Our problems are a call to use our greatest powers.

A THINK WALK is the practice of thinking on your feet to stimulate the mind. Walking gives us time alone, removes us from the whirlwind of our day and any interruptions, and provides a sanctuary from chaos where the mind can soar to greater heights. Throughout history, a number of noteworthy people have mentioned the positive results of solitary think walks.

"The moment my legs begin to move, my thoughts begin to flow," said Thoreau. "All truly great thoughts are conceived by walking," wrote Friedrich Nietzsche. "Never trust a thought that didn't come by walking."

While great thoughts are never certain, walking seems to lead to my best thinking. I only discovered this phenomenon after a hip strain, when, unable to run for a year, I turned to walking for exercise. I found that ideas flowed during this time. Solutions and inspirations effortlessly came to me. I felt in touch with an inner wisdom in nature. Now I never face a major life decision, adopt a new strategy, or try to solve a problem without first mulling it over on a think walk.

"We should take wandering outdoor walks," said Seneca, "so that the mind might be nourished and refreshed by the open air and deep breathing."

Admittedly, there is no doubt that people can think and solve problems just fine without walks. Our mental faculties obviously work when we are sitting in a chair, pacing in an office, or driving a car. But walking creates moments of isolation, and in this age of distraction, a walk can be a ritual to remove us from the buzz.

While walking may not be crucial to thinking, it provides time and space from the whirlwind of life and its distractions. A walk creates a rhythm of movement that synchronizes the body, mind, and spirit. It provides the time to ponder, evaluate, and strategize our lives.

"I have walked myself into my best thoughts, and I know of no thought so burdensome that one cannot walk away from it," said Kierkegaard. "Thus if one just keeps on walking, everything will be all right." Enlightened thinking happens if only we make time to think.

THE LIFE LESSON: THINK WALKS

When trapped in the struggles of the middle class,
I found my best solutions during my focused think walks.

LESSON 4-37 · PRUDENCE

*Prudence: Regard for self-interests; caution
in practical matters; discretion.*

A prudent man doesn't make the goat his gardener.

HUNGARIAN PROVERB

An emotional mind makes mistakes, reflected the Wealthy Gardener, while a rational mind makes money. Let passion give way to reason when dreaming gives way to planning.

By March, Jimmy had been at the new real estate agency for five months, and he was frustrated. His ambition had become a double-edged sword: It pushed him, but it had also led him to impulsively change brokerage firms to receive a higher income. In a short span, he saw that ambition without prudence can lead to setbacks.

He had received a text the previous night from his boss, who wanted to meet with him first thing in the morning. Jimmy now entered the arrogant man's office and sat opposite his massive desk.

"I've been looking over your numbers," his boss said, "and you've been underperforming during the past three months. We need to talk about it."

"The winter months are always the slow season," Jimmy said.

"And due to your underperformance," the man continued, "we will need to renegotiate your contract. Until your sales pick up to a satisfactory level, I aim to eliminate your higher-than-normal commission rate."

Jimmy remained poker-faced despite the sudden shock.

The winter season had been sluggish. He was starting anew since moving over to the firm, but he was still the top-listing real estate agents at the small agency. He had even recently expanded into a new territory that was closer to the city. But with no administrative help at the agency, every new listing bogged him down with immense paperwork. And the demands of paperwork stifled the growth of his business. In his mind, he suspected that this renegotiation wasn't about slow sales—it was intentional deceit from the outset.

Jimmy eyed his boss evenly. "What if I refuse to renegotiate?"

"Then you're free to leave," the man replied, "without your clients."

"If you violate the present contract, I could get an attorney."

"You can do that," replied the owner, looking smug. "But he will see that you signed a contract that allows me to change your commission rate."

Jimmy nodded silently. He would review the contract details later, but in the meantime, he assumed this claim was true. With thirty new listings at this agency, he surely didn't want to start over again.

"What are the terms of the renegotiation?" Jimmy asked.

The owner smiled. "Regular commissions, just like everybody else. If you start to produce, then we will renegotiate again. You can take it or leave it."

Jimmy was silent for a long moment. "I'll think about it."

"Don't think too hard, kid. And don't forget the lesson, okay?"

Jimmy smiled tersely. "What's the lesson?"

"The devil's in the details," the man said, smiling.

Jimmy nodded, stood, and let himself out of the room. It was evident that his own lack of precaution had caused this mess, and he was determined not to repeat the mistake. He would remain calm and think without an emotional response. He needed to calculate his next move.

And by lunch, he had decided to stay at his current agency. Sure, it would feel good to abandon that jerk, but what end would be served?

Ambition told him to bolt, ego told him to shout, but wise judgment told him to think of his self-interest. He did a final gut check, and while he didn't like the arrogant owner, he felt it was best for him to bide his time for now.

. . .

PRUDENCE IS WISE CAUTION with regard for self-interests. It is self-control, detached objectivity, and practical calculation that leads to steady financial direction and a richer life.

"Wisely and slow," wrote Shakespeare, "they stumble that run fast." "All enterprises which are entered on with indiscreet zeal may be pursued with great vigour at first," Tacitus said, "but are sure to collapse in the end." Let those without discipline act without reason.

I once had a patient who retired at sixty-two but wasn't ready to be idle. To occupy his many free hours, he volunteered in the community. His church group offered weekly spaghetti dinners, and it wasn't long before this man was helping in the kitchen. He found that he loved this activity and valued serving others.

He also spent many weekend hours at an outdoor park and campsite. One day he befriended the owner of a concession booth in the park who planned to sell his little operation. My retired patient bought the small booth. He served hot dogs, ice cream, candy, pizza, and drinks to weekly campers and daily visitors.

It was a mildly profitable little venture.

And then a restaurant owned by a fellow church member came up for sale. My patient, now the happy owner of the concession booth, was given the first opportunity to buy the restaurant before it was exposed to the marketplace.

Curiously, the retiree asked my opinion. As I listened, my intuition told me that he was about to ask if I would be willing to invest in his venture. He explained all the upsides of the restaurant, but as I listened, I could see nothing but the enormous financial risk.

"Well, what do you think?" he asked.

"Maybe I'm just fearful," I told him, "but I don't think I could live with the worst possible outcome. But if you can survive the worst, maybe, then, you should consider it."

What I meant was that only if his financial situation allowed him to survive the loss of the restaurant should he consider buying it. But I also hoped to make it clear that due to my own financial situation, I was not interested in being an outside investor.

He eventually purchased the established restaurant operation. I watched admiringly, since I saw in him the spirit of a man who, despite his age, wasn't done living. Here was a dreamer who was young at heart and still daring greatly.

On the other hand, it is always wise to be prudent. Those without prudence often learn the pain of misjudgments. Wealth requires strategic thinking with a calm respect for the worst consequences.

A year later, the restaurant was empty. Two years later, in anguish and with tears in his eyes, he openly told me that he had used all his life savings to buy the restaurant and his cash reserves were running out. He was a great guy, but he was devastated. Once again, I sensed he wanted an outside investor to help his cause.

"I have no money," I said. "My own cash is tied up in real estate."

In the end, he took out a home equity line of credit and bet his retirement on a business that failed. It is always in one's best interest to pause long, think calmly, and consider the worst-case scenarios before making a decision.

"It is better to be careful a hundred times than to be killed once," a wise saying tells us. "Think like a man of action, act like a man of thought," said Henri Bergson. "I think we should follow a simple rule," said Dr. Joyce Brothers. "If we can take the worst, take the risk."

THE LIFE LESSON: PRUDENCE

I saw that emotions led to financial setbacks,
But detached objectivity prevented foolhardy mistakes.

LESSON 4-38 · ESSENTIALISM

Essentialism: Narrow focus on one thing;
use of energy and time on a sole task.

If you spread the water across many, many seeds, you
don't have as much water for one seed.

TYLER PERRY

Prosperity requires saying no to almost everything, considered the Wealthy Gardener, and saying yes to only a few things. Wealth rewards a narrow focus on potent activities.

He met Jared on the weekend to take a walk through the vineyard. After stomping out of their secret meeting earlier that week, Jared had called to apologize for his rash behavior and now wanted to support his dad's lifelong aspiration.

"So what is really going on with you?" the Wealthy Gardener asked.

Jared sighed. "If I'm being honest, it seems like my whole life is spiraling out of control. A few years ago, I was an engineer with direction. I now work sixty hours a week, spend every dime, and have no time to call my own. And now there's a baby on the way."

They strolled for a minute without speaking.

"Do you have a plan to overcome your situation?"

"I don't even know where to begin," Jared admitted. "I feel trapped. I have daily responsibilities and I can't handle any more on my plate."

"What are the obstacles holding you hostage?"

Jared thought about it. "I think my obstacles are time and money. I have neither, and so I'm powerless to change. It's harder to get ahead compared to previous generations. You'll call it an excuse, but I barely break even."

"I am not saying that prosperity is easy," acknowledged the Wealthy

Gardener, "but isn't it true that in every garden, we always find several tomato plants that are outproducing the others?"

Jared seemed annoyed as he thought about it. "Okay, what the hell does that mean?"

The Wealthy Gardener chuckled. "You may not be aware that I've won Best Tomato at the county fair for the past two years. And the way to get an award-winning tomato is by pruning the plant's branches. I constantly pinch off the nonfruiting branches, and I leave only one tomato on the plant."

"Isn't that fascinating?" Jared snorted.

"And you may be interested to know that in the garden of life, the same rule applies to growing our wealth. The people who win prosperity give their strength, energy, and attention to just one fruit—their personal net worth."

"And how am I supposed to do that?"

"Prune the nonfruiting branches," said the Wealthy Gardener. "Cut the frivolous and mundane pursuits that waste time. Focus your power. If you want to control your affairs, you'll need all your energy going to one tomato."

"You mean spend all my life in pursuit of money?"

"If wealth be the goal, get your mind off distractions and onto your one thing. Those who acquire wealth in the future must prune the nonfruiting branches today. You choose the goal, but then make it your one tomato. And as for choosing a life of prosperity, it's not so bad for you. In the end, wealth can be a tasty tomato."

Jared grinned. "So the key to wealth is giving my life for it?"

"If your goal is wealth, then yes, that is what I'm saying. Get your mind off distractions and onto your one thing. One hundred percent of your potential looks like an obsession. But it will awaken the Silent Power that exists in the garden and works behind the scenes to make the plants grow."

"Well, what exactly should I do to help my dad?"

"The vital task is to secure a location to force him into action."

"Consider it done," Jared said. "What should I do after that?"

"Decide exactly what you want in your own life," said the Wealthy Gardener. "I mean *exactly* what you cannot live without. And then decide the number of weekly hours you're willing to give to this purpose. And finally, fight for those hours as if your life depends on it."

ESSENTIALISM IS A NARROW FOCUS on one thing, the use of energy and time on a sole task. It requires saying no to almost everything and saying yes to just a few things. It is an effort so rare that it appears to be an obsession, a dedication so full that it seems to exclude all else.

In my late forties, I was invited to a golf outing by the president of a midsize bank that had financed my two largest real estate deals. I was paired with a big-time developer who built luxury homes. Our foursome that day also included the bank's private attorney and its chief commercial lending officer.

We stepped up to the first tee. The attorney smacked a perfect drive straight down the middle of the fairway. The commercial lending officer cracked a gorgeous drive straight away, fifty yards farther than the attorney's ball. I stepped up and sliced my ball into another fairway. My partner, the luxury home builder, swung and missed the ball. Everyone burst into laughter.

"You guys really suck," joked the commercial lending officer.

"You should be glad we don't golf as much as you do," I snapped.

"You're right," he said, and laughed. "Keep working hard to pay your loans."

It's a funny story with a meaningful lesson. The wealthy of the future must prune the nonfruiting branches of today. They must give 100 percent to productive activities that move them toward the accumulation of riches. The leisure time will follow this reward.

"Deciding what not to do," said Steve Jobs, "is as important as deciding what to do." Michael Porter agrees: "The essence of strategy is choosing what not to do."

But how can a person say no to their duties? What does obsessive effort look like in the life of an average person?

Work, work, and more work—like your life depends on it—on things that produce monthly savings. If that seems like too much, wealth is not for you. And neither is any worthy achievement.

"I suggest that you become obsessed about the things you want," said Grant Cardone. "Otherwise, you're going to spend a lifetime being obsessed with making up excuses as to why you didn't get the life you wanted." A devotion and commitment to one thing—essentialism—is the key to unlocking our dreams.

I had a treasured friend while I was an undergraduate at college. After undergraduate school, I went to chiropractic college while my friend opted for a more rigorous direction. He graduated and moved on to medical studies, which often required ninety-hour workweeks.

He woke up at five o'clock in the morning, six days a week. On Sunday, as a treat, he would sleep in until seven o'clock. He worked as a medical student seven days a week for six years. His official duties during this time ended at six every evening, at which point he brought a lot of paperwork home to review until midnight.

Medical school is a life of pure essentialism.

After six years, his challenges intensified; he started doing rounds at a hospital as a medical intern. More years passed, and he suffered from sleep deprivation. And worse, while he sacrificed every waking hour, my friend amassed staggering personal debt in student loans.

In the end, he temporarily gave everything—100 percent dedication to an all-consuming goal—to get exactly what he most wanted.

Rare achievement always requires obsessive dedication, whether the aim is to be a medical doctor, get out of massive debt, or attain financial independence. It's work, work, and work. But obsessions lead to rewards, and my friend is now a respected anesthesiologist.

"I'm glad I did it," he joked later, "but I don't think I could survive it again." It's a common refrain among those who recall with pride their times of obsessive effort.

Essentialism is singular focus that uses a steady parade of hours on a concentrated purpose. It is claiming hours from the grip of the mundane. It is seeing hours as the cause of direction, and then fighting for those hours as if our lives depend on them. It is using time so that each day counts as progress toward a worthy cause.

"The difference between successful people and really successful people," said Warren Buffett, "is that really successful people say no to almost everything." Pick your own goal, but then make it your one tomato.

THE LIFE LESSON: ESSENTIALISM
....

I always used an ambitious to-do list to get things done,
But finally embraced fewer activities to accumulate wealth.

LESSON 4-39 · FLEXIBLE PLANS

Flexible plans: Adaptable means to an end.

There are no gardening mistakes, only experiments.

JANET KILBURN PHILLIPS

The road to wealth has many detours and setbacks along the way, the Wealthy Gardener reminisced, and that is why all earned riches require a fixed goal with flexible plans.

Jimmy's plan was simple enough. At the small agency, he was overburdened by paperwork that prevented his growth. He acted boldly and hired an associate to manage the back-office duties, freeing him to dedicate more time to obtaining new listings, the most lucrative impact activity. But lately he was battling new competition.

Jimmy reviewed his problems with the Wealthy Gardener during their weekly breakfast together at the local diner. He explained that his initial momentum in the business was now gone due to a team of twin brothers who were aggressive real estate agents in an adjacent town.

These brothers had a strategic advantage: They worked for a discount agency that charged less to sell a house. Sellers could save thousands by choosing the discount real estate agents, and the twins seemed to be everywhere all at once.

"Do you have a strategy to overcome this new obstacle?"

Jimmy sighed deeply. "At the moment, unfortunately, I don't."

"Then that's the problem," said the Wealthy Gardener. "You need a new plan. Have I told you about how I won Best Tomato at the county fair the last two years?"

Jimmy chuckled quietly. "Yeah, only twenty times, but who's counting? And each time you remind me to choose one goal, then prune all the other branches and make it my big tomato."

"Well, I can't recall who I tell anymore," griped the Wealthy Gardener. "But there's another secret to my award-winning tomatoes, and I'll let you in on it. I entered my first contest five years ago and won first place. But the next year I got sacked pretty good. When I got home, I tried to figure out what went wrong."

Jimmy smiled but offered no response.

"One evening, I was outside. I saw that my tomato plant, positioned in the corner of my garden, missed an hour of sunlight each day when the sun moved behind a nearby tree. You see, I had picked the perfect spot for the plant the first year. But a year later, it was the wrong spot because that tree had grown several feet and now blocked some of the plant's sunlight. And because of the shade, I had a loser tomato. Do you see how this applies to you?"

Jimmy sighed. "When times change, we adapt, or we fall behind?"

"It's vital to focus on one goal and track results," said the Wealthy Gardener, "but stay flexible with your plans. The only certainty on the road to wealth is that you will need to constantly improvise plans. You will meet with setbacks, and you'll make mistakes, but you can always change your strategy. Adaptation is necessary to prosper in life."

"So how do I decide on the best response to the twins?"

"Focus on your desired outcome and wait for hunches, ideas, and thought flashes. You'll find that guidance comes to you in the form of sounder plans. And the source of your inspiration, in my master gardening opinion, is the same source that grows my prize tomatoes."

FLEXIBLE PLANS are adaptable means to an end or objective. In a business or a career, failure is when we run out of money and can't get any more. Anything less is feedback. Our results are the feedback that tells us if we're doing the right things, and if we're doing them well enough. We need to be fixed with our goals, open to feedback, always tracking results, and flexible with strategic plans.

"All failure is failure to adapt, all success is successful adaptation," said Max McKeown. "Intelligence is the ability to adapt to change," said Stephen Hawking. "Adapt or perish, now as ever, is nature's inexorable imperative," wrote H. G. Wells. Insanity is doing the same things over and over again without success. Persistent struggle calls for one thing only—a sweeping change of strategic plans.

The middle class's challenges are (1) how to earn enough money to amass savings, and (2) how to continue earning a surplus in changing economic climates. Our plans need to change with the seasons.

I'll never forget being confronted with my own lack of sound strategy in my late twenties. A lady once asked me, "What's your plan to get more time and money?"

"Just keep working hard and hope it gets better," I replied.

"Is that really a sound strategy?"

I was speechless, unable to think of anything to say in response. The woman had smacked me with reality. I was in over my head, busy as I could be, and earning a decent living while saving very little. My current strategy wasn't working to provide financial direction.

"You're going to tell me how to get rich quick?" I asked her.

"I can only tell you my story," she said. She was a dentist in my town who was now working with a network marketing company. In several years, she'd built a residual income of more than $5,000 per month. Regular people bought household products through the company, she got a commission, and so did others in uplines and downlines. All I could think about was the $5,000.

"And we have a ninety-seven percent retention rate," she said. "Our customer satisfaction is off the charts. This is the strongest aspect of our business."

I signed up. Within two months, I was the number one sales associate in the eastern United States. I enthusiastically enrolled my family and friends. But four months later, it was clear that something was amiss. Customers were dropping out of the program and discontinuing their product orders by the boatload. It was a devastating mass mutiny!

In time it became very clear that the retention rate was a sham. The dropouts remained "customers" who could order products at a higher price. While they never reordered, they were "retained" in a database as virtual customers.

I was embarrassed and ashamed. What a dope I had been to fall for it and to bring my most trusted innermost circle into the scheme. The business idea was sound, but the company's facts were false.

I ended my association with the organization.

As I look back over my life, I now see that time as part of my flexible plans toward my stubborn goal of financial freedom. I beg every reader to never be ashamed of failed attempts when you have stood up for yourself and taken a swing. It's only in moments of audacity that you show the strength of your soul.

My journey to financial freedom was a course of misses, blunders, surprises, humility, setbacks, mistakes, misjudgments, missed goals, and slim escapes from financial disasters. But every time the result—the feedback—was poor, I found the solution for upward mobility in a new strategy. We must be open and willing to adapt our plans.

"All you need is the plan, the road map, and the courage to press on to your destination," said Earl Nightingale. Nancy Thayer said, "It's never too late, in fiction or in life, to revise." Our plans are always adaptable. As Napoleon Hill said, "It's always your next move."

THE LIFE LESSON: FLEXIBLE PLANS

I gained prosperity despite setbacks and misfortunes,
By being stubborn about goals and flexible about plans.

LESSON 4-40 · LEARNING CURVES

Learning curve: The process of increasing knowledge,
competence, wisdom, and/or understanding.

Gardening is learning, learning, learning. That's the fun
of them. You're always learning.

HELEN MIRREN

Our lifetime earnings, pondered the Wealthy Gardener, correlate with
our lifetime learnings. Those who increase their knowledge expand their
options.

He surveyed the classroom at the reformatory with deep concern.
These naive youngsters had no idea what troubles lay ahead of them. For
any hope of a better future, they would need to earn income, control
spending, and save money. And the statistics showed that most of these
boys would return to society and do none of those things. Could this
outcome be changed by knowledge?

"Attention, please," said the Wealthy Gardener. As was his customary
practice, he started the class by reviewing past lessons. "We've talked
about how every life has many problems, and how winners consistently
handle them. We've discussed calm thinking and how emotions can sab-
otage self-interests."

He slowly walked to the center of the room. "We've reviewed how
goals require time and energy on vital actions, and we've talked about
claiming the hours in a day as if our life depends on it. Last, we've talked
about staying stubborn on goals but flexible on plans. And finally, today,"
he said, "we'll discuss personal finance and the psychology of wealth accumulation."

The classroom was silent, and he had their attention. Watching from
a chair, Jimmy was thinking about his own financial problems.

"We must start with the math," the Wealthy Gardener said. "If we make ten dollars and spend nine, we obviously have one dollar to save. Most people know the simple math, and yet always spend without saving. Why is that, exactly?"

"My dad said he never had any money at the end of the month," said a kid in the front row. "He worked all his life in an office just to survive."

"What did your dad do to earn money?"

"He was the manager of a hotel," the kid said, "and he was frustrated. He always said that life is unfair for the hardworking middle class."

Another kid scoffed at the boy's statement. "He should try the lower class!"

The classroom grew loud as the kids talked and joked about their meager backgrounds, and their conversation quickly digressed into a debate of who had it worse in life. The Wealthy Gardener waited silently until the commotion died down.

"I don't mean to shame your families," he said at last, "but I do want to challenge you to break the financial patterns of your pasts. And the way to gain your own financial security is to educate yourself out of scarcity."

The classroom was quiet as he viewed their puzzled faces.

"What I mean is," he said gently, "while I don't know your families, if they claim life is unfair, then I imagine they have one thing in common. I would bet my last dollar that they haven't learned about personal finance or money management. And I also suspect they don't own any books about wealth."

The kids were silent as he watched them consider this truth.

"If you want to break old patterns," he continued, "the way is through knowledge. If you want to be the exception of the family, you will need to read books on personal finance and wealth. You are starting your life at a disadvantage, but education is an equalizer. It's your way to a better life."

"My parents have no books on wealth," a kid offered, "but I don't see what good books would do them. There was never enough money to save."

"And that is a problem," agreed the Wealthy Gardener. "Will you just settle for the same scarcity? The more you focus on solving a problem, the quicker you'll discover a solution. Trust me on this—you will never find a wealthy person who did not study wealth."

The classroom was silent as the boys digested this information. Jimmy considered his own lack of formal education and contemplated how his next strategic shift would indeed require a tremendous new learning curve.

"You'll stay where you are in life," continued the Wealthy Gardener, "or you will grow yourself into greater capabilities. To reach your full potential, you must rise above your raising. You must stretch beyond your current understanding of things. Your life will be the result of choices, and the best decisions result from deeper knowledge. Learning expands the future."

"Where do we begin to study wealth?"

"Give me a few months and maybe I'll have an answer for you. I'm currently trying to organize the information you will need for success. If I were to assemble this knowledge, by a show of hands, who would use it?"

The hands went up, one after another, until the response was unanimous. The Wealthy Gardener nodded in silence, as Jimmy watched with intrigue.

A LEARNING CURVE is an education to improve ourselves. Those who increase knowledge expand options. My cousin and I attended the same college. She earned a business degree and, within two months of graduating, found employment at a small business with nice owners.

Within several years, however, the joy of earning income gave way to the realization that there was nowhere to go in her position. The firm was tiny, with just half a dozen employees. Without direction, she was unfulfilled. She had the option to settle for average or to educate herself for a brighter future.

It was not an easy decision to return to college for an MBA, since there was little assurance that this expensive degree would result in a new job. This discomfort bridge would require sixteen-hour workdays plus schooling. Family argued strongly against her pursuing this additional education, but she was determined to try.

"If you are not willing to learn, no one can help you," said Brian Tracy. "If you are determined to learn, no one can stop you." We can earn our way out of unwanted conditions by methodically expanding our knowledge base. Winners have a growth trajectory.

To condense this story, after earning her MBA, my cousin was hired by a Fortune 500 company and traveled the world for decades as a regional executive. What would have been her fate if she had refused to study, educate herself, and expand her horizons?

"To earn more you must learn more," said Robin Sharma. "An investment in knowledge," wrote Benjamin Franklin, "always pays the best interest."

Though I started at the same undergraduate college, my career path was different than my cousin's. I was in the entrepreneurial lane where education is often gained through self-learning. As a small business owner, to survive I had to offer value to others. I learned money management and cash flow control for profitability. I studied my field and immersed myself in books on personal finance and wealth. But before I could save, I needed to earn more.

I will try to avoid being redundant, but wealth, for me—the core of the matter—was foremost about learning to control my thoughts. The reason I believe so many people deride goal setting is because they haven't built the mental muscle to regulate the mind to radiate absolute faith, all the time, day after day, as long as it takes to win. It's easier to be cynical. It's easier to disbelieve. It's easier to fail the test of everlasting vigilance of thought—keeping the mind free of doubt, worry, fear, and negativity—than it is to gain this level of self-mastery.

And so the first life-changing learning curve of my economic reality was training my mind to concentrate on goals and radiate absolute faith. At the same time, I learned the practical value of momentary pauses in the days to consult my inner wisdom for guidance. I own volumes of books on the power of goals and mental clarity as proof of a learning curve that was vital to getting money in the bank.

After the learning curve of self-mastery over thoughts, I then studied every book I could find on money that seemed intelligent and legitimate. In my home office, the bookshelves look like an archeological dig from past immersions about money strategies and tactics; these books are grouped into categories: the stock market, entrepreneurship, real estate investing, buy-and-hold investing, landlording, saving money, getting out of debt, and personal finance.

I was always on a new learning curve in total immersion to better myself, to improve my knowledge, to know more about wealth. I studied wealth to become wealthy.

I can't stress enough the impact of learning curves in my life. Education is the path of upward mobility. A friend once made a statement that gave me pause. He complimented me by saying, "What I admire about you is that you are always reinventing yourself."

I was surprised because I never saw my evolution as reinvention, but it evidently looked that way as I had opened a chiropractic practice, developed a rental business, started buying and selling houses, and became the author of a book. And each reinvention—if that's what it was—was nothing more than a steep learning curve.

We *earn* our way out of unwanted conditions by *learning* our way out of them. Former Vanguard Group CEO Bill McNabb saw this truth firsthand and expressed it as follows:

We've actually tracked senior leaders here at Vanguard and asked why some did better in the long run than others. I used to use the word 'complacency' to describe the ones that didn't work out. But the more I reflect on it, the more I realize that's not quite it . . . The people who have continued to be successful here have stayed on a growth trajectory. They just keep surprising you with how much they're growing.

Billionaire Mark Cuban shares a similar view: "In this world, you have to learn how to learn and get in the habit of always wanting to learn. Most people won't put in the time to get a knowledge advantage." Once when Elon Musk was asked how he got into space travel and rocket technology, he answered, "I just started reading books on it." When the mind expands, the possibilities multiply.

THE LIFE LESSON: LEARNING CURVES

I found that my earning correlated with my learning,
And as my knowledge increased, so did my options.

Self-mastery: Control of focus, emotion, and thought.

A man sooner or later discovers that he is the master-gardener of his soul, the director of his life.

JAMES ALLEN

The molder of internal conditions, considered the Wealthy Gardener, is the shaper of external conditions. We master our money by mastering ourselves.

Jimmy sat in the passenger's seat of the pickup as they drove home from the evening class at the reformatory. "I was on a winning streak for a while, but that momentum is long gone. It's all falling apart."

"And that's called life," said the Wealthy Gardener, chuckling. "When times are good, it is easy to be optimistic. When times are bad, we see who can keep the faith. The winners of fortune must master the self."

Jimmy thought about it. "What do you mean by master *the self*?"

"Self-mastery is a lot of things," said the Wealthy Gardener. "But we are talking about financial success, and so it's about an obsessive devotion to our goals. When times are tough, we need a goal to stay on course. When times are good, we need a goal to keep the momentum. Goals focus our thoughts, and our focus determines our plans. Goals also center the inner wisdom that seeks to guide us."

"So mastering the self is just having goals?" Jimmy asked.

"Self-mastery is the ability to know *exactly* what you want and the discipline to carry your goals with you during your days. It's also feeling and acting like a person who is *already* successful. If you can maintain this ongoing mentality, you'll have attained the ultimate level of daily self-mastery—and you'll be guided if only you remember to remember to pause and listen to your own inner voice."

Jimmy was silent. He had been neglecting his morning rituals but didn't see the need to confess this to the Wealthy Gardener. He had not been exercising. He had not glanced at his goals in two weeks. He had not read any affirmations. And he could not deny that, with all the problems at work, his daily attitude was one of exhaustion.

"I'm thinking about rental property management," he finally admitted.

The Wealthy Gardener raised an eyebrow. "What do you like about it?"

"I think it's a big hairy problem for rich people who own apartments," Jimmy said, "and so that makes it needed. It would put me near wealthy people. I also like that it would offset the cyclical nature of real estate commissions. And since I've hired two real estate agents on my personal staff, we could easily expand our business."

"I like your reasoning," replied the Wealthy Gardener. "Study a venture before you leap into it. And in the meantime, keep your mind on wealth throughout every day—focus on being the successful person who already owns it."

Later that night, Jimmy lay in bed reviewing his goals and feeling financial freedom. Upon awakening the next morning, he forced himself to run two miles to achieve a peak emotional state. The exercise was followed by a review of affirmations, goals, and a detailed schedule of the day's hours.

"Financial freedom," he repeated as he drove to work, fixating his mind on his singular goal. When doubts or worries appeared, he refocused on being a successful person. Throughout the day, he controlled his emotions and he paused to stay attuned to his inner wisdom.

"Financial freedom."

SELF-MASTERY IS CONTROLLING our internal state regardless of external conditions. It is mental transcendence. It is the stubborn command of thought, intention, and emotion. It's the firm resolution to perform any action for as long as it takes to earn results. It's doing things we should be doing and avoiding things we should not be doing. It's the discipline, self-control, and resolve to rise above our financial conditions.

"Okay, I get it," one might say, "but how do I master thoughts?"

"Achieve self-mastery over your thoughts," wrote Napoleon Hill, "and constantly direct them toward your goals and objectives. Learn to focus your attention on the goals that you want to achieve and on finding ways to achieve those goals."

In my own life, my upward mobility has relied on my daily capacity to hold a clear goal of wealth in my mind and to believe I would achieve it despite all evidence to the contrary. Negative feelings and doubts arose during soul-crushing setbacks, of course, but my attention has always veered back to my goals. Goal focus is the ultimate essence of self-mastery—and the battle of the mind is waged anew every day.

The second essential element of self-mastery is continuously striving to feel accomplished. "Be as you wish to seem," said Socrates.

Before achieving financial freedom, I strove to be the person who had already attained great wealth. In my mind I was a resounding success even when trapped in the struggles of an ordinary life.

Earl Nightingale said, "Hold your goal before you; everything else will take care of itself." William James added, "Act, look, feel successful, conduct yourself accordingly, and you will be amazed at the positive results."

In my twenties, I was overwhelmed with the duties of a single business. During my forties, I juggled the greater responsibilities of three small businesses, while also raising a family and entering triathlons. And I also maintained a more optimistic and expectant daily attitude.

What was the difference? Studies suggest that grit ripens with age. But still, it should not be overlooked that by my forties, I had adopted my daily rituals.

In my forties, I was crazy enough to read my goals aloud with the in-tent of driving them into my subconscious mind. I was weird enough to sit alone in a sauna every night and feel like a person who already had wealth. I would imagine my wishes fulfilled—security, wealth, and lifestyle freedom. I was open-minded enough to trust that Universal Intelligence would notice if I stirred up a burning gratitude for an outcome. And I was nutty enough to consider that feeling successful in my days mattered in my quest for wealth.

Year after year, one day at a time, I mastered myself; I focused on one goal. I controlled my mind to stay on one task. My mind then compelled me to take action. And my own inner wisdom emerged.

"I am, indeed, a king, because I know how to rule myself," said Pietro Aretino. We control thought, or we control nothing. We control money by controlling ourselves. "Self-control," said George Bernard Shaw, "is the quality that distinguishes the fittest to survive."

Self-mastery is transcendence. It is fixating our thoughts on a target throughout life and then trusting that everything will take care of itself. It's knowing that the right actions spring from a focused mind.

It's having faith that a deliberate daily focus attracts ideas, people, situations, and events to support our goals. It's learning that self-mastery engages the aid of the Universal Intelligence.

The essence of self-mastery is the clarity to know *exactly* what we want, the discipline to *carry* our goals with us during our days, and the awareness to *feel* and *be* a successful person in advance of our crowning achievements.

THE LIFE LESSON: SELF-MASTERY

I learned to master my intentions, emotions, and actions,
And by controlling myself, I gained control over money.

LESSON 4-42 · REMARKABILITY

Remarkability: An impression worthy of remark;
standing out by surprise or due to a rare quality.

If you've never experienced the joy of accomplishing
more than you can imagine, plant a garden.

ROBERT BRAULT

Meeting expectations earns a paycheck, the Wealthy Gardener contemplated, but surpassing expectations earns upward mobility.

A week later, Jimmy sat alone in his cubicle, poring over a book on property management long after the other agents had gone home. In addition to reading books, Jimmy had been using his free time to think up solutions to deal with the twins who were stealing his business.

They had the benefit of being cheap, but he had the advantage of being successful. He had been called the "newcomer to watch" in a trade journal, and Newcomer of the Year by the local real estate commission. He had also been the top-listing agent at two separate agencies. Since Jimmy had been remarkable in the past, he could tout his outstanding record, while the twins could only offer a price discount.

As part of a new strategy, he'd assembled a portfolio designed for prospective new clients. Inside the packet were past news articles about him, his awards and achievements, and his sales figures. A poignant slogan was printed on the front of the packet: *You can hire cheap Realtors, or you can hire a top-selling Realtor.* This key strategy was designed to turn the twins' primary appeal into their handicap.

Within a week of launching his new campaign, the plan produced results. He had signed two listings and his frustrations had eased with this success. He now planned to double down to win back the lost territory.

Simultaneously, he studied the rental property management business during nights and weekends. While anybody could sell a house, the satisfactory execution of property management was a rarer skill.

From his research he found that most commercial real estate owners tended to be dissatisfied with their property management. This was a positive sign, and an indication of the need for better service.

Jimmy plotted his strategy, immersing himself in a steep learning curve to understand everything about the business. He would assemble a team for repairs and master property management software. He would start with small apartments, offering cutthroat discounts to gain business. He would also offer better service for half the price. Just like in his role as a real estate agent, he would win business by being remarkable.

And if he were remarkable, his business would grow by word of mouth. He could then tout his own outstanding record as a rental property manager, causing a snowball effect to monopolize the trade.

REMARKABILITY IS STANDING OUT by surprise or due to a rare quality. My practice boomed during a span of three months due to the smallest act of kindness: I started writing two thank-you notes per day. Simply writing "thank you" raised my income due to remarkability.

For example, I'd write different thank-you notes depending on the situation: "I want to thank you for choosing me as your chiropractor. I promise to treat you like family." "Thank you so much for your kind words." "I appreciate you trusting me with your referral . . ."

It took just minutes a day to write these notes.

I learned that handwritten notes did more than generate loyalty and goodwill; they left an impression that got people talking. Patients told friends and family about the notes—and my services—because this small gesture was so unexpected. I was shocked by how a minor deed created this response; that is, until I was on the other end of it.

I once went to a world-renowned skin surgeon for a Mohs surgery, which is considered the most effective technique for removing skin cancer. This specialist had actually practiced with Dr. Mohs and was considered the top skin cancer surgeon in the world. I asked him what it was like to be regarded as the best in the world in his field. He paused in thought and then said, "It's a lot of responsibility."

A week after my surgery, I received a phone call. It was the doctor calling to ask how I had been feeling since the procedure. I told everyone about this gesture (as I'm doing now). Why? Because that phone call was surprising and remarkable.

You will observe that I didn't tell anyone about the technical procedure to remove skin cancer. It was expected that this medical service would be provided. But it was unexpected that the surgeon would be so generous as to personally call me to see how I was doing. Of course, my patients must have felt the same. I was being paid to fix their backs, necks, or sciatica. But a handwritten thank-you note was surprising. It is the unexpected that is most remarkable.

"The key to finding your remarkability," advises Mark Schaefer, "is to think about what makes you surprising, interesting, or novel." Your financial security is about what makes you remarkable compared to the competition. Give people a reason to remark about you.

When I was slugging it out for decades in my chiropractic practice, one of the benefits I offered patients was a massage with each visit. I employed massage therapists on my staff, and for a time I was the only one doing this. Why did it work? It was an unexpected service of going the extra mile. It was remarkable.

Remarkability is absolutely essential for thriving in a small business, but it is equally important for employees climbing the ladder in larger companies.

A close friend of mine had been stuck in middle management at a utility company for years. During his forties, he was promoted step-by-step to his present-day position as vice president. I asked him about his ascent and how he got recognized in such a huge company.

"Everybody is always overly busy," he told me, "but then a boss would have a new task that needed to be done. It's another responsibility on top of the everyday jobs we already can barely handle. He would ask, 'Who can do it?' Everyone would grow quiet. I was always the one who volunteered. And so I just slept less than my colleagues. I think the extra effort got me noticed." In a corporate setting, volunteering for extra work was remarkable.

"What's wrong with being unremarkable?" one may ask.

Well, nothing, if you can accept obscurity. You may feel good about your work, but you'll be passed over for promotions. You'll see that others don't seem to notice your efforts. You'll feel lucky to hang on to your job. You won't find any new opportunities. You'll have big dreams, but without personal impact, your hopes will fade. You'll become jaded about success. You'll work as hard as everyone else, but you'll feel unappreciated and undervalued at your job.

The opposite of being irrelevant, of course, is being remarkable.

In a work environment, we must be so remarkable that it is never a choice for a supervisor or boss to know who deserves the promotion. "Be so good they can't ignore you," advises Steve Martin.

Go the extra mile. Do more than you are paid to do. Work longer than expected. Show genuine interest in others. Be the solution. Aim for excellence. Help your boss. Give your best effort. Strive for perfection. Don't complain. Never allow average. Unify the team. Obsess over quality. Make a small dent in your working universe.

"By definition, remarkable things get remarked upon," said Seth Godin. "Remarkable doesn't mean remarkable to you. It means remarkable to me. Am I going to make a remark about it? If not, then you're average." We are either remarkable, or we are replaceable.

THE LIFE LESSON: REMARKABILITY

I found that meeting expectations earned a living,
But surpassing expectations earned prosperity.

LESSON 4-43 · LEVERAGE

Leverage: One's ability to influence negotiations.

To dream a garden and then to plant it is an act of
independence and even defiance to the greater world.

STANLEY CRAWFORD

The prosperous seek negotiations, the Wealthy Gardener reflected, and
realize that options equal power. Leverage is the ability to award benefits, impose losses, or walk away from a compromise.

Jared waltzed into the human resources office during his lunch hour.
The head of the HR department was a middle-aged woman with a gruff
demeanor. She oversaw the daily problems of the 380 employees at the
packaging plant.

"What do you want?" she growled as he entered.

"I came to ask for a raise," Jared said, mustering his confidence. His
financial situation was tight, and with a baby on the way, he was worried.

"Have a seat," she said. Jared sat in a chair beside her desk. She asked
for his name, typed it into the computer, and then studied the monitor.

"You've been here a year, and you've already had two raises?"

"A little over a year," Jared clarified. "I manage a team of—"

"So now you're asking for a raise of how much?"

Jared shifted uneasily. "I want $30 per hour. I'm getting married and—"

"What qualifies you for another raise?"

This meeting was not going according to plan, Jared thought. He sat
up straighter in the chair, trying to stick to the script he had practiced,
but his heart was racing.

"Well, I have an offer from another company," he lied in a steady voice. "I'm asking you to match it. I would rather stay with your company."

"That's very kind of you," she said, studying the computer screen. "Okay, if that's everything, I'll talk to my boss and get back to you."

Later that evening, the Wealthy Gardener opened the door to his front porch and was surprised to see Jared waiting for him there. Over the past month, Jared had not returned his calls. Worse still, he had not lifted a finger to contribute to his dad's future day care center. Jared was always the victim, rationalizing failures with no accountability.

"I need to talk to someone other than my parents," Jared said, running his fingers through his hair. "I lost my job today. And I have no backup plan."

The Wealthy Gardener paused, then said, "Well, come on inside."

As they walked to the couch, the Wealthy Gardener guessed that the baby was due in four months. Jared was likely broke and now without an income. In no time, Jared was explaining what had transpired that day at the HR meeting.

"I needed some leverage," he sighed, "so I invented a story of an offer from another company. I asked them to match it, but then they called my bluff."

The Wealthy Gardener exhaled heavily. "And you were fired?"

"I was advised to take the other job. I couldn't admit I was bluffing, and so I walked out of the office. I'm unemployed, but no longer living with my parents. I was trying to be smart by negotiating a pay raise."

The Wealthy Gardener slowly digested the news. "Until you're like a tractor to a farmer," he said finally, "you'll have no financial security. You'll have leverage only when others fear losing your services."

"So I've learned," Jared said tersely. "What should I do?"

"Lay your cards on the table," said the Wealthy Gardener. "You need to eat humble pie, if not for yourself, then for your family. Swallow your ego and get your job back before they find a replacement—if it's not already too late. You need them more than they need you."

LEVERAGE IS THE POWER or ability to influence negotiations. We hear too much poor advice on the necessity of reaching successful negotiations. If we must agree to terms, we are at a disadvantage from the start. The power to walk away due to our options is our leverage.

But how do middle-class folks gain leverage in negotiations? Career leverage is earned by providing a useful skill with an excellent attitude. It is being so good that an employer can't afford to lose you without serious inconvenience. It is being so remarkable and competent that other employers will want you. And then it's about investigating all employment options and being willing to walk.

Financial security is gained with quality options.

For example, my good friend Pat is a wealth manager for a handful of the wealthiest individuals in the Pittsburgh area. He serves "old money" clients with the aim of wealth preservation, as opposed to wealth generation. It had always looked like a dream career from my vantage point of sixty-hour workweeks.

But he earned this outcome through leveraged negotiations.

In college he worked as a waiter at a prestigious country club that exposed him to the lifestyles of the rich and famous. He graduated from a state college with a degree in business and finance. One of the wealthiest patrons from the country club invited him to apply for a job in corporate banking.

Pat got the job, and this wealthy man became his boss and mentor. He advised Pat to stay on the investment side of the banking business and avoid the retail side; this advice was golden. In time, however, a competitor reached out and made Pat a lucrative offer. Pat met with his boss to discuss the situation and to perhaps renegotiate his contract.

One might say that Pat was showing disloyalty to his mentor by considering an alternative option. Is it wise to confront an employer for a raise? Pat wasn't too worried about his employer, he told me. In a free market society, we're never paid an unfair salary. We will only be paid our true market value.

Pat's employer and mentor refused to negotiate, and in that moment Pat became a "free agent" in the financial services ballgame. During the next twenty-five years, he moved up the ladder by accepting similar offers. He didn't accept every offer, of course, but he always considered his choices.

At last, after he had amassed a base of personal contacts, he launched his own wealth management company, exercising the option to work for himself.

"No issue can be negotiated," said Saul Alinsky, "unless you first have the clout to compel negotiation." This is a key point. Pat had options because he had earned respect in the financial industry. Still, it is wise to observe that during many negotiations, his current employers often said no. Due to his options, however, these failed negotiations led in positive new directions.

While our options are vital to negotiations, they don't always need to be exercised for us to win. Like a free agent testing the market in a sport, shopping one's services on the open market may command increased pay on the same team.

A family member of mine worked in computer software design and management for a large bank. In his thirties he shopped his résumé around like a free agent, testing the market to determine his job options. An unexpected offer came to him for $25,000 more than he was earning at his current bank position. It was a substantial raise and, with a family of five, next to impossible for him to resist.

Mulling it over, he saw no point in trying to renegotiate his contract with his current employer. Over the previous decade, they had offered only modest pay increases to keep his annual wages in line with rising inflation.

He accepted the new position and turned in his two weeks' notice. His current employer, however, was not about to be outdone. Within days he was offered a raise of $30,000 to remain with the company in the same position.

He was astounded by the sudden turn of events.

He ultimately decided to stay, but not without learning a key lesson. For a decade he had been extremely competent, well-liked, and ignorant of his true value. With just one good option, however, he received what he was worth.

"My deepest lifelong regret," he joked, "is that I think they would have gone higher. I should have claimed my other offer was for forty thousand dollars more!"

"You never get what you deserve," says Jalen Rose, "but only what you have the leverage to negotiate." Our options equal the leverage in negotiations.

"Negotiating isn't about getting what you want or giving in to what the other party wants. It's about having both parties walk away satisfied." Such statements are common lore among business consultants. With all due respect, I couldn't disagree more with such wisdom.

In most cases successful negotiation is about meeting somewhere in the middle of opposing aims, wherein both parties are mildly dissatisfied with the deal. The right price for a house is more than a buyer wants to pay and less than a seller wants to receive. The right salary is more than an employer wants to pay and less than an employee wants to earn. That's reality in a free market society. And only the option to walk away gives us any power in these negotiations.

THE LIFE LESSON: LEVERAGE

I struggled in vain to influence financial outcomes,
Until I saw that options are the leverage in negotiations.

LESSON 4-44 · RELATIONSHIPS

Relationships: The connections between people.

The very best relationship has a gardener and a flower.
The gardener nurtures and the flower blooms.

CAROLE RADZIWILL

Personal success and inner fulfillment, reflected the Wealthy Gardener, depend on our daily interactions with others. Good relationships enrich the days, while poor relationships bankrupt the spirit.

Jimmy had two real estate agents working on his team, and today they gathered in the conference room for a midweek meeting. In addition to regaining their momentum by acquiring new listings, the team had been canvassing the area nonstop during the past two weeks, interviewing apartment owners.

"You two are both killing it," Jimmy said. "And I want you to know that I appreciate your hard work. So now tell me: What is the attitude of the apartment owners?"

"They do nothing but bitch," Jen snapped. She was a gregarious personality in her late twenties. She now leaned back in a chair with a wry grin. "They are a wonderfully disgusted bunch of rich people!"

Jimmy smiled. "And their disgust is based on what exactly?"

"The usual headaches of landlording. They complain of unqualified tenants and subsequent evictions. They believe the apartments are being neglected. They don't receive the monthly reports promised by their management companies. And most of them have high vacancy rates. It's a bloody mess! And I see no loyalty to the current managers."

Jimmy chuckled. He could best connect with Jen's sharp mind through humor and joking around. But his newest assistant, Brad, needed straight communication. He had only been on the team for a month and was not comfortable with Jen and Jimmy's quick banter. His personality was serious. Brad was a computer guy with an accountant's mind, more comfortable in the back room than in sales. He was inclined toward the organizational requirements of property management. Despite their differences, Jimmy saw, both agents responded favorably to his courtesy and respect. And a little appreciation never hurt, either.

"Are you finding the same responses, Brad?"

"I agree with her assessment," Brad said soberly. "Most owners could be convinced to switch to a cheaper management service at the end of their current leases."

Just then, the door swung open and the agency owner barged into the room. "So you are having a private little meeting today?"

Jimmy nodded. "Do you need the conference room?"

"No, but I'm definitely feeling a bit excluded," the owner said contemptuously. "What is the purpose of this meeting?"

"Well, we're real estate agents," Jen said. "So what's your best guess?"

Before the owner could rebuke her, Jimmy intervened. "We're meeting here to coordinate our efforts to make more money."

It was a true statement that clearly threw the owner off balance.

"There's a rumor," he muttered, "that you're considering property management. I'd like to remind you that you are all bound by a noncompete clause."

"We would never forget our contract," Jimmy said with a long pause. "And you can be sure we are operating within the rules."

The owner eyed him. "Just making sure you're aware of it."

"Got it, boss," Jimmy said, and the owner stomped out of the room.

Jen closed the door behind him. "Why do you kiss his ass?"

"You call it kissing ass." Jimmy shrugged. "I call it managing a bully. A man with a big ego is easy to control, and I see no need to stir him up. Now listen, I've looked into this noncompete clause and we are not competing if we get into property management before him. We now have a critical goal to find a duplex to manage."

RELATIONSHIPS ARE THE CONNECTIONS between people. Our daily interactions with others can influence our financial success as well as the deeper reward of our personal fulfillment.

"Your career success in the workplace of today, independent of technical expertise," said Harold M. Messmer Jr., "depends on the quality of your people skills."

By the end of my house-flipping career, I was getting the best deals from many real estate agents. The deals came to me because I'd gained favor with the agents. I had gained favor because I was mindful to treat them with courtesy and respect. It wasn't a manipulative ploy, but an attitude of sincerity. We had personal relationships. I knew these agents as people—their hobbies, their families, and their stories.

I believe that everyone can win at relationships. Too often we tend to think that relationships—connections between people—are dependent upon inborn qualities like charisma, charm, personality, emotional intelligence, good looks, social grace, etc. These are all good excuses for not holding ourselves accountable for our relationships. I gained favor with real estate agents due to my courtesy and respect.

"Hey, John," I'd hear on the phone. "I got one for you to look at."

"Hey, my friend," I'd reply, "I'll always look at *your* deals."

This type of dialogue was common during my wealth building years when I counted every minute. I showed respect to another person and it didn't take a whole lot of effort to do so.

By contrast, it's sad how much is lost due to a lack of courtesy.

During a summer weekend, I was talking with a vice president of an international company. He was a guy who had come from a middle-class family and risen to the top, and so I asked a question.

"How does someone like you rise in such a huge company?"

His answer was quick. "It's really about relationships," he said bluntly. "A lot of stars get tripped up because they can't get along with each other, or with their bosses. It's the single biggest pitfall."

Since he called these people "stars," I had to assume they had many superlative qualities. But they couldn't master the simple attitude of showing courtesy and respect to others. What a waste of potential.

"You don't have to be friends with everyone you work with," writes Karen Rancourt. "Embrace 'have-to' relationships for what they are—functioning, but not emotionally close. The main goal of a have-to relationship is to create and maintain civility and cordiality."

What does civility and cordiality look like in the workplace? It is being a good person. It is being supportive of others. It is asking a coworker if he's feeling okay, and then listening. It is paying a sincere compliment. It is recognizing strong effort. It is giving credit. It is withholding criticism. It is forgiving others for mistakes. It is being patient when a person irritates you. It is choosing to remain calm. It is finding the right words. It is an attitude that makes others feel good around you.

Relationship building is about how we make people feel during our time with them. "People will forget what you said and did," says Carl W. Buehner, "but they will never forget how you made them feel."

If this statement is true at work, it is even truer at home.

In my own life, I've struggled like most parents. The more I loved my family, the more I strove to protect and provide for them. And to provide for them, I needed to work a lot and make sacrifices. How did I maintain strong family relationships despite coming home late at night?

I worked long hours, but I always shared my financial fears and hopes with my wife and kids. They knew my income, my expenses, my worries, my dreams, my wins, and my losses. I tried to express how my sacrifices would help pave a brighter future *for all of us*.

My son once relayed to me how his friends envied our relationship. He had told them how I was completely transparent with him about everything. I always revealed my vulnerabilities. They, in turn, envied him because their family dynamics were not so open.

And because I openly shared my vulnerabilities with him—instead of pretending that I had it all figured out as an adult—my blunt honesty helped him understand what I was facing. It was no different with my wife. She supported my sacrifices because she knew my intentions.

She understood *why* I was sacrificing our time.

My work supported the family. But it was my job to make abundantly clear to them the reasons for my sacrifices. To do so, I had to speak to them as partners and equals, whether it was my forty-year-old wife or my teenage children—I had to treat my family with courtesy and respect, without pride. I had to communicate from my heart.

When loved ones know we're all on the same team—and understand how sacrifices help the family unit—they'll support us almost always. When they don't understand the sacrifices of achievement, it's usually due to poor communication on the part of the ambitious one.

We need to be vulnerable at times to gain support. We need to show courtesy and respect to others. We don't need to fawn over people; we only need to choose civility and cordiality in our daily interactions.

People respond favorably when we support them in words, deeds, or attitude. When we support other people, we gain their support of us.

THE LIFE LESSON: RELATIONSHIPS

I gained the cooperation of others by being courteous,
And found that supporting others led to them supporting me.

LESSON 4-45 · SOUR ADVERSITY

Sour adversity: A bitter difficulty or misfortune.

The strongest oak of the forest is not one that is
protected from the storm and hidden from the sun. It's
the one that stands in the open where it is compelled to
struggle for its existence against the winds and rains and
the scorching sun.

NAPOLEON HILL

Adversity befalls every winning life, reminisced the Wealthy Gardener,
but achievers know that nothing is final until the heart stops beating. As
long as we have breath, we have hope.

He was struggling deeply this morning to shape his manual of success
into meaningful words and stories. Alone in his study, he finally stood,
sighed audibly, and walked to the bay window.

Outside he saw a picture of tranquillity: a sunny landscape with lush
green lawns, flowers, azaleas, and rhododendrons in their fullest spring
bloom.

He saw Fred next door with his puppy, walking toward the mailbox.
Getting the mail was a daily routine that occurred at precisely ten thirty
every morning. The man was a creature of habit, perhaps to his own
detriment, thought the Wealthy Gardener. Fred was a prisoner of the
known and the predictable. Unable to venture past his familiar routines
into new endeavors of risk or uncertainty, he was trapped by the patterns
of his habits.

Walking back to the house with his mail in hand, Fred suddenly stag-
gered to his left. He stumbled on wobbly legs for several strides, then
stopped on the lush green lawn. He seemed to recover his balance, but
then froze in place for several seconds before falling to his knees. The

Wealthy Gardener bolted from his room and raced next door. When he arrived at his neighbor's yard, Fred was gone.

The burial service was three days later. In the last row of chairs, the Wealthy Gardener surveyed the scene of familiar faces and the anguish of loss. The pastor of Fred's church recited Bible verses, and Connie's and Jared's shoulders shook in the front row. Family members sobbed openly. Jimmy sat in one of the middle rows with friends from work.

After the service at the cemetery ended, people clustered in groups before driving to the winery for lunch. Seeing Jimmy standing alone by a tree, evidently deep in thought, the Wealthy Gardener sauntered over to him.

"I know we're all going to die," Jimmy said softly, "but I can't help thinking how Fred died before he took a shot at the day care center."

"Fred had more than enough chances," snapped the Wealthy Gardener, "but the old fool delayed his action until 'someday'—and someday is a dangerous time. Come with me," he continued, motioning for Jimmy to follow him. They eventually stood at the closed casket, which rested under a makeshift tent.

"Here lies a man with unfulfilled potential," said the Wealthy Gardener, "who chose safety and ease over discomfort, who opted for excuses over sacrifices, who waited until it was too late and in doing so denied the world the gift of his beautiful dream. Learn from a fool who chose comfort, and vow to never ignore your own inner wisdom."

Jimmy stared at the coffin. "I won't ignore it."

The Wealthy Gardener motioned toward Jared, who was sitting alone on a bench. He looked wrecked, maybe even drunk, and had been conspicuously apart from his fiancée throughout the service. She was now driving away.

"Sadder still," the Wealthy Gardener said, "is a thoughtless life."

Jimmy followed the Wealthy Gardener's gaze toward Jared.

"Observe the grief of a superficial existence, the fate of one who lives only for the day," the Wealthy Gardener said coldly. "It's the face of self-absorption and the regret of wishing he had lived more intentionally. He now cries for time lost with his father, but he'll cry one day for an even greater loss. He'll mourn the time of living without aim. He lets time pass without impact, and in turn allows a life without significance. Woe to the one who wastes time and then defends aimlessness. His alibis secure his future regrets."

SOUR ADVERSITY is a bitter difficulty, a great misfortune. I once faced an adversity so soul-crushing that I wondered if death would be preferable to the fate I seemed destined to suffer.

At age forty, I was making financial progress. My mind was focused on my goals, my practice was booming, and my rental business was steadily growing. In contrast to my meager years of financial insecurity, I was now saving as much as the average chiropractor was earning in profits. Financial freedom was still far away, but I had a plan and direction. My clinic was busy ten hours every weekday.

I was doing so exceptionally well, in fact, that I attracted the attention of a major insurance company. I received a phone call from my local insurance representative requesting a meeting. At that time this insurance company accounted for 80 percent of health insurance coverage in my area.

The representative sat down with me and kindly explained that I was seeing too many patients.

"What do you mean?" I asked.

He explained that my practice was billing far more than an average chiropractic clinic in my area. I told him that was because I worked many more hours than the average chiropractor in my area.

"Be that as it may," he said, "if you don't get in line, you will be audited."

I was told to see fewer patients and bill less, or face consequences.

I drove home after this meeting in a state of mental numbness. As previously discussed in the book, an insurance post-payment audit review was the most feared threat in medicine at the time I was practicing. These audits were not aimed at finding fraud or illegalities, but rather were intended to review treatment notes. If the insurance company deemed my notes inadequate, I would be forced to pay back hundreds of thousands of dollars without recourse or arbitration.

I had taken steps to prepare for such a situation, but in Pennsylvania, no chiropractor had ever won an audit. The cards were stacked against me. The insurance company served as judge and jury, and it received the settlement money.

I thought about my options: Should I slow down my clinic at the extortion of an insurance company that controlled my financial cash flow? If so, it would be the end of my quest for financial freedom. I would have no money for real estate growth. I would continue earning a living but have no excess money above my living expenses.

Or should I stand up for what was right? I had nothing to hide. But as William McFee once warned, "Doing what's right's no guarantee against misfortune." Should I stand my ground at the risk of losing everything?

I decided to be defiant. I stayed busy and ignored the threat.

Two months later, I found a large envelope in my mailbox. The audit had arrived, and I was staring down the barrels of my greatest fear. They were requesting patient records dating back five years. I was asked to supply these records within two weeks, and then the insurance company would decide my fate.

There will be times in every life when one faces an adversity that does not have a silver lining. It hurts and inflicts hardship. The truth is that the worst adversities are sour, distasteful, and often soul-crushing. They are repugnant storms that seem to be nothing more than tests of endurance. They are trials of misery.

I would like to say that I faced this adversity with unflagging bravado. In truth, I was terrified. If I lost this audit, I would have a new life. With no skills for other work, I would be stocking shelves. If I lost, the insurance company would withhold all future payments to offset its fine. Like a fort surrounded by an imposing army, I would die slowly of financial siege.

I sent the requested records and awaited my fate. Months passed with no response. My hair thinned, and I looked gaunt. Sleep was impossible. I was helpless, worried, and vulnerable. After six months of torturous anxiety, however, I slowly came to a profound awakening. I was facing a crisis beyond my physical capacity to handle, but no future result could extinguish the Inner Light.

Within each of us is a light. It is pure love. It is gratitude for being alive. This light is the essence of the soul. When I was reduced to my worst nightmare, on the brink of losing it all, I realized that nobody has the power to take this light from me. I'd continue. I would survive. I could endure anything life threw at me without it breaking my spirit.

Only death extinguishes the Inner Light. And we can choose to love and be happy no matter what. I decided to trust the mental disciplines I had practiced so often in my past, this time radiating thoughts of a perfect outcome. I fixated daily on a total victory.

"Faced with crisis, the man of character falls back upon himself," said Charles de Gaulle. "In times of adversity and change," said Howard Schultz, "we really discover who we are and what we're made of." A wise old saying tells us that adversity introduces a man to himself. I agree. It is in our suffering that we find our souls.

Eventually, a single-page letter came back in reply to the audit. It had been buried in a stack of insignificant mail on an uneventful day: *Your records have passed the audit.* I read this sentence, unable to speak due to the lump in my throat. When I told my attorney, he was shocked by the news. I was the first chiropractor ever to win an insurance audit in the state.

Napoleon Hill wrote, "Every adversity carries within it the seed of an equal or greater benefit." But what was the benefit of this sour adversity?

I learned that adversity can either break the spirit, or it can reveal the spirit. We can discover the Inner Light, protect it during stormy seasons, and then allow it to guide us through the darkest days until the clouds of our adversity pass.

Sometimes the lesson of adversity is one of endurance. We learn to simply outlast crisis. It is a trial of misery with little benefit, other than introducing us to our strongest selves. And we learn that in the end, the only things we ultimately control are our thoughts and attitude.

When it was all over, I had a more accurate understanding of my resilience. And maybe this inner strength is the benefit that comes from sour adversity.

"Let me embrace thee, sour adversity," wrote Shakespeare, "for wise men say it is the wisest course." But it is a wise course only if we retain our hope, love, and joy of living.

THE LIFE LESSON: SOUR ADVERSITY

I met with adversity that nearly broke my spirit,
But found an Inner Light during my darkest hour.

LESSON 4-46 · ACQUIESCENCE

Acquiescence: The reluctant acceptance of something,
without protest, in order to change it or adapt to it.

If you enjoy the fragrance of a rose, you must accept the
thorns which it bears.

ISAAC HAYES

The want of ease leads to suffering, thought the Wealthy Gardener, and
causes a life of undue frustrations. Accepting "what is" may be the first
step to improving one's financial problems.

In the backyard garden a few days after the funeral, the Wealthy Gardener contemplated his life. Fred's death had stopped the world for a
week. It had also provided the Wealthy Gardener with a harsh reminder
of his own mortality.

His cancer was terminal, he had been told, and it was a fact that he'd
reluctantly accepted. He had tried chemotherapy, but one treatment had
left him muddled and exhausted for five days afterward.

The only person who knew of his cancer was Fred, and he was now in
a grave. Well, there's a time and a place for everything: *A time to laugh*
and a time to cry, a time to live and a time to die . . .

Fred was a gardener who never fully shaped his plot of land. What
had his indecision cost him? He had lived and died without realizing true
happiness or satisfaction, due to his inability to act on a dream.

The Wealthy Gardener thought about his own dream—the unfinished business of writing a financial guidebook for the boys at the reformatory. He would use his remaining days to live with purpose for this
final crusade.

Just then the doorbell rang. He didn't move from his chair, and a moment later Connie and Jared approached on the pathway to join him in

the backyard. Jared carried a cookie platter that had been dropped off at their house. They were soon sitting with him eating cookies, their chairs in a circle.

"So how are you holding up?" asked the Wealthy Gardener.

"It's been chaotic," Connie admitted. "It hasn't sunk in yet."

"I feel the same way. I'm expecting the old geezer to show up for cards tomorrow night. But he won't show up, and I'll need to get used to it." The Wealthy Gardener looked at Jared. "How about you, son?"

Jared sighed heavily. "I've been beating myself up about being so busy during the last year, and how I didn't make time for him in my schedule."

The Wealthy Gardener studied him for a long moment in silence. "There are some things, in the end, that we can do nothing about," he said at last. "And when we face those times, it is then that we learn to accept even our past mistakes."

Jared made no response, but his face was stony.

Connie spoke up. "I haven't seen you gardening lately."

"I have some unfinished business that I'd like to wrap up by the end of the year," said the Wealthy Gardener. "And I have an unforgiving deadline."

"I haven't seen you at the winery, either," Jared offered.

The Wealthy Gardener looked at him. "After your father's death, I've come to accept that life is short. And this leads me to want to make the best use of my own remaining days."

ACQUIESCENCE IS THE RELUCTANT acceptance of something, without protest, in order to change it or adapt to it. Accepting our life's current reality is the first step to improving our financial conditions. It's facing financial stress, not ignoring it, in order to grow more secure.

"Expecting that life is hard and accepting that ultimately results in it being less painful," says Stephen Josephson, PhD. "We can't necessarily get rid of pain, including the pain of losing a job or having to move, but we can get rid of suffering, and suffering is failing to accept what is."

During the audit described in the previous lesson, I acquiesced to a situation I considered unfair and senseless. If I had lost the audit, I had no better options for gainful employment than a high school teenager. A bully was punching me for being productive, working long hours, and serving too many people. In the end, my opinions didn't matter. I was in a fight, and I had to accept it.

When I finally accepted the reality that I had absolutely no power to control the outcome of the post-payment audit review, when I gave up my attachment to the outcome, when I accepted that this unfair situation was my current life, the suffering eased by several degrees. When I acquiesced to the unwanted situation, I then regained the power of my fullest mental resources.

I stopped fighting against the present reality and started thinking clearly. I could focus my mental concentration on my goals. I could radiate a positive outcome, find the Inner Light, and feel grateful in advance for winning. My acquiescence freed me to focus on better things. I gained time and energy for mental practices.

"Suffering is basically the mind's refusal to accept reality as it is," said Marcus Thomas. "Accept—then act. Whatever the present moment contains, accept it as if you had chosen it . . . This will miraculously transform your whole life," advises Eckhart Tolle.

Of course, such advice is easier said than done.

In modern times, we may need to accept that we can't save money working a forty-hour job; that we can't have both financial freedom and live in the house of our dreams in an affluent neighborhood; that weekends aren't always for leisure if we want upward mobility; that the highest-paying jobs are stressful and require solving big problems; and that prosperity requires daily sacrifices, inconveniences, and unglamorous work over many long years.

During the audit, I accepted that innocence was no shield against dire consequences. "Expecting the world to treat you fairly because you are a good person is a little like expecting the bull not to attack you because you're a vegetarian," said Dennis Wholey.

In the end, the audit vindicated me. My life should have returned to normal. But the insurance rep paid an unexpected visit to congratulate me on the great outcome. Upon leaving, he mentioned how "things may not go so well next time." Was this a threat? I wasn't sure by his tone, but I was wary.

How should I have responded after getting bloodied in the ring?

Throughout life, I have always used the expression "This is X." It is a reference point on maps that say *YOU ARE HERE*. There is always an arrow pointing to an X in our lives. When we find ourselves suffering, we need to accept X. We need to deal with it. We must get our head around it. We need to get on with the business of making plans and taking actions. The sooner we acquiesce to the facts, the quicker we regain our inner resources.

"Wisdom . . . is knowing what you have to accept," said Wallace Stegner.

Resistance to unpleasant situations is the root of suffering. But acceptance of unpleasant situations is the first step to overcoming them.

I had a bully threatening me after whipping me in the ring, and I decided that it was unwise to get into this fight again. I may have won the audit, but the insurance company won the war. I slowed my clinic volume down to be more uniform with all the other chiropractors in my area. What good came from it all?

We are told too often that success is about throwing hard punches, but in many situations, it is about *taking* hard punches. It is about survival. We can only win the war if we can stay alive to plan and fight another day. I retreated from the fight to retrench.

The unwanted reality was that I now had a substantially reduced income, and I didn't need to like it. I only had to digest it, readjust myself, and accept it.

"Every adversity, every failure, every heartache carries with it the seed of an equal or greater benefit," claimed Napoleon Hill. But what was the benefit of this reduced income?

Given my new circumstances, I had only one choice. I would cut back my hours at the clinic, which would then free up more time for my real estate flipping business. I gave thirty hours every week to each business for the next year.

During that initial year, I earned $150,000 through flipping real estate and $95,000 through my chiropractic clinic. The total income greatly exceeded my best year ever in my clinical practice.

Acquiescence was the start of a whole new direction.

"The resistance to the unpleasant situation is the root of suffering," wrote Ram Dass. And the problem of resistance is that it occupies our mental energy and distracts our attention when we need our fullest powers the most.

"Acceptance of what has happened," said William James, "is the first step to overcoming the consequences of any misfortune." There's always an arrow pointing to an X in life. When we suffer due to reality, we need to accept X.

While I was writing this book, my father, who was on vacation at the time, sat down on a couch one day and died. Death is the ultimate X, and since my father's passing, we've been adjusting. We accept that life is finite, and his death reminds us to respect the passage of time.

THE LIFE LESSON: ACQUIESCENCE

I caused my own stress by resisting my problems,
But found that accepting reality was the start of progress.

LESSON 4-47 · EMOTIONAL GUIDANCE

Emotional guidance: The sensory pull of a silent voice.

Gardeners must dance with feedback, play with results,
turn as they learn . . . Wise is the person whose heart
and mind listen to what Nature says. Time will tell, but
we often fail to listen.

MICHAEL P. GAROFALO

Our reasoning and intuition, considered the Wealthy Gardener, make a powerful team. It is best to get them in agreement, but there will be times when inner wisdom knows things that reason can't grasp.

It was a summer night with a star-filled sky. Dozens of small tents and campfires dotted the farm's grounds. About fifty attendees were gathered at the annual Eagle's Club Retreat. As in years prior, the attendees were either current students or past graduates of the reformatory for troubled teens. Since a newspaper article about the event had drawn the attention— and concern—of nearby residents, several policemen were present as chaperones.

"I get paid in satisfaction when I get it right," said the Wealthy Gardener to the others around the campfire, "and it's a form of compensation that guides me." The current topic of conversation was prosperity and the inner voice.

"I wish satisfaction paid my bills!" laughed a cynical former student in his twenties. He had graduated from college and was now a family counselor.

"Are you sure it does not?" asked the Wealthy Gardener.

"What do you mean?"

"I mean, are you worried about survival? Are you anxious about a job loss? Are you bored with the work you do? And do you always hate Mondays and dread the thought of your work?"

The young counselor smiled. "Well, I'm not that bad off!"

"But people do have these issues. Compared to them, you have satisfaction in your employment. All our negative feelings—fear, worry, boredom, dread—are an emotional guidance system screaming at us to change. And if we fail to listen, the inner voice will slowly fade."

There was a thoughtful silence around the campfire.

"I think it's important to make a distinction," Jimmy said. "I think fatigue, or a weak state of mind, can cause negative emotions like despair or a feeling of being overwhelmed."

The counselor studied Jimmy intently, and the Wealthy Gardener felt a fatherly pride in his protégé. "What do you suggest, then?"

"I'm all for listening to the inner wisdom," Jimmy said, "but I can't trust my emotions until I produce my best state through exercise, rest, meditation—whatever gives me strength. Only then can I know the guidance is real."

"It is wise advice," said the Wealthy Gardener. "Not every emotion should be followed with impulse. Still, we can learn to recognize our true emotional guidance system that speaks to us through feelings like boredom, worry, frustration, doubt, despair, insecurity, and even hopelessness, especially when they become overwhelming."

"And these feelings can guide our lives?" asked a boy.

All eyes drifted to the Wealthy Gardener, who was deep in thought. "Let me tell you the parable of the scarecrow," he said to the boys around the campfire. "It was made of straw, wore a flannel shirt—normal in every way, except that it had a brain, a heart, and the ability to walk. For several years after it was planted, however, it acted like all other scarecrows. It stayed motionless in its familiar field.

"As you might imagine, after a few years the crows lost all fear of the scarecrow. Soon they were occupying the same fields. One day a bold crow perched on the arm of the scarecrow and took a peck at him. It flew away with a piece of straw. It returned the next day and took another peck. And so began the start of a daily decline of the scarecrow's strength.

"At first, it felt wrong to the scarecrow. There was a vague sense of vulnerability, worry, and fear of survival. Worse, the scarecrow sensed a strange pull to leave this field, but also felt uncertainty about walking away into the unknown. It was a scarecrow, after all, and this meant it was reasonable to act like one.

"But each day, the scarecrow died a small death. It didn't happen all at once, but slowly and persistently, it lost a piece of itself to the pecking crows. It never budged and, choosing to ignore its emotional guidance system, the pecking soon felt normal. And the heart that once beat, well . . . it just faded until the scarecrow stopped feeling anything at all. The crows took the straw, and the scarecrow slumped forward without ever using its fullest innate abilities."

The Wealthy Gardener looked around the campfire. "Use your hearts, minds, and ability to choose," he said. "Never disregard the guidance of emotions. Stay close to the Source of your feelings. Be mindful to pause and listen every day for inner wisdom."

EMOTIONAL GUIDANCE is the sensory pull of a silent voice. When our thoughts are on what we want most, an emotional guidance system forewarns us of impending dangers and, conversely, pulls us like a gravitational force into opportunities.

I had a patient who lost her job after twenty years at a factory. This employment setback, however, gave her the long-awaited opportunity to pursue her life's dream. Kim loved animals, and she always wanted to start and run a pet grooming business.

I'll never know what happened, but after six months she eventually found another assembly line job. Given the chance, she didn't act. She knew it was wrong not to follow her heart, but in the end Kim simply acted like the scarecrow. And she now admits to a vague sense of dullness, lassitude, and despair. If only she had paused long enough to listen for the silent voice of emotional guidance.

"Feelings are really your GPS system for life," Oprah Winfrey said in a commencement address. "When you're supposed to do something, or not supposed to do something, your emotional guidance system lets you know."

It may be the inner voice speaking loudly when we feel boredom, worry, doubt, frustration, a sense of being overwhelmed, despair, financial insecurity, and hopelessness.

"A lot of what passes for depression these days is nothing more than a body saying that it needs work," said Geoffrey Norman. Work is easier than worry. And surprisingly, work can cure despair.

Through decades of business dealings, I have learned to rely on an intuitive sense, along with reasoned calculation, to arrive at accurate decisions. In my broader life directions, I have learned to view satisfaction as a green light that signals *GO*. And I have come to see the feeling of dread as a red light that signals *STOP*. Satisfaction or dread has guided the direction of my life.

"For the past thirty-three years," said Steve Jobs, "I have looked in the mirror every morning and asked myself: 'If today were the last day of my life, would I want to do what I'm about to do today?' And whenever the answer has been 'no' for too many days in a row, I know I need to change something."

While working on this book, a person asked me why I was writing it. As explained in an earlier lesson, after reaching my goal of financial freedom, I started feeling a sense of melancholy that I associate with my inner wisdom. I view this melancholy as a call for a new direction, a deeper understanding, or a rebalancing of my priorities.

It is a signal to pause and consider life.

I eventually followed this emotional guidance system to write out my lessons for my son, who was a college senior at the time. This melancholy gave way to a feeling of satisfaction when I commenced to write the book. And every week we would talk about the lessons.

We eventually finished all the life lessons and ended our weekly interactions, but then I felt the melancholy return once again. Was this melancholy my emotional guidance system urging me to push onward and develop these lessons into a polished book for publication?

I paused to consider my inner wisdom. I felt a strong intuition, a pull, to take this last step—I felt compelled to get the book published.

In stillness I sensed that this direction was right, and I trusted this sense. And that is exactly the essence of following our emotional guidance system—it leads us by an inner pull.

The challenge for me is that it leads into the unknown. We don't always get to see the destination when we choose our direction. Sometimes a feeling is all we will have to guide us on the way.

"Whenever you feel stressed, anxious, worried or uneasy about any part of your life, it's nature's way of telling you that something is wrong," said Brian Tracy. "It's a message that there's something that you need to address or deal with. There's something that you need to do more or less of. There's something that you need to get into or out of. Very often you'll suffer from what has been called *divine discontent*. You'll find dread in your days."

In my business ventures and financial pursuits, I have learned to move away from dread and toward satisfaction even when I can't clearly see where the new direction leads. It's not easy to follow the heart, but sometimes we must. Since the eyes can't always see what the heart can hear, it is sometimes wisest to close our eyes.

THE LIFE LESSON: EMOTIONAL GUIDANCE

I was inclined to think only with rational logic,
But found more success when I consulted my inner voice.

LESSON 4-48 · ACCOUNTABILITY

Accountability: Full responsibility for all that is.

Life is a garden. You reap what you sow.

PAULO COELHO

We are all self-made, believed the Wealthy Gardener, but only the prosperous admit it. One's conditions are the grade of one's past.

On a weekday morning, Jared walked his dad's dog before lingering in the backyard of his mom's house. The Wealthy Gardener emerged to water his flowers, and soon they were standing on either side of the picket fence.

"You're upset with me," Jared said. "You don't say it, but I can sense it."

The Wealthy Gardener paused to consider his best response, knowing this might be Jared's most-needed life lesson. "Do you really want to talk about this subject?" he asked candidly.

Jared nodded slowly. "I'm ready to listen."

A moment later they were seated in the Adirondack chairs, facing each other. "How exactly can you sense that I am upset with you, Jared? You claim to distrust Intangible Forces like sensing thoughts."

Jared shook his head without answering.

"As you may recall, I keep an acorn on my desk to remind myself to never think I know it all," said the Wealthy Gardener. "When I look at a dormant acorn, I am reminded of its potential, and I am humbled by the mysteries of the Universal Intelligence beyond my understanding."

Jared stared into the distance. "I suppose this leads to God talk?"

"Your mind is like an acorn," continued the Wealthy Gardener. "On my desk, it had potential within it. But the acorn on my desk sat for more than ten years, and nothing became of it over this time."

Jared looked thoughtful but didn't respond.

"Now, consider the mystery of Nature," he said. "When I took that seed and put it in the moist soil, it magically came to life. A seed that was dormant for ten years mysteriously grew into a live oak tree. And this sapling will produce thousands of acorns like the one from which it grew."

Jared breathed deeply and exhaled. "And the point is?"

The Wealthy Gardener motioned to a six-foot sapling in front of them. "See what has become of the acorn in soil?" he said. "In the same time, what has become of you?"

Jared was quiet for a minute. "I don't see the connection."

"In the garden of life, we are growing or dying. And our mind is the Unseen Power, the essence of our potential, the core of our being. We control it, or we control nothing. A controlled mind is the force that compels the actions, choices, work, and struggles behind every worthy achievement. An unfocused mind is like the acorn on my desk. We each have a Godlike potential in our minds, and we are accountable for it above all else. We honor it, or we waste it."

"I feel trapped by past mistakes."

"And you are the cause of it all. You are trapped by your lack of aim, and you'll always be trapped until you stop making excuses. You need to control your mind to focus on outcomes and become the power that grows acorns into oak trees. You have within your mind that potential of Universal Intelligence to shape your conditions."

Jared sighed. "But I don't even know what I want in life."

"And now you face the root problem. So I must ask: Are you doing anything to gain clarity, or have you stopped thinking altogether?"

Jared closed his eyes and sighed. "Where do I even begin?"

"Accept full accountability for your conditions," said the Wealthy Gardener. "Your conditions are the sum of your waking hours. Control your mind, and then let your inner wisdom direct you."

After Jared walked away, the Wealthy Gardener sat for a moment to reflect. We may have an inner wisdom, but we are free to ignore it. He decided to stroll to the farm next door, wondering if Jared would ever change his ways. People can change, but old habits die hard.

As he approached the farm, he smiled at the thought of its current owner. They hadn't spoken for way too long, and the Wealthy Gardener needed to enlist the aid of a reliable man.

After greeting Santos in his office, the Wealthy Gardener asked, "Do you recall when I put you in charge of my operations during my long absence?"

"Yes, of course."

"And what did you learn?"

"That my daily efforts matter on the farm, but the harvest is how I'll be judged. The world is impartial to talent, brains, character, or intentions. But focus of daily hours is the equalizer of men. I've discovered this truth, and I now live it every day."

The Wealthy Gardener smiled. "I'll be going on another journey, only this time for a much longer stay. And I would like to offer you the same deal in my absence. I need you to care for my operation along with your own, and if you manage both well, you will then be gifted my remaining businesses."

Santos gasped. "Your farm, vineyards, and winery?"

"Where I am going, I won't need much. And you are the one person who can keep my operations healthy," said the Wealthy Gardener. "I need a strong leader to ensure the welfare of the employees. Are you up to the challenge?"

"It would be the honor of my life, and you can count on me."

FULL ACCOUNTABILITY is taking responsibility for all that is—everything. There was a time when my life savings dwindled to half its value in the stock market crash of 2000–2002. I had invested at the peak of the dot-com boom, and then watched my cash vanish. Surely this financial calamity was due to forces outside of my control. It wasn't my fault, right?

In my view, I was fully responsible for the loss of my savings. A wealthy uncle once advised me to never put money in the market that I could not afford to lose. Why? Stock market money is not guaranteed to retain its value.

I don't recall anybody forcing me to invest my savings. I willingly entered this arena of risk. I was accountable for the loss. Internal thinking—not external forces—causes most failures. I had put the money in the market, and now it was gone.

"It is a painful thing to look at your own trouble and know that you yourself, and no one else, has made it," said Sophocles. "Mistakes fail in their mission of helping the person who blames them on the other fellow," said Henry S. Haskins. When we blame outside events for our failures, we lose our ability to change.

I have an acquaintance who owned a flooring business. In his sixties, however, the business failed. He filed for bankruptcy and retired in defeat with little money. His family and friends blamed his wife for the company's failure. She had handled all the cash flow, after all, and the owner—a simple man with little need for wealth—asked only for a weekly allowance. His wife ruined the business, they claimed, while the owner himself was a good guy who got raked by a gold digger. She divorced him, they said, and got his remaining money.

To this day I am speechless, unable to articulate a response to this man's family and friends. Business owners who do not guard their cash flow deserve all future miseries!

"The fault, dear Brutus," wrote Shakespeare, "is not in our stars, but in ourselves." Full accountability is a belief that empowers.

We may miss our goals due to external factors, but our daily thinking ensures our end victory.

"Ninety-nine percent of the failures come from people who have the habit of making excuses," said George Washington Carver. Due to my stock market misfortune in 2000, I gradually pivoted into real estate investing. We are always responsible and accountable.

I confided that during the first year of my business, I faced an inability to produce income. I could have blamed excessive competition. I wanted to excuse myself as a victim of the economy, my profession, my location—anything.

But I refused excuses and grew desperate enough to try using mental practices. I visualized patients calling the clinic, controlled my thoughts, radiated gratitude, and concentrated intensely on my goals. And I witnessed the phone ringing off the hook.

After that experience, it was impossible for me to believe in powerlessness. We cause our conditions, for better or worse, by our choices, our hours, and our thoughts. When I controlled my mind, I then gained the power of an inner wisdom that guided the way.

We are never unaccountable for our financial conditions. Staying in the wrong career is our fault. Living with insecurity is our fault. Having too little time is our fault. Not amassing savings is our fault. We allow it all, and we must own it all. When we blame others, or the conditions surrounding us, we give up our power to change.

Even during the crisis of my insurance post-payment audit review, I could blame only myself for my adversity. I knew the threat existed, but I didn't change careers to avoid it. Like a sailor heading into dark skies, I did not alter my course to miss the tumultuous storm.

Tony Robbins once said, "You always succeed in producing a result." It is a bitter pill to swallow when our results are poor, but this bitter pill is the best medicine for improving a condition. Earl Nightingale offered a memorable quote on accountability when he said, "We are all self-made, but only the successful will admit it."

THE LIFE LESSON: ACCOUNTABILITY

I saw that my financial conditions were my own doing,
And any other belief was a waste of my brain cells.

LESSON 4-49 · DIRECTION

Direction: The course along which someone moves.

One of the most delightful things about a garden is the anticipation it provides.

W. E. JOHNS

The way to wealth is a steady forward direction, the Wealthy Gardener believed, which happens to be the way to life satisfaction.

Jimmy stared into his new laptop on the desk at the agency. The numbers suggested upward momentum in both his real estate business and the property management operation. In fact, he could now turn his daily focus to saving his extra money. He hoped to begin a steady climb toward his long-term goal of financial freedom.

But as he studied his paltry $19,000 checking account balance, he felt a growing disenchantment. This was a full year of savings. Using this figure as the starting point of his net worth, he calculated how much he'd need to save over various interims to reach his goal.

Jimmy realized he needed deeper insight, and he knew exactly where to get it. He stood up from his desk, got in his car, and drove to his mentor's house. Minutes later, he walked around the house to the rear garden and found the Wealthy Gardener tugging a weed from the dirt. He was muttering under his breath as he worked.

Jimmy sat down in a chair without detection. "It's when the plants cuss back at you that you should be alarmed," he joked.

"Well, you sneaky son of a gun!" bellowed the Wealthy Gardener. "You're quieter than a church mouse. What are you doing here?"

Jimmy smiled quickly. "Just stopped by to talk for a minute."

The Wealthy Gardener stood slowly and straightened his back.

"These weeds are winning the war, but I just countered with a major of-fensive," he said, sitting down next to Jimmy. "Talk about what?"

"About financial freedom," Jimmy said, and then he explained how he was feeling discouraged despite his recent momentum. For the first time in his life, the twenty-three-year-old had done the math and saw that the numbers just didn't add up to his future aspirations.

"It was a lot easier to believe in my financial dream," Jimmy admitted, "before I used a calculator and a spreadsheet to plot it out."

"Let's take a walk and discuss it," said the Wealthy Gardener.

They got up and strolled through the vineyard, stopping once they reached the crest of a hill. There was a panoramic view of the neighbor-ing farm. The corn stretched as far as the eye could see.

"It's an impressive fall harvest," said the Wealthy Gardener, "and in-deed it's a miracle when you consider that none of it existed in this ground just eight months ago. Do you know what the farmer had to do to produce this bountiful harvest?"

Jimmy frowned. "He stayed moving every waking hour?"

"That's not too far from the truth," the Wealthy Gardener agreed, chuckling. "And it's the effort required on the farm. But that's only the visible part of the farmer's achievement. It's not really the absolute cause of the harvest, is it?"

"I don't know what you mean."

"The farmer planted in the spring and worked all summer, but through it all he trusted the seeds to grow. He could only do his own small part, and that meant using each day in the direction of the harvest. Every farmer is an optimist who works with the laws of Nature."

"I suppose that's true."

"You now have a clear idea of what you want in life. Use your days for direction and don't fret over it. You will see your dreams take root if you do your part and water them with daily attention. Trust prosperity to grow, knowing that plans always spring up from a conditioned mind.

The fall harvest unfolds when our thoughts are filled with purpose and faith. Opportunities will arise that you cannot imagine. With clarity and trust, the seeds of wealth will grow in the right seasons."

DIRECTION IS THE COURSE along which someone moves. Choosing our life direction is sometimes the only strategy that makes sense when our goals seem impossible. Direction gives us a sense of purpose. It fills us with daily satisfaction. And it leads to new opportunities.

"The road is always better than the inn," Cervantes said, but he surely meant that the road was better when we're heading in a direction of our own choosing.

When I turned thirty, my wife and I held hands and walked along a tree-lined street. We strolled past countless homes, and I recall thinking that every home was owned by someone. And every homeowner had a job, and each one of those jobs paid enough to own one of those houses. My income repaid my college loans during prosperous months, but it barely paid the bills during meager months.

Working for survival is motion without direction. Paying back student loans may be direction, but it's a lot like paying a mortgage on an invisible house. And so I then decided to pursue financial freedom—a goal so out of reach that I could only pursue its direction.

"Know what you want to do, hold the thought firmly, and do every day what should be done, and every sunset will see you that much nearer the goal," said Elbert Hubbard. Marian Wright Edelman wrote, "We must not . . . ignore the small daily differences we can make which, over time, add up to big differences that we often cannot foresee."

To pursue direction, I began by saving a dollar a day. I obtained a two-foot-tall plastic Coke bottle with a slotted lid for depositing money. This first step of saving a dollar a day was the start of an accumulation that led to my financial freedom.

Saving a dollar each day, trivial as it may seem, had a transformative effect on me. This simple act developed my wealth consciousness. When excess money came into my possession, it went into the plastic bottle. I occasionally emptied the bottle and deposited its contents at a bank. It gave me direction. But far more important, this little step gave me hope.

"Nobody made a greater mistake than he who did nothing because he could do only a little," observed Edmund Burke. "Success is the sum of small efforts, repeated day in and day out," said Robert Collier. "One thing at a time, all things in succession . . . That which grows slowly endures," wrote Josiah Gilbert Holland. "Happiness is a direction, not a place," said Sydney J. Harris.

My fondest memory of this crucial time is that, as I moved in the direction of prosperity, I felt like my workdays had meaning. Sure, there were many challenges along the road to independence. But the start of any journey, even before the first step, is a choice of direction. And from there it's just steady progress.

When choosing a direction, if we consider only those destinations that can be calculated and plotted, we limit our goals to the realistic; we downsize our dreams to the sensible. To reach our potential, we must never cower from the bigger goals that are out of reach. We only need to set a steady direction toward our aspirations and then trust the Universal Intelligence to assist our dreams according to our faith.

We can always change our lives by altering our direction. Any job can be left behind by aligning steady actions with a future goal. Poverty and financial insecurity are no match for consistent steps on a prosperous pathway. It is the use of days, and the impact of hours, that provides the foundation for the achievement of prosperity.

"It is by attempting to reach the top at a single leap that so much misery is produced in the world," said William Cobbett. Aesop said, "Plodding wins the race." "I find the great thing in this world is not so much where we stand," said Oliver Wendell Holmes Jr., "as in what direction we are moving."

THE LIFE LESSON: DIRECTION

....

When wealth was impractical and beyond my reach,
I focused on using each day to gain steady direction.

LESSON 4-50 · SELF-DISCIPLINE

*Self-discipline: The will to do unpleasant, difficult, painful,
exhausting, dreadful, and uncomfortable tasks.*

Every garden is a chore sometimes, but no real garden is
nothing but a chore.

NANCY GRASBY

Wealth requires sacrifices, mused the Wealthy Gardener, but mediocrity requires insecurity. The one with discipline will work in free hours, but the one without discipline will never be free.

He surveyed the classroom from behind the podium. "All right, everybody," he said loudly, "can I have your attention? We have covered a lot of ground this year, mainly on the theme of your financial success. We have talked about how to earn money and gain financial security so that you'll never have to rely on forces outside of your control. Now today, I want to discuss your main advantage to succeed in this competitive world of employment."

The classroom was quiet as he wrote on the chalkboard:

Success is hard—it's your advantage!

"You'll graduate this year," he continued, "but your success outside these walls will be earned through the payment of sacrifices. Success is hard, and most people won't tolerate the hardship. But you will go into this world and be like warriors, willing to endure suffering to gain satisfaction. You will not shrink from hard challenges. You will think big and you won't settle. You will fight without yielding to opposition. You will accept fear but never self-pity or excuses. You will seek the toughest paths to earn rewards, and you will be happier for it. Mediocrity is the hardest life of all, and it is not for you."

Jimmy glanced around the classroom, believing that the kids seemed both mesmerized and intimidated by this bold lesson of future hardship.

"Your goals will be earned by trials that others won't bear," continued the Wealthy Gardener. "And you should be glad they're hard, because that means you can win. Your critics will be silenced by the show of your discipline."

He turned, walked to an easel, and removed a blank sheet of poster board to reveal one with the following words:

HAPPINESS = DIRECTION

Direction in life comes from discipline.

- *Do what you* **resist**: *All growth requires resistance.*
- *Push past hard: Glory is found* **beyond comfort**.
- *Go for* **failure**: *Challenge your current capabilities.*
- *Suck it up:* **Pain is an ally** *that eliminates the weak.*
- *Set* **bigger** *goals: Stay uncomfortable by thinking huge.*

The classroom was dead quiet as all eyes scanned the five points. One of the boys sitting in the middle of the room sighed audibly.

"It doesn't look like fun," he said. The other kids laughed.

"It doesn't need to be fun," agreed the Wealthy Gardener, "but it leads to a better and happier life. Now, can somebody please tell me the first rule of discipline?"

A hand went up in the front row. "Do the things we resist?"

"That's remarkably accurate," chided the Wealthy Gardener. "Do what you resist. Choose the path of most resistance. Self-discipline builds strong habits. Do the dreadful things first every day, without exception! Now, who knows the next rule of discipline?"

"Push past hard?" a kid said, reading the poster board verbatim. "Glory is found beyond comfort!"

"You are psychic today!" the Wealthy Gardener shouted dramatically. "It's like you are in my head. And yes—in every worthy endeavor, there's a point when you hit the wall. But there's no growth in the comfort zone.

Growth and glory are only achieved by what you do after you push into the suffering phase."

"So we should challenge ourselves by going for failure?" one student asked, reading from the board again. The kids laughed, and even Jimmy smiled at the upbeat atmosphere.

"Well, that is an astonishing question!" the Wealthy Gardener yelled. "I was about to say that very thing. People don't know their potential because they don't fail enough. If you do ten good push-ups, you gave a good effort. But if you do push-ups until you can do no more, you gave it your all. In our work, we should push to failure. People don't do this, however, because extra effort and temporary failure are uncomfortable. What's the fourth rule of discipline?"

"Suck it up!" the kids shouted in unison.

"You got that right!" the Wealthy Gardener shouted back. "Pain is your ally—it eliminates the weak. Accept it and be glad. There is no such thing as an easy life that contributes much to a worthy cause.

"Both successful people and unsuccessful people hate discomfort, but successful people suck it up and do the work anyway. They don't need to like it. They just do their jobs. Doing the things that suck separates the successful from the average."

The kids were laughing uproariously now.

"What is the last rule of discipline?"

"Set bigger goals!" the class shouted.

"And why not? Goals are your future. Don't water them down. Make them big enough to scare you. Choose goals that make you uncomfortable. The bigger the goal, the better. If you will only dare to dream and then endure with a rare discipline the temporary discomforts, you will stand out among the masses."

SELF-DISCIPLINE IS THE WILL to do unpleasant, difficult, painful, exhausting, dreadful, and uncomfortable tasks. The day came when financial freedom was mine. The quest had been a stealth mission since my life had appeared as one of steady work and humble choices.

When the day finally arrived, I was close to my fiftieth birthday. This was the age I had written for my goal completion; I had visualized it a million times. And when it happened, I then had time to think.

I realized that maybe I was just a big fish in a small pond. On the other hand, moving forward in my life, financial freedom was life-changing. I had lived and worked in the middle class, starting out deeply in debt, but I somehow managed to retire by fifty. It was an uncommon outcome in life, especially given my humble beginnings.

I valued my prize.

But more important, I cherished its price.

In hindsight, what counted was the struggle. I earned self-respect and deep satisfaction by enduring daily discomforts and hard challenges over decades. My fondest memories were those of conquering the worst of times with unrelenting discipline.

"The one quality which sets one man apart from another—the key which lifts one to every aspiration while others are caught up in the mire of mediocrity—is not talent, formal education, nor intellectual brightness," said Theodore Roosevelt. "It is self-discipline. With self-discipline, all things are possible. Without it, even the simplest goal can seem like the most impossible dream."

Self-discipline is needed to choose discomfort.

"Success is a comfort awarded only to those willing to do the uncomfortable," said Darren Hardy. "Growth requires a constant state of discomfort so get used to it."

Success is hard. But so, too, is mediocrity.

I never enjoyed the daily pain during the years I built my wealth, but I was rewarded by conquering it. Discipline is doing what needs to be done, when it needs to be done, whether we want to do it or not. It is swallowing our pride, choosing wisely, resisting impulses, and maintaining a steadfast focus.

"Resolve to perform what you ought," said Benjamin Franklin. "Perform without fail what you resolve." Discipline is a battle to be fought anew each day, and it requires a lonely walk on the path less traveled. "Live like no one else now," Dave Ramsey reminds us, "so later you can live and give like no one else."

Discipline is choosing between what we want *now* and what we want *most*. It is impulse control over our feelings and suffering. Self-control is the quality that distinguishes the fittest to survive.

"A professional is someone who can do his best work when he doesn't feel like it," said Alistair Cooke. "The ability to delay gratification in the short term in order to enjoy greater rewards in the long term is the indispensable prerequisite for success," said Brian Tracy. We must choose the hard life to earn our comforts.

Among all disciplines, however, there is one that governs the rest. It is the easiest of them to perform and perhaps the easiest to forget as well. It is the discipline of living with daily purpose.

"Your ability to discipline yourself to set clear goals, and then to work toward them every day," said Brian Tracy, "will do more to guarantee your success than any other single factor."

"Small disciplines repeated with consistency every day," said John C. Maxwell, "lead to great achievements gained slowly over time." Discipline liberates us to be who we want to be, to do what we dream of doing, and to have the things we hope to have in life. And Jim Rohn said it best: "We must all suffer one of two pains: the pain of discipline or the pain of regret."

THE LIFE LESSON: SELF-DISCIPLINE

I wondered if wealth required too much sacrifice,
Until I saw that mediocrity required too much worry.

LESSON 4-51 · IMPACT STATISTICS

Impact statistic: A measurable input that advances
a successful outcome; an action goal.

Don't judge each day by the harvest you reap, but by the
seeds that you plant.

ANONYMOUS

Wealth is built on results, reflected the Wealthy Gardener, and it grows
from steady impact that can be measured in the passing days.

Jimmy and the Wealthy Gardener drove home together in the truck,
as was customary after a lesson at the reformatory. They talked about
that evening's general message and the kids' reaction.

"I just don't get one thing," Jimmy said. "I have the self-discipline to
outwork the other agents. But there are some weeks when my work produces no results. And so success is not just about work ethic."

The Wealthy Gardener smiled. "I see where this is going," he said,
steering into his driveway. They went inside and, minutes later, were
seated on kitchen stools facing two bowls of ice cream. "What causes
your best results?"

"It's the impact of the work," Jimmy said. "I mean, on some days, no
matter how busy I am, I just don't get a lot done. Other days I get a ton
of important things done. In both cases, my effort is the same."

The Wealthy Gardener nodded. "We see that people can work identi-
cal hours with vastly different results. Busy is normal but impact is rare.
Work results is a subject we'll need to discuss in the classroom."

Jimmy nodded. "But now how do I ensure my own results?"

"Let me tell a story that may help clarify the subject of targeted effort," said the Wealthy Gardener. "I once coached a youth basketball
team. I told the kids to hustle, to do their best, and to outwork their op-

ponents. But my advice only made them busy, frantic, and exhausted in their games. They became victims of unrewarded hustle.

"And so I made a chart of key statistics," he continued, "and I tracked the stats of impact for their games. Now the kids had objectives. They stopped being busy and frantic, and they started to grab rebounds, take charges, steal the ball, and care about shooting percentages. By tracking these key statistics, it was clear that some players ran around on the court with no impact in the games, while others made huge impacts, as measured by those key statistics."

The Wealthy Gardener leaned back, satisfied he'd made his point.

Jimmy nodded. "I could use impact statistics for my work."

"We only have so many hours in a day," said the Wealthy Gardener. "Without objective measures, we are like my players, who believed hustle was their only goal. Our impact is the goal. Many adults never grasp the difference between hustling and contributing. Statistics clarify it."

Jimmy leaned back with an enlightened expression. "It would explain why my results vary despite giving the same effort during my ten-hour days."

"It is as you say," agreed the Wealthy Gardener. "In all pursuits, there are vital activities that produce winning results. These are the objectives of work. We must focus on impact statistics to direct our work on the winning."

"It makes perfect sense," Jimmy said. "I'll start tracking my inputs."

IMPACT STATISTICS ARE INPUTS that advance a successful outcome. Wealth arises from consistent, result-producing efforts that can be measured. These impact activities can be tracked in hours, while other inputs are best tracked by tasks completed.

We track our impact statistics to focus our exertions, and to separate everyday hustle from the key hustle that wins the game. If we rely on memory alone, we're all superheroes of effort. But if we keep track of impact statistics, we will often see the true reality of our efforts.

"Nothing is easier than self-deceit," claimed Demosthenes.

The importance of tracking effort became apparent to me while I was working as a chiropractor. I dreaded the weekly imposition of insurance paperwork. I detested the follow-up on past billings. I groaned about checking for denied claims. The critical objective of insurance work is full reimbursement for services rendered to patients. The work is dull, monotonous, frustrating, and never ending. Sadly, I could not delegate this unwanted task to someone else.

I hated this work so much that I lumped all paperwork into Wednesdays— I would suffer all day without interruption. And I did an amazing job of almost doing what I should've been doing to win the game.

I gave six hours every Wednesday to this weekly torture. But on those days, I'd also clean the floor in the waiting room. I'd do paperwork and go for a run. Sometimes I would drive to a store to buy materials for my latest real estate project. Patients would often call and, since I was at the clinic, I'd tell them to stop in for a visit. I was always busy, always getting stuff done.

When I began tracking my time spent on actions that got results, I had to first clarify which activities drove my key results. I called these my impact activities. In this case, I started to focus on the impact activities that were most vital to insurance collections. And then I tracked my weekly hours spent in total immersion on these critical impact activities.

How can we identify which impact activities of our daily work will contribute most to winning the game? Ask yourself one question: If you could offer only two hours a day for a critical work outcome, which tasks would fill this limited time? This question, with its imaginary time constraint, forces deeper clarity.

A second question may help provide clarity as well: Which activities, if *not performed* today, would result in the worst consequences? Which two impact statistics are most vital to winning the game?

I recorded my key impact statistics for Wednesdays by tracking my time spent on these vital actions using a desk timer. The desk timer was running while I was planted in my chair, immersed in one of the critical tasks related to insurance reimbursement. When I performed any other task in the day—and this included using the restroom—I paused the desk timer.

On the first day, I clocked seventy-four minutes at my desk during my six-hour day at the office. Most of my time that day had evaporated into minutes related to real estate, eating lunch, exercise, seeing patients, and taking phone calls. I was shocked! Without keeping track, I was overestimating my actual input. Busy is normal, but impact is rare.

Within a month, I was able to log six hours devoted to this dreaded task every Wednesday. Did tracking my efforts increase results? That year my insurance collections increased $24,000 despite similar billings the previous year. It's humiliating to admit that I was not collecting this money due to a lack of focus and, worse still, a lack of full effort. I was misjudging my own inputs.

Being busy means doing stuff. Being productive means getting stuff done. Being effective means getting the most important stuff done. When we track tasks that produce critical results, we shed light on the real contribution of the work hours in our weekly schedules.

"Follow effective action with quiet reflection," said Peter Drucker. "From the quiet reflection will come even more effective action." I found that financial freedom required a lot of hustle directed by vital impact statistics.

THE LIFE LESSON: IMPACT STATISTICS

I learned that busy is normal, but impact is rare,
And results skyrocket by tracking impact statistics.

LESSON 4-52 · ASKING

Asking: Making an inquiry that can open doors.

Because a garden means constantly making choices,
it offers almost limitless possibilities for surprise and
satisfaction.

JANE GARMEY

"Ask and you shall receive" may not be an absolute maxim, thought the Wealthy Gardener, "but not asking is the absolute way not to receive."

The Wealthy Gardener and Jimmy were sitting on Adirondack chairs facing the garden. The leaves on the oak trees were a brilliant reddish orange; the evening autumn air was crisp and invigorating. "So what's your end goal?" asked the Wealthy Gardener, his voice raspy. "Five years from now, that is, where do you see yourself?"

"Let me think about it," Jimmy answered slowly. "Why five years?"

"Why not five years?" the Wealthy Gardener asked. "In five years, you'll be a new person with new conditions that are unrecognizable from now. I never plan farther than a five-year horizon. It will always be a new garden every five years."

"Okay, in five years," Jimmy said, "I'll be a real estate broker, and then I'll employ ten to fifteen real estate agents. I also expect the property management business to grow to four hundred units. And last, I want to help the cause against drunk driving to atone for my past mistake."

The Wealthy Gardener paused, thinking of Jimmy's accident. He'd always believed Jimmy needed to forgive himself, but now chose to avoid this taboo subject.

"That's an ambitious plan indeed," the Wealthy Gardener said simply. "But now I want to ask a favor of you. I'm leaving for a retreat and will be gone a very long time. Would you be willing to take over the classes at the reformatory? You are my best student, and I think you're ready now. Teaching these kids would be natural for you."

Jimmy hesitated. "I'll need time to think about it."

The Wealthy Gardener looked serious. "You can say no, but I think you'll regret it in the future. And if I don't ask you now, I know that I'll surely regret it."

Jimmy stared into the distant landscape.

"There's no rush for you to decide," added the Wealthy Gardener. "I have two months before I leave on the journey. Just consider it. You are free to decline. But it is my job to ask, and not presume I know your answer."

"Fair enough," Jimmy said. "Now, let me ask you a question. During the past four months, you've virtually been a hermit. You look sick, you've lost weight, and your voice is raspy. Why don't you tell me what's up?"

The Wealthy Gardener sighed. "I suppose you should know. I've been working on a book for you to use at the reformatory. Since I won't be around next year, I was hoping to leave it behind with you. It may be an old man's folly, but I'm creating a syllabus. This project consumes my waking hours."

"Is that your unfinished business?"

"Yes, it is," the Wealthy Gardener said, nodding, "and it must be finished before I leave this place. But it's slowly sucking the life out of me—as you can see."

Neither spoke as they sipped iced tea. A gust of wind hurled through the overhead tree branches, causing some leaves to flutter toward the ground.

"How long have you been a real estate agent now?"

Jimmy did the math. "About eighteen months."

"Within six months, you'll complete your two-year apprenticeship," said the Wealthy Gardener. "You'll then be able to be a real estate broker, and own your own business."

"Well, yes. I can do it legally, but it's not really practical."

"And have you approached your owner to see if he's willing to sell?"

"Willing to *what*?" Jimmy asked, taken aback. "He'd never sell to me. And besides, I don't have the resources to even consider a purchase."

"My best student still has much to learn," the Wealthy Gardener said, sighing. He paused, staring at the horizon, then continued. "Is it wise to answer the question for your boss without giving him a chance?"

Jimmy looked dumbfounded. "You believe it's possible?"

"What is required to make it possible? That is a much better question."

"I'd need an owner willing to sell," Jimmy said, "and I'd need a pile of cash to pay him. And, oh, by the way, I'd need both in less than six months!"

"And you believe it's impossible?"

Jimmy appeared defensive. "What am I supposed to believe? Should I naively think anything is possible, on any deadline, despite any obstacle?"

"Maybe not, but you're forgetting a thing called asking," said the Wealthy Gardener. "Little hinges swing big doors. Asking for what you want in life is a little hinge, too often ignored, that can swing the mightiest of doors."

Jimmy stared at him, and then his gaze softened with understanding. "Would you finance the purchase of it?"

"Yes, indeed I would," answered the Wealthy Gardener. "This option awaited only your request. Our dreams are lost for want of asking. Opportunities in every life vanish in the silence. Questions open doors."

"Okay then," Jimmy said, grinning. "Let's talk turkey. Would you like to fork over several million bucks as a generous gift between good buddies?"

"I would not," chuckled the Wealthy Gardener. "But you would be wise to notice that my rejection causes no harm. A question denied is rarely a setback. It's just a swing at the plate with no strike called."

. . .

ASKING IS THE ACT of making inquiries that can open doors. Dreams are lost for want of asking. Lives remain stuck for lack of bold questions. What do you want, and what is required to make it possible?

During my business career, I have experienced the power of bold questions. I would not be financially free if not for asking for what I wanted. And I've learned it is my job to ask the question—not to answer it for another person.

"You get in life what you have the courage to ask for," said Oprah Winfrey. "Ask for what you want! Give other people the opportunity to say 'yes.' Stop saying 'no' for them," said Roger Ellerton. And Peter Mc-Williams advised, "Learn to ask for what you want. The worst people can do is not give you what you ask for which is precisely where you were before you asked."

For many years I have continually asked audacious questions that required courage, planning, and a lot of discomfort.

I asked to buy a coveted clinic building with no money down. I offered to pay for it over five years, including a final balloon payment. The sellers were speechless, but then they said yes. To me it felt just like paying rent. Since the "rent" went toward the future buyout, the building was virtually free.

What would I have gained if I hadn't asked for it?

In an earlier lesson, I detailed how I made an offer to buy a block of duplexes at a 50 percent discount. The real estate agent didn't want to present my "lowball" offer to the sellers. He was shocked when it was accepted. I was glad it was his job to ask the question, not to answer it for them. I then asked the bank for a refinance loan. I received a loan for my total investment plus $140,000 more, so these six duplexes were cheaper than free to me. And they net a positive cash flow of $3,000 per month.

What would I have gained if I hadn't asked for it?

A foreclosure property came on the market at $190,000. I made an offer of $75,000. It was unrealistic to expect the bank to drop to this price. But, again, it was my job to ask, not answer for them. I reasoned that renovations on this distressed property would amount to an additional $75,000. And I wasn't working for free—I fixed houses for profit. From my point of view, it was a legitimate offer. But the bank refused to even respond to it. That is, until the day they asked my real estate agent if my offer was still on the table. I live in this house today.

What would I have gained if I hadn't asked for it?

It is crucial to note that every major financial advancement during my life has followed a bold question. There were always many other factors involved, but these other factors varied according to the situation. The only constant in these life-changing leaps of progress was a bold question. Bold asking preceded every big break.

"Many things are lost for want of asking," states an English proverb. If we fail to speak up for what we want, doors will fail to open on their own. The best opportunities are reserved for those of us with the courage to give another person the chance to say yes.

Doors will remain closed for the silent majority.

"If you don't go after what you want, you'll never have it. If you don't ask, the answer is always no. If you don't step forward, you're always in the same place," wrote Nora Roberts. Bold questions are the keys to opening doors that would otherwise remain closed.

THE LIFE LESSON: ASKING

I found that asking led to leaps of progress,
And a bold question preceded every big break.

LESSON 4-53 · AFFLUENCE

Affluence: The state of having a great deal of money.

Watching something grow is good for morale. It helps
us believe in life.

MYRON S. KAUFMAN

The rich may get richer, pondered the Wealthy Gardener, but only because they once managed their income and expenses to gain an advantage. Wealth arises from passing sacrifices that yield rewards.

They sat on the stone patio, as Jimmy summarized his attempt to buy
his boss's business. "So my boss said he'd sell if the price was right, but
then a week later he came back with an outrageous number. I told him
the price was too high, and so I pulled out of the deal."

The Wealthy Gardener raised an eyebrow. "I'm impressed by your
restraint, and your protection of money. It's a good sign for your financial prospects in the future."

"What do you mean?"

"Those who protect money, and learn to grow it, will gain advantages
over a lifetime." There was a pause, then the Wealthy Gardener stood up
and led Jimmy to a goldfish pond built into the stone patio. They began
feeding the fish.

"In every goldfish pond, we always find several specimens that are
disproportionately larger than the others. At the start, these large goldfish had a slight advantage. Maybe they were just born bigger, but their
huge size today is due to this slightest size advantage in their past."

Jimmy nodded without comment, watching the fish gulp the food.

"Due to their size advantage, the bigger fish ate more food each day.
In turn, they grew even larger. And in time, it became a self-perpetuating

cycle. The larger these advantaged fish became, the more food they ate each day, and so the larger they grew."

The Wealthy Gardener paused for effect, watching the fish swim in circles.

"Your wealth is very much the same," he said slowly, "in that it grows from the smallest of advantages. We hear people complaining that the rich get richer, but these complainers are failing to earn their own small advantages."

"And that is how you became wealthy?" Jimmy asked. "You rose by gaining advantages?"

"I had to earn financial advantages by managing my income and expenses," he said, "and then I managed my advantages to amass my wealth. The postponement of luxuries, combined with the acceptance of long hours, allowed my wealth to outpace others'. While my friends lived for pleasure, I grew into the largest goldfish in the pond. And so the start of my wealth was born from small advantages. You must acquire excess money and use it to grow your own advantages."

"Well, you have given me an advantage with your generosity," Jimmy said. "My greatest fear now is blowing my one chance."

"We all have more than one chance. Smart money always seeks a home. You will always find investors if you can ensure the safety of their money and show them a successful track record. But now what's your plan? Have you found another real estate agency to buy?"

Jimmy paused, sighing audibly. "I've changed course. If I buy a business, I want it to be a property management company. It's a safer operation to evaluate due to the predictability of future cash flow. I found an owner who's willing to sell, but the problem is that it will cost twice the amount we discussed."

"And what can be done to make it possible?"

"Well, I'd like to show you an investment that I think makes sense."

The Wealthy Gardener grinned, and they reviewed the business for the next thirty minutes. Jimmy believed the price was fair, based on past tax returns and a capitalized earnings valuation method. The Wealthy Gardener delved deep into the profit-and-loss statements, year-to-year earnings, consistency of gross income, and net operating income after taxes.

"Now, if you own this business, what will matter most to you?"

"The net profits and cash flow," Jimmy said. "But my goal would be to get more doors under management to build the gross income."

"How much will you pay yourself as the owner?"

"Well, that's not exactly clear," he admitted reluctantly. "Since it's my business, I could claim all profits after taxes. And it looks like I can take home maybe five thousand a month, based on the current spreadsheet."

"What will you do with this money?"

Jimmy laughed. "I haven't decided just yet."

"Oh really?" countered the Wealthy Gardener. "But I thought your goal was financial freedom. If you want to be wealthy, the use of excess money is never a decision for the whims of your desires. All surplus is saved to build your financial prosperity."

"Save every dime of my profits?"

"Maybe not every dime," said the Wealthy Gardener. "But you will need to sacrifice, and if you can survive on your real estate commissions alone, then these profits are untouchable. It is seed money for a harvest that will grow and produce more seeds, and those seeds will grow to produce seeds of their own, and so on."

"I can do that." Jimmy smiled. "I'll use my profits to start seeding my fortune."

AFFLUENCE IS THE STATE of having a great deal of money. In my thirties, I was in the middle of my struggle for wealth but still a million miles away from the finish line. One evening I was at a niece's birthday party with thirty family members and friends. The kids were playing, the women were talking, and the dads were drinking heavily.

At the end of the night, an attorney friend of mine walked over and put his arm around me. "You're the smartest one of us," he said. "I'm watching what you're doing. You work your ass off. And you live below your means. The rest of us spend our money. You're going to end up richer than all of us."

He surely wouldn't recall his words the next day, but I never forgot the impression he left on me. He saw that I was quietly gathering capital and increasing my financial advantages; I was earning money and protecting it. I was saving it and investing it. Behind the scenes, I was quietly amassing a financial snowball for the future.

My growing affluence required sacrifices of time. It demanded risk, but only when the odds were good and when the rewards aligned with my goals. And it required me to swallow my ego.

Vanity is a luxury for the broke.

"Thrift is not an affair of the pocket," said S. W. Straus, "but an affair of character." "Men who make money rarely saunter; men who save money rarely swagger," said Edward Bulwer-Lytton. But is the sacrifice worth it?

As one who has been on both sides of the fence and has struggled in the middle class, I can give testimony to the power of capital and the advantages available to those who will sacrifice and delay gratification to amass it.

Many years later, in my forties, I was finally approaching my goal of financial freedom. One day I met with the president of a large bank and its chief commercial lending officer. I was anxious but also prepared for the meeting. I had created a folder to leave with them along with a detailed proposal for a critical loan—it included a net worth statement that showed I was worth $2.4 million. For years I had saved, and throughout that time I had maintained a relationship with this bank.

I brought my son, Mike, a college finance major at the time, to witness the transaction. We were greeted at the front door by my loan officer, Linda. She welcomed us easily and then escorted us on an impromptu tour of the main bank offices. At each door, she introduced us to the employees. The staff members stood to shake our hands. They were respectful, acting as if we were royalty.

For ten minutes I felt like I was experiencing someone else's life.

And even the top brass of the bank continued the red carpet treatment. Not only did I get the loan, I experienced a moment that fathers dream about: I had brought my son to show him a skirmish for money, but instead he saw the fruit of hard labor, the reward of sacrifice, and the esteem that is showered upon those who prove themselves worthy to be safe stewards of capital.

"A bank is a place that will lend you money if you can prove that you don't need it," joked Bob Hope. Banks lend to those with proven track records. This is because financial records reflect patterns of behavior and choices.

I always drove used cars, but I paid cash for two college educations. I lived in a moderate house in a rural town, but own over a hundred rental units with positive passive cash flows. I operated a chiropractic clinic in the basement of a veterinarian clinic for years, but I now own the best professional building in town. I worked weekends and evenings instead of relaxing, drinking, or golfing—but I enjoyed the quiet exhilaration of amassing money for financial freedom.

I gave my time and energy to build a fortress of capital. And when I had a few rough years, the fortress was resilient enough to withstand any crises.

My daughter unexpectedly needed $9,000 while in college, and I easily paid cash. My son required $14,500 after graduation, and I wrote a check. A family car died, and I bought another one for $25,000. A roof needed to be replaced, and I doled out $14,000. I was disabled for three months but managed to live comfortably on my passive income. My wife wanted to earn a teaching degree, and her tuition was recently paid—without loans—from the steady flow of residual income.

I know that my loved ones never need to worry due to the power of affluence—I am their safety blanket. And the power of capital provides this refuge. The ultimate blessing of having enough money is never having to worry about having enough money. Peace of mind is priceless.

Affluence alone provides these real powers, and nothing can take its place.

When we are broke, we must give our life to create a money snowball that grows on its own. But in time the money becomes a genie that has no equal for granting wishes.

"Each day acquire something to fortify you against poverty, against death," advised Seneca. "Try to save something while your salary is small; it's impossible to save after you begin to earn more," joked Jack Benny.

The start of my savings was a dollar a day, and the journey required two decades of steady progress, delayed gratification, and a swallowed ego. It was often dull and mundane. It was slow plodding. It was not all passion.

But when I look back, I see temporary sacrifices to gain slight advantages. And as I worked, these tiny advantages became greater in power. In the end I gained the upper hand, not over others, but over my life's financial condition. "Money," said P. T. Barnum, "is a very excellent servant, but a terrible master."

My drunken lawyer buddy was right: I was unlike others in my small community. I had taken Dave Ramsey's advice to live like no one else now, so I could later live like no one else. And during the climb, I knew no friend more loyal to me than my growing affluence.

"If your outgo exceeds your income," said Bill Earle, "then your upkeep will be your downfall." But conversely George S. Clason reminds us that, "Wealth is power. With wealth many things are possible." Wealth expands options.

THE LIFE LESSON: AFFLUENCE

I saved my dollars to gain a financial advantage,
And then managed my advantages to amass my wealth.

Self-forgiveness: Letting go of guilt, remorse, shame, self-hatred, or self-contempt for failures or mistakes.

A gardener learns more in the mistakes than in the successes.

BARBARA DODGE BORLAND

What most people never suspect, mused the Wealthy Gardener, is that wealth involves personal mistakes, wrong choices, and even humiliations. And the challenge of inner peace—the greatest treasure—is the maturity to forgive ourselves for our regrets and imperfections.

He finished his morning meditation and blew out a candle. At exactly nine, there was a knock on the door. Jimmy was about to enter, but instead, the Wealthy Gardener stepped outside. "Today I'd like to go for a walk."

"Okay." Jimmy shrugged. They traipsed steadily along a pathway that meandered through the vineyard. They spoke of trivialities until they arrived at a serene pond on the edge of the property. They could see Mary's tombstone on the nearby knoll.

"I have one last bit of unfinished business," said the Wealthy Gardener. He paused as the cold wind cut through the air. "My upcoming retreat is a permanent stay. I will soon join Mary in eternity."

Jimmy's eyes widened slightly. "I knew it—you're going to die."

"I have terminal cancer. I've known it for a year. The treatment did nothing but make me sick. I chose to accept my fate instead of adding six more months of illness to my dying days. And I'm sorry I didn't tell you sooner."

Jimmy appeared frozen by the news. "How much time is left?"

"Weeks, or possibly days, I don't know for sure."

"Why didn't you tell me sooner?"

The Wealthy Gardener sighed. "I know you, Jimmy. If I had told you a year ago, my illness would have taken you from your own life affairs."

"Maybe that was a decision best left to me."

"I beg your forgiveness," answered the Wealthy Gardener. They sat on the bench by the pond; the wind blew, causing ripples on the water that startled the ducks.

"I brought you here for another reason," he continued cautiously. "I need to talk to you about Mary's death. You've paid your penance, son. And before I die, I need to know you will let it go. I must know that you will forgive yourself."

Jimmy didn't speak for a minute. "I can't do that," he said coldly. "That accident is a part of me, and it's my own burden to bear in life."

The Wealthy Gardener was silent for a long moment.

"When Mary died in the accident," he began, "Fred helped me to get up and moving—to find a cause outside of myself. It was his idea to meet the underage youth who'd driven the other vehicle.

"But when I walked into the reformatory to gain my closure, I found only a scared teenager inside those walls. You weren't the animal I'd imagined. You were just a vulnerable human being who had made a re-grettable mistake. But you had the strength and decency to approach me and apologize."

The Wealthy Gardener turned to look at his protégé.

"I lost my wife in that tragedy, Jimmy, but I gained a son. By finding you, I found meaning in my later years. And since the day we met, you've been the blessing of my life. You healed me, and now I need you to for-give yourself. In my final days, it is the only favor I ask."

Jimmy shook his head slowly. "I can't do that for you."

"I ask you to do it not for me," said the Wealthy Gardener, "but for you. Yours was the mistake of a child, but it doesn't define who you are now. My days are behind me, but yours are still ahead. A bright future awaits you, but only if you forgive yourself for the mistakes of the past. I forgive you. And you can be sure that Mary has forgiven you as well."

Jimmy took a deep breath to steady his voice before he spoke.

"I erased her from every special occasion in your life," he said at last. "I caused her death, and I can't forget it. I deserve the guilt and pain. It's my scar, and I won't let it go. I want to use it to prove that my own life matters. And to one day make you proud of me."

"Take these last words to heart," said the Wealthy Gardener, his voice shaking. "I accept you without conditions. I love you beyond measure. No man has ever been prouder to call someone a son."

Jimmy seemed like he was about to speak but swallowed his words. His head dropped and he struggled to retain his composure.

The Wealthy Gardener reached over and grasped his hand. "Don't let your wounds turn you into someone you are not. You're not your mistakes, son. You have nothing to prove to me. You are already forgiven." The Wealthy Gardener leaned closer to him. "Now forgive yourself. That is my only dying request for you."

Jimmy closed his eyes, and a single tear rolled down his cheek. He slowly put his face in his hands and sobbed. It took him an hour to cry it all out.

SELF-FORGIVENESS IS LETTING GO of guilt, remorse, blame, shame, self-hatred, or self-contempt for past offenses, mistakes, and failures.

At fifty-two, my brother lay motionless in a parking lot. A car had veered off the highway, caromed over a median, and swerved toward where he was standing. At the last second, he realized the vehicle was coming straight at him. He ducked behind his own car for protection. But the out-of-control vehicle smashed into his car, hurling it into him. The impact sent him airborne. He landed twenty feet away, dead on the scene.

An eighty-year-old woman had been unconscious behind the wheel of the car. As it turned out, she had fallen into a diabetic coma while driving. The passenger in the vehicle was her blind husband. After the accident, the woman was taken to the hospital but checked out okay. She was reportedly unconcerned over the dead victim.

The police launched a full investigation. The elderly woman was charged with vehicular homicide. It turns out that she'd been at a local bank before the accident and, while there, had nearly passed out from low blood sugar. Her husband had argued with her not to drive, but she had driven anyway.

And a minute later, my brother was dead. I wouldn't know it until three hours later. My mother called with words that will echo within me forever. "Joe was in an accident," she said, her voice breaking. "And he's gone."

Many emotions swirl in the aftermath of a nonsensical accident. Our inner family suffered and grieved the unfair loss of a loved one. But we didn't entertain the emotions of bitterness or revenge for too long. We refused to press charges.

We chose to forgive, but not for the sake of the elderly lady.

We chose to forgive for the sake of ourselves.

Only by forgiveness can we suffer tragic loss or soul-crushing failures and come out unscarred and undamaged. Forgiveness does not mean ignoring the pain; it means deciding that the pain will not control what's left of our life. Forgiveness heals the wounds of the soul. It gives us closure.

If we could only be so generous in forgiving ourselves.

One of my close friends was trained extensively in a career field with few local opportunities. After applying to a number of positions, he landed a coveted interview for the perfect job. The vital interview came by way of a referral from a colleague.

On the morning of the interview, however, through no fault of his own, my friend experienced a freak panic attack. It gripped him like a seizure; he couldn't move or think. Going to the meeting was impossible. He stayed home and missed the interview.

He hadn't chosen the panic attack, but he has never forgiven himself for it. He didn't bring it on, but he clings to blame and shame. He holds on to the memory in merciless self-torture for missing his big shot. He will not forgive what he calls "the big choke."

"If your compassion does not include yourself, it is incomplete," Buddha said. When we forgive, we heal. When we let go, we grow. "Forgive yourself for your faults and your mistakes and move on," said Les Brown.

Another friend of mine acted on her lifelong dream of owning an antiques business. She found a space on a busy thoroughfare. She rationalized that all the traffic would be good for business and the store's visibility, so she agreed to pay an exorbitant rent.

Within two years, her business was closed. Her money had run out. She took the failure personally, and she lives with remorse. People didn't care to buy what she had for sale, and the congested traffic almost assured the store's invisibility.

"People in heavy traffic focused on staying in their lanes," she said, "not on my sign." She is glum talking about it and won't let herself off the hook. She stepped up to the plate, took a good swing, and missed the ball. It happens. But her worst mistake is that she allows her failure to define who she is today. She hasn't moved on. She still beats herself up. And she hasn't risked again.

"Forgive yourself for not having the foresight to know what now seems so obvious in hindsight," said Judy Belmont. The challenge of failure is to forgive yourself for not knowing what you didn't know before you learned it.

"As I walked out the door toward the gate that would lead to my freedom," said Nelson Mandela, "I knew if I didn't leave my bitterness and hatred behind, I'd still be in prison . . . Forgiveness liberates the soul."

"There are many aspects to success," said Deepak Chopra. "Material wealth is only one component . . . But success also includes good health, energy and enthusiasm for life, fulfilling relationships, creative freedom, emotional and psychological stability, a sense of well-being, and peace of mind."

It's always time to forgive yourself for whatever you keep beating yourself up about. When you feel the need to replay a negative situation in your mind, consider reading the following passage about forgiveness to help you let go of the past:

God, grant me the serenity to stop beating myself up for not doing things perfectly, the courage to forgive myself for mistakes of the past, and the wisdom to know that yesterday's regrets do not define who I am today.

THE LIFE LESSON: SELF-FORGIVENESS

I used to beat myself up over mistakes and regrets,
But I found that self-forgiveness allowed my brightest future.

Habit: A behavior pattern followed until
it has become nearly inescapable.

Habits are like a garden full of seeds. Some grow into
flowers; others into weeds.

MARIE CIOTA

Jimmy called off work to sit beside Mary's tombstone the following day.
He watched the ripples on the water, the white clouds floating in the sky.
He felt remorse, but he also sensed an unfamiliar peace.

At noon the Wealthy Gardener approached from behind him and laid
a hand on Jimmy's shoulder. "Would you mind some company?"

"I'm kind of busy," Jimmy said, turning with a smile.

The Wealthy Gardener chuckled and sat on the ground beside him.

"Can I ask you a question about death?" Jimmy asked.

"Okay, but just keep in mind I haven't done it yet."

Jimmy grinned. "Now that you're dying, what's your final advice
to me?"

The Wealthy Gardener sat a long moment in silence. "It's not easy to
come up with one bit of final advice," he admitted. "But I'd say, if pressed,
that one should never play leapfrog with a unicorn."

Jimmy laughed. "Come on—I'm serious!"

"Okay then, I'd have to tell you to form successful daily habits. We
first make our habits, and then our habits make us. It's the ultimate life
strategy."

Jimmy looked at him curiously.

"Prosperity may be a way of life," he continued, "but it's a way of
life that's built on doing the right things. The longer we do the right

338

things, the more these right things become our habitual patterns. It's not that habits lead to effortless achievement, but that our most-repeated activities—over time—will become almost involuntary. Habits compel us, and eventually they control us."

Jimmy didn't say anything as he thought about it. He considered how he wrote down his goals every day and how the ritual felt natural to him. He knew it was a habit because it seemed he was compelled to do it. He always felt better after writing his goals. But when he skipped this ritual, he felt worse.

"And one more thing," added the Wealthy Gardener. "Life is difficult alone, Jimmy. Stay close to the Source. Be aware of silent promptings. Direct your thoughts; heed your inner wisdom. You will find that Universal Intelligence always responds to clarity and faith."

Jimmy nodded. "And I'll have your guidebook for the kids at the reformatory?"

"I believe this is true, but only you can determine it."

"Aren't you going to give me the book?"

"If you're prepared for it, you don't need me to give you the book," said the Wealthy Gardener. "If you are ready to receive it, the book will find you."

"I'll need a few years to figure that out," Jimmy joked. "But seriously, in the meantime, it seems to me that I know little about personal finance. All we talk about are the behaviors that lead to wealth."

"And that's because behavior is the main obstacle. But still, I see your point," said the Wealthy Gardener. "Set aside an hour each morning to meet with me. I will teach you the ten seeds of wealth."

HABITS ARE BEHAVIOR PATTERNS followed until they become nearly involuntary. I have always felt a deep contempt for the power of habits. It seemed like a philosophy for slackers, for those without the iron discipline or sheer willpower to plow down obstacles. Success habits seemed like a copout for the weak—until the power of habit finally beat me into humble submission.

It is evident to me that the dominant trait of my character is raw discipline. I worship the hallowed ground of self-discipline because it has been behind my daily goals, work, mental practices, self-control, daily meditation, sacred efforts, and, ultimately, financial freedom.

Discipline has been the skill that makes up for many of my average qualities and ordinary weaknesses. But there was a period in my life when this trait mysteriously vanished.

It is a humbling story that taught me the power of habits. While this example centers around exercise, it is ultimately about actualizing our full potential. It is about assuring prosperity by making success habits part of our physical brain.

Due to a busy work schedule in my later forties, my time for exercise shrank to thirty minutes a day. I had previously developed a post-workout ritual of lounging in the sauna or whirlpool for ten minutes. With a tighter schedule, however, I couldn't exercise for thirty minutes and then relax for another ten.

It is important to study the psychology of the following changes.

At times I swam for a full thirty minutes and skipped the whirlpool. At times I swam for twenty minutes and used the whirlpool. Some days I ran for thirty minutes and skipped the sauna. On other days I ran for twenty minutes and used the sauna. And after a year of this, I found that I had no willpower for thirty-minute workouts!

What in the world was wrong with me? By the age of fifty, I was pretty set in my ways. I knew my strengths, and I knew I could always drive myself to do whatever needed to be done, regardless of temporary suffering.

But now it required a Herculean effort to exceed twenty minutes of exercise!

Had turning fifty somehow made me soft and lazy? I didn't think so, because I still had the capability to write for ten hours straight every day. And I still had the stamina to outwork my thirty-year-old contractors in the labor of real estate. So what was going on in the exercise department?

With deeper insight, I realized that I had trained myself to choose the short workout. It had taken about a year, but over time, I had rewired my brain. Like Pavlov's dog, I had given myself a treat for every short workout, withheld the treat for every longer workout, and trained my brain to control me.

"All bad habits start slowly and gradually," said Zig Ziglar, "and before you know you have the habit, the habit has you." It was true. But it was also true that I could transform my bad habits into good ones. For the next year, I steadily rewired my brain with "rewards" after thirty-minute workouts.

We make our habits, and our habits make us. And, at last, I understood a humbling truth about my financial success: It was the power of habit that was behind my daily goals, work, mental practices, self-control, meditation, sacred efforts, and, ultimately, financial freedom.

"Motivation is what gets you started," said Jim Rohn. "Habit is what keeps you going." Our repeated activities—over time—become almost involuntary.

"Once you understand that habits can change, you have the freedom and the responsibility to remake them," wrote Charles Duhigg in *The Power of Habit*. "Once you understand that habits can be rebuilt, the power of habit becomes easier to grasp, and the only option left is to get to work."

THE LIFE LESSON: SUCCESS HABITS

I erred in thinking that habits were for weaklings,
But saw that my own prosperity was built on daily habits.

Chapter 5

THE 10 SEEDS OF WEALTH

LESSON 5-1 · THINK WEALTH

Wealth: An abundance of possessions or money.

He who hunts for flowers will find flowers; and he who
loves weeds will find weeds.

HENRY WARD BEECHER

"Any fifth grader can grasp the strategies required to be rich," the
Wealthy Gardener said to Jimmy on the first day. "It is human behavior
that leads to failure of the masses."

Jimmy thought about it. "Wealth is a matter of self-discipline?"

"Yes, but not entirely. What matters most is knowing what you want—
clear, definite goals with a specific attainment date—and knowing why
you want it. Wealthy people know why they want to be wealthy. They
have deeper reasons. Discipline will wane when the climbing gets steep,
but a compelling purpose for the money fortifies our determination."

"Are you saying that rich people are clearer on why they want wealth?"

"I am indeed. The masses may want wealth, but their desires compete
with many other wants. The accumulation of money comes to those who
seek it and sacrifice their contradictory desires. It eludes those with scat-
tered focus. The wealthy tend to narrow their aims and direct their time
and effort. They avoid mindless pursuits because they want money and
the lifestyle it can afford them."

"Like a Lamborghini?" Jimmy grinned.

"Whatever gets your pot boiling," said the Wealthy Gardener, smiling. "But in reality, most people who achieve wealth have a humbler lifestyle. They are accumulators, not big spenders. They are focused on the
long game. Their reasons for wanting wealth vary, but the wealthy all
wanted wealth."

"Doesn't everyone want wealth?" Jimmy asked, almost to himself.

"Yes, but average people want it without the sacrifices required to accumulate it," said the Wealthy Gardener. "The wealthy think about money more seriously. They will sacrifice the luxuries of today for the promise of tomorrow due to their greater vision. They know what they want, and—"

"And they know why they want it," Jimmy interrupted, smiling. "You seem to be implying that so much of wealth comes down to thinking."

"Thinking of wealth leads to behaviors that lead to accumulation." The Wealthy Gardener closed his eyes. "Regardless of the causes behind it, what we think about tends to become our reality. The outer world is but a reflection of our inner world. This has been the constant truth of my life."

Jimmy raised an eyebrow. "Isn't high income correlated to future wealth?"

"It would seem logical, but substantial wealth tends to elude any person, regardless of income, who does not make wealth a priority. The gathering of riches requires actions and choices that are compatible with its buildup. The wealthy think of accumulation. They are wired to think differently."

"They are different in what ways, exactly?"

"They think about their direction. They know their goals. They spend time alone in reflection. They read about wealth. They study and plan ways to grow richer. They know how much they are worth, how much they earn, how much they spend, and where the money goes. The wealthy are happier due to their progress. And they are always trying to find more profits by increasing their earnings while decreasing their expenses."

"So the first seed of wealth is to think a lot about wealth?"

The Wealthy Gardener smiled. "And to know why it is important to you."

345

. . .

WEALTH IS AN ABUNDANCE of possessions or money. People who eventually gain wealth think a lot about it. "You must walk to the beat of a different drummer," Dave Ramsey said. "The same beat that the wealthy hear. If the beat sounds normal, evacuate the dance floor immediately! The goal is to not be normal, because normal is broke." You need a clear goal and a big why.

"All riches have their origin in Mind," said Robert Collier. "Keep your best wishes close to your heart and watch what happens," said Tony DeLiso.

Keep a vision of wealth close to your heart. Write goals and read them at night and in the morning. Feel amassed money in your possession and see yourself performing services to earn this reward. In your quiet time, assure yourself that wealth is your destiny. Feel prosperous until it feels natural. Drive wealth deep into your mind. Build a faith that displaces all doubts.

"A prosperity consciousness," Brian Tracy said, "attracts money like iron filings to a magnet." The days pass and, with focus, our wealth grows.

Thinking of wealth will influence the mind to make better choices. "If you would be wealthy, think of saving as well as getting," said Benjamin Franklin. "The wealthy buy luxuries last," said Robert Kiyosaki, "while the poor and middle-class tend to buy luxuries first."

Tomorrow's wealthy are the accumulators of today. They are focused, self-disciplined, steady earners with contempt for spending. They think about wealth and what it will mean for their lives. They forgo luxuries today.

The knowledge of why one wants wealth—a greatest desire or a worst fear—is vital to the perseverance that precedes any substantial accumulation. Our reasons anchor our resolves. The wealthy know why they want riches.

For example, George Orwell had a clear motive for wealth: "Lack of money means discomfort, means squalid worries, means shortage of tobacco, means ever-present consciousness of failure—above all, it means loneliness."

Warren Buffett and Charlie Munger knew why they needed wealth. "Like Warren, I had a considerable passion to get rich," said Munger, "not because I wanted Ferraris—I wanted the independence. I desperately wanted it."

Accumulation of wealth, before actions and choices that lead to it, requires uncommon thinking. The wealthy must want wealth more than they want comfort, luxury, or social status. Wealth finds those who clearly know what they want—and why they want it—and spend a lot of time thinking about it.

THE LIFE LESSON: THINK WEALTH

Since I tended to get what I thought about in life,
I concentrated daily on wealth and why I wanted it.

*Frugality: Spending very little money and only
on things that are really necessary.*

By sowing frugality we reap liberty, a golden harvest.

AGESILAUS

"Trying to become wealthy without curbing expenses is like trying to lose weight without cutting calories," said the Wealthy Gardener on the second day. He was lying on the couch, looking frail and weak; Jimmy sat in a nearby rocking chair.

"It's hard to argue that one," Jimmy said, amused at the comparison. "But I see wealthy people who drive expensive cars and live in beautiful houses."

The Wealthy Gardener eased into an upright position. "Do you really?" he asked. "And how is it that you know these people have amassed wealth?"

Jimmy didn't respond to the question.

"The truth is, you don't know, do you? You only see their spending—not their bank accounts. You see high-income earners consuming 'prestige products.' But the more visible their spending, the less likely it is that they're saving."

"Maybe they can afford these possessions and still save."

"It is not impossible," agreed the Wealthy Gardener, "but it is unlikely. The reason is, most people, regardless of other factors, tend to raise their spending to their incomes. I'll stress this more tomorrow, but it explains why so few people end up with wealth. In the end, they give it all away. This tendency is especially prevalent among high-earners with status jobs."

Jimmy considered it. "But you own a lot of things."

"The stuff I own earns money," the Wealthy Gardener said, chuckling. "And my expenses never kept pace with my rising income. I'm a farmer by trade, and farmers turn income into savings better than most professionals. Frugality has been easy for me because my needs have been few. I like simplicity."

Jimmy agreed. "I like simplicity and freedom."

"Says he with the new car parked outside my humble abode," said the Wealthy Gardener, raising an eyebrow. "Says he who lives in an expensive townhouse with a swimming pool, fitness center, and tennis court."

Jimmy stiffened in response. "I needed a car and a home."

"Of course you did," agreed the Wealthy Gardener. "But only the wise distinguish between needs and wants. You needed a car, but you wanted a new one. You needed a home, but you wanted a luxury townhouse. If you earned no more than $25,000 a year, however, financial constraints would teach you the difference between your needs and your wants. As it is, you were able to choose more than your basic needs. This is the expanding lifestyle trap."

Jimmy sighed audibly. "But I don't want to live like a poor man."

"Only you can choose," agreed the Wealthy Gardener. "Just don't deceive yourself. Spending is fun, but frugality leads to freedom. Spending is instantly gratifying, but it can lead to wage slavery. Luxury cars and expensive homes come at a price—they deplete wealth."

Jimmy didn't respond as he contemplated these words.

"Everybody wants a cure for financial problems," said the Wealthy Gardener, "but nobody likes the medicine. Frugality is the medicine."

"I have no problem with sacrifice," Jimmy countered. "I just may be more inclined to increase my earnings in order to win the game of wealth."

"Personal finance without thrift is like a dam with many leaks," said the Wealthy Gardener. "Water cannot accumulate despite the generous flow of the river. Likewise, a lifetime of income without frugality always depletes."

Jimmy smiled begrudgingly. "Okay, I'll dam up the damn river!"

. . .

FRUGALITY IS SPENDING very little money and only on things that are necessary. An Ashanti proverb tells us, "One cannot both feast and become rich." "Beware of little expenses; a small leak will sink a great ship," wrote Benjamin Franklin. In the old days, a person who saved money was a miser; nowadays, the same person is a wonder. Frugality is rare.

So is the accumulation of wealth.

It is estimated that less than 3 percent of the US population will become first-generation millionaires. Those who make the grade rarely do so until they are in their fifties. They credit hard work and discipline. They are not borrowers. Most live in middle-class neighborhoods. The average millionaire is not likely to display wealth. Friends and family usually have little clue that these millionaires are rich. Most of them drive used cars. Often, their strong defense helps them outscore their competition, even those who have a superior income.

Financial defense requires a bit of modesty, mixed with a dash of humility, added to a whopping pound of independent thinking. Rich people stay rich by living like they are broke; broke people stay broke by living like they are rich. Future millionaires control expenses. They delay their indulgences.

Delayed gratification is the key to financial accumulation. You must not think of yourself as too good for any task, nor think that you're entitled to free time, entertainment, comforts, status symbols, or showy extravagance. Instant gratification prevents long-term wealth.

"Allocating time and money in the pursuit of looking superior often has a predictable outcome: inferior economic achievement," wrote Thomas J. Stanley. "What are three words that profile the affluent? FRUGAL FRUGAL FRUGAL." The amassing of wealth is earned through work and thrift.

Financial achievement is the result of hundreds of small efforts and sacrifices that no one ever sees or appreciates. It's not about how much we make, but how much we keep—that is what determines our financial gains. How much we keep requires both offense and defense. It requires frugality.

THE LIFE LESSON: FRUGALITY

I faced daily choices between spending or saving,
And gained upward mobility through sacrifice and modesty.

LESSON 5-3 · PROFITABILITY

Profitability: Ability to generate excess money.

Wealth, like a tree, grows from a tiny seed.

GEORGE S. CLASON

"Wealth is built on profit-*ability*," said the Wealthy Gardener. "It's the ability to earn money and spend money in a way that results in excess money to save."

"You're referring to discretionary income?" asked Jimmy.

"Bingo—that's the stuff. In a business, an owner who spends profits on luxuries will usually end in failure. In life, the same tendency causes underaccumulation. Spending money on nonessential items leads to vulnerability. We need to have excess money to be wealthy."

Jimmy thought about it. "I think most people get the idea that they need to save and invest money. The common problem is they don't have money at the end of the month."

The Wealthy Gardener frowned. "Household economy is the first issue to resolve. It takes a good offense, or earning more, and it takes a good defense, or spending less. The wealthy do both to win. Profits result from a balanced game plan."

"What if people have a ceiling on income?" countered Jimmy. "And what if their monthly income barely covers their fixed living expenses?"

"Then they are chained to a life of financial insecurity," said the Wealthy Gardener. "They are prisoners of wage slavery. They live to meet living expenses and to pay taxes."

Jimmy sighed, thinking there was no worse fate.

"What we need are financial constraints," said the Wealthy Gardener. "We need to set aside a portion of every paycheck to create a condition of forced scarcity. This plan reduces our capacity to spend. It is the way to assure the behavior that leads to wealth."

Jimmy sighed. "I have absolutely no clue what you mean."

"For example, recall the discussion we had yesterday about you earning $25,000 a year. If you could earn no more, don't you think your spending would be different than if you earned, let's say, $125,000 annually?"

"I'd admit that's true."

"Well, the difference in your spending is due to a constraint. When you exist in an environment of economic scarcity, it ensures your frugality. Right?"

"Yes," Jimmy said, sensing he was being led into a trap.

The Wealthy Gardener continued. "Have you ever heard the phrase *pay yourself first?*"

"Sure—save first and spend what's left."

"The reason it works is because it imposes an artificial environment of scarcity. With little money to spend, we clearly choose our needs—not our wants. And somehow we manage to always survive while saving money."

"You followed this plan?"

"You can be sure of it," said the Wealthy Gardener. "It's the only way to get real money in the bank. It ensures we don't fall for Parkinson's law."

Jimmy smiled, knowing he was now being baited. "What is this law?"

"Glad you asked," said the Wealthy Gardener with a wry smile. "This law says that no matter how much money people earn, they tend to spend the entire amount and a little bit more besides. Their expenses rise in lockstep with their incomes. Many people today earn several times what they earned at their first jobs. But somehow they seem to need every single penny to maintain their current lifestyles. No matter how much they make, there never seems to be enough. It explains why most people are broke."

"And why spending is the cause of failure," Jimmy said. "But paying myself first will create a spending constraint to assure my monthly profitability."

PROFITABILITY IS THE ABILITY to generate excess money. Broke people will argue against setting aside money at the start of each month. "How can I set aside money at the start of the month," they ask, "when I have no money left over at the end of the previous month?"

It's a logical question, but accumulators think differently than people who are broke. They may set aside one hundred dollars, for example, and then save incrementally higher monthly amounts over time. They accept lifestyle changes. They cut back. A lifestyle of financial insecurity must be transformed into a lifestyle that creates monthly profits.

"But what if I cut back and my income still does not produce enough to save?" you might ask.

"He that will not economize," Confucius said, "will have to agonize."

Profitability may require earning more. The forty-hour workweek is for survival income. Wealth won't grow from minimum efforts. Accumulation requires sacrifice—working smarter, harder, and longer—and this explains its rarity. More income may require working two jobs, pursuing more education to increase earning capacity, or running a side business.

If you want more, work more. "Work is a surefire money-making scheme," said Dave Ramsey. "Without labor nothing prospers," said Sophocles.

"But I don't have time to work more," is a common refrain.

"A television costs you about $40,000 a year," said Jim Rohn, "not to own it, but to watch it. What else could you do with that time?" How about working, earning, or learning? Time wasted is money lost and wealth abandoned.

When we use all our waking hours, we will have money to save. If we allow our expenses to increase at a slower rate than our incomes, and we save or invest the difference, we can become wealthy during our working lifetimes.

THE LIFE LESSON: PROFITABILITY

I struggled for years with no success in saving,
Until I developed a strong offense and a stingy defense.

LESSON 5-4 · GET OUT OF DEBT

Debt: An obligation to pay or repay; a state of owing.

Interest on debts grows without rain.

YIDDISH PROVERB

"If you ever want freedom," said the Wealthy Gardener, "you must break free of debt. It is the slave master in a free society, the obligator of drudgery. Debt robs the future of time and money. It chains the worker to the wages."

"Slavery is a pretty strong comparison," Jimmy countered.

"What would you call working for nothing but food, shelter, clothing, and debt obligations?" asked the Wealthy Gardener, shaking his head. "It is surely a form of slavery. Where is the hope for a better condition in such a life?"

"The hope lies in earning more," Jimmy said, "to pay down the debt."

"It is exactly as you say," agreed the Wealthy Gardener. "Debt is so easy to fall into but so difficult to climb out of. Debtors come to realize that their futures have been sold to their creditors. And they are trapped. Their lifestyles may appear okay, but the interest payments devour their profits. When monthly wages are consumed by debt payments, the soul always grows weary."

"I'd rather die than exist like that," Jimmy said. "I would work three jobs as long as it took. There is no way I would allow debt to control me for life."

The Wealthy Gardener smiled, leaned forward, picked up a clump of papers from the coffee table, and handed them to Jimmy. It was a business loan for $585,000 at a 6 percent interest rate with a twenty-year amortization schedule.

"Welcome to debt," said the Wealthy Gardener, chuckling. "I now own you."

Jimmy thumbed through the paperwork. This was the loan he would use to buy the large property management business. "So the monthly payment is $4,191," he said. "I can handle that much and still earn my own profits."

"Yes, and we have reviewed the numbers. Any debt that earns a profit is good debt. But tell me, are you aware of the amount of this loan?"

Jimmy looked surprised at the dumb question. "It's $585,000."

"That's not even close," said the Wealthy Gardener. "You are obligating yourself to pay $1,005,869 with interest over twenty years. That's your real cost. It's shortsighted to only consider the monthly payments."

"Well, it seems to me the business will be paying it—not me."

"I agree that the interest matters less when it's paid by profits," said the Wealthy Gardener, "but too many people take on personal debt based solely on monthly payments. It is an especially dangerous practice in the purchase of an education, home, vehicle, or even furniture. The payment system is the devil in disguise."

"But if it's affordable—"

"What's affordable today may not be affordable tomorrow. Who has the wisdom to know the conditions of the future? Can you be sure of a steady income, good health, and prosperous times? Debtors are most harmed in an economic downturn. To free yourself of worries—free yourself of debt."

"Okay, but everyone needs a home and a car."

"Just keep your mortgage under twice your annual realized income," the Wealthy Gardener advised. "As for cars, you don't need one that costs over $30,000."

Jimmy silently calculated his townhouse's mortgage, concluding that he was within this general formula. But then his expression changed.

"What will happen to this loan," he asked delicately, "when you pass—"

"I drew up this loan as an education about the debt process," the Wealthy Gardener said. "But when this lender dies, the debt will be forgiven. You will have a great start at a very young age. How will it change your life?"

Jimmy shrugged. "I'll have an additional $4,191 to save every month."

"You are doing it right if the world can't see your progress. Every time you pay off a debt," said the Wealthy Gardener, "you have that much more to pay off other debts and, in the end, to eventually save toward your wealth."

DEBT IS AN OBLIGATION to pay or repay, a state of owing. It has been theorized that the only reason a great many American families don't own an elephant is because they've never been offered an elephant for a dollar down and a number of low monthly payments.

Earl Wilson observed, "Today, there are three kinds of people: the haves, the have-nots, and the have-not-paid-for-what-they-haves."

There is no worse enemy for our profitability than debt, and without profits, there is nothing to save and no hope for wealth. Debt robs the future to pay for the wants of today.

"Debt is the worst poverty," said Magnus Gottfried Lichtwer. "A man in debt is so far a slave," wrote Emerson. "The greatest enemy of financial well-being is not poverty but debt," said Kent Nerburn. "It is the debtor that is ruined by hard times," said Rutherford B. Hayes.

Get out of debt and get out of danger.

The way to gain freedom is by temporarily giving up all freedom. Use each day's waking hours to pay the price for debt reduction. An extra job can yield a realized income of $1,000 a month to pay down the principal.

Pay off debts in order of their size. It may be financially wise to start paying off those debts with the highest interest rates, but it is psychologically wise to attack the smallest debts first and gain a few wins. Get the small wins, and each paid debt will increase your free cash to pay off remaining debts.

Debtors suffer the pain of sacrifice or the pain of slavery. Debt is a cruel master who accrues interest while we sleep. Dave Ramsey summed up the life of the debtor: "I owe, I owe, so off to work I go." Work off the loans.

"Getting out and staying out of debt is key," advises Ann Wilson. "Debt is the biggest barrier, a parasite to wealth." And thereby it enslaves.

THE LIFE LESSON: GET OUT OF DEBT

I realized that debt enslaved me to duty,
But a life without debt was a life without chains.

Saving urgently: Getting cash in the bank as the top
priority; imperative monthly accumulating.

It is only the farmer who faithfully plants seed in the
spring who reaps a harvest in the autumn.

B. C. FORBES

"I can't promise that saving money will make you fabulously rich," the Wealthy Gardener admitted, "but it will make you happier and richer."

Jimmy laughed. "I thought money couldn't buy happiness?"

"Quite the contrary," the Wealthy Gardener said, chuckling. He was lying on the couch under a blanket, looking frail on the fifth day. "Worry is misery. Without savings, you're guaranteed to be worried. With savings, this condition improves."

Jimmy thought about it. "Okay, but I think people know to save a portion of their money—they just don't do it."

The Wealthy Gardener gazed out the window. "People live for the day," he said, "but forsake the future. They haven't found the proper balance."

"Some people will criticize the savers," Jimmy reflected. "They see the pursuit of wealth as a superficial life, and so they think it's best to spend and enjoy."

"We each choose our ways," said the Wealthy Gardener. "But anyone who advises against saving money is a fool to be disregarded for further advice."

Jimmy nodded without replying.

"In my days, I was busy like everyone else," the Wealthy Gardener continued, "but my goals focused me. In turn, I urgently saved a portion of my earnings. And due to my savings, I gained admission to an exclusive banquet that wasn't available to those without cash of their own."

Jimmy looked at him oddly. "What banquet?"

"The banquet of ownership and investing. To become wealthy, we must transition from consumers into owners and investors. Ownership of stocks, bonds, real estate, a business—this is the way to wealth. Without savings, this banquet is not for you. With enough savings, the doors open."

"Is this why you became richer than others?" Jimmy asked.

"The difference between me and my friends was not our starts in life," continued the Wealthy Gardener. "We attended the same schools. But I saved urgently—and it made all the difference. I saved while they spent, and this increased my options. The others knew they should save, but it wasn't urgent for them. And without urgency, their attention was on other things."

"I bet they don't see their spending as the cause of mediocrity."

"I'm sure you're right. It's the economy, or taxes, or stagnant wages. Nobody accepts blame. My friends call me lucky," said the Wealthy Gardener. "In their eyes, I grew rich by chance. But if luck is when opportunity meets preparation, then preparation is a pile of cash when opportunity knocks."

Jimmy smiled. "And a pile of cash is the price of admission to the banquet of opportunity. But why were you able to save while they couldn't?"

"I've thought about this quite a bit. It seems we wanted different things, and our desires took us in different directions. I always wanted power over my affairs in life. This need for control drove me to urgently save money while others didn't seem to care as much about monetary accumulation.

"I also kept my lifestyle simple. I saved money, lived on the rest. I enjoyed my gardening. I chose a modest existence while my friends incurred debts on extravagance. The mortgage, cars, country clubs, and luxury furniture stole their excess. They worked to pay expenses while I saved and invested.

"In the end, small financial advantages allowed me to grow at a different pace. Like the goldfish with a slight size advantage in the small pond, due to my advantages, I was able to double and triple my growth rate compared to my peers. I became an owner of assets while they remained consumers. I, in turn, got the breaks."

"And lucky breaks were because of your savings?"

"My financial breaks were due to a lot of small things along the way," clarified the Wealthy Gardener, "none of which would have happened without saving money. I wanted control over my life. My friends got caught up in their busy everyday lives. They failed to save money because retirement never seemed urgent, until it was too late."

SAVING URGENTLY MEANS BANKING excess income as the top priority. Without urgency to save, we spend arbitrarily and then wonder where the money goes. Urgency is vital because an empty bank account causes hopelessness, vulnerability, and dependence. Worse, it causes smart people to fear losing thankless jobs.

Money in the bank changes life quite a bit. Saving money provides a cushion against catastrophe. It is the power to absorb hard punches. It requires a discipline that, when mastered, qualifies one to attend a greater banquet.

"Save money and money will save you," goes a Jamaican proverb. "If you wish to get rich, save what you get," advised Brigham Young. "A fool can earn money; but it takes a wise man to save and dispose of it to his own advantage." If we don't save, we stay broke no matter how much we earn.

Gaining wealth is a marathon made up of consistently saving small amounts—all the days of our lives—to one day gain access to the banquet of ownership. And once we gain access to opportunities, we gain financial advantages.

"Never give up on a dream because of the time it will take to accomplish it. The time will pass anyway," said Earl Nightingale. Save at the start of each month using an automatic savings draft from every paycheck. Such a plan will create a sustainable structure for spending while you accumulate wealth; it ensures progress without willpower. Since you can't spend what you don't see, it's important to move the money into the bank before you have access to it.

Saving now is the way to wealth, while saving someday is the way to scarcity. "If you cannot save money," said W. Clement Stone, "the seeds of greatness are not in you."

THE LIFE LESSON: SAVE URGENTLY

I saw that an empty bank account left me powerless,
But a pile of cash offered security and possibilities.

LESSON 5-6 · KEEP SCORE

Score: An objective measure; a metric to judge success.

If we are unhappy with the harvest we're reaping, we
should sow different seed.

PHIL PRINGLE

On the Wealthy Gardener's suggestion, Jimmy and he were meeting on a Saturday. Jimmy wasn't sure, but he suspected that they were racing against time.

"The reason to keep score," said the Wealthy Gardener on the sixth day, "is to gain insight and discipline over the daily choices that impact your wealth. Net worth is the single most important financial metric you can track; it represents the sum total of your financial reality in one convenient number."

Jimmy nodded. "It's our assets minus our debts, right?"

The Wealthy Gardener winked. "That's exactly right, and it is a moving score based on what you earn this week, what you spend this week, what you do with your profits, and what your investments do for you. Net worth is a single snapshot of your wealth, and its moving parts, frozen in time."

"Okay, so how do I find my net worth number?"

"Well, let's go through it. What are your debts?"

Jimmy thought about it. "I got the new car financed by the dealer for $38,500. The townhouse was $150,000, but, as a first-time home buyer, I was eligible for a loan of $145,000. Other than that, I financed my home furniture for $3,500. And I now have a business loan for $580,000."

The Wealthy Gardener nodded. "Those are your liabilities. Add them up."

A moment later, Jimmy said, "I'm $766,500 in the hole."

"Okay, now what do you own that could quickly be sold?"

Jimmy looked confused. "All the same stuff, I guess. The car is worth $38,000, according to its current estimated value. The townhouse was appraised at $150,000. The furniture cost me $3,500. And the property management business is valued at $600,000."

"How much money do you have in the bank this week?"

Jimmy thought about it. "It was $15,000 yesterday."

"Add it all up. These are your assets."

A moment later Jimmy said, "The total is $806,500."

"So tell me, what is your net worth as of this minute?"

Jimmy used a calculator on his phone. "It's $806,500 minus $766,500 for a total net worth of $40,000."

"Now allow me to split hairs on one item. The furniture you bought for $3,500, do you really think you can sell it used for your purchase price?"

"No, but I chose that number because—"

"I don't care why you valued it wrong. An asset is only worth the cash you can get for it today. Cut the estimated value of your furniture in half."

Jimmy recalculated. "Okay, my net worth is now $38,250."

"And with such an accurate score, you can weigh the impact of your choices. If you save $500 next month, or pay down $500 of your debt, your net worth will increase by that amount. If you buy a $30,000 indoor swimming pool that adds $20,000 to the value of your house, your net worth will shrink by $10,000. If you use $3,000 from your savings for a vacation, your net worth will decrease by $3,000. A net worth statement is like an X-ray of the moving parts of your financial condition."

"I see how this would be useful in making decisions."

"A current financial scoreboard is imperative for many reasons," agreed the Wealthy Gardener. "It shows day-to-day progress on a grand scale. There are tools available online to keep it simple. Tracking your net worth lets you see the direction of your wealth during your marathon of accumulating money."

"And progress in life fuels determination," Jimmy said.

"I believe a sense of direction is vital," said the Wealthy Gardener, sipping his tea. "Keep working, keep saving, keep investing, keep repeating. These are the gears of our wealth. The one who seeks the direction will usually stay the course."

A SCORE is an objective measure of performance, a metric to judge success. "What gets measured gets done," said Tom Peters. "What gets measured gets managed," said Peter Drucker. "What gets measured gets improved," said Robin Sharma.

What gets measured certainly gets our attention. If you want financial accumulation, measure it. Keep a running tally.

Keeping financial score monitors wealth building during the chaotic whirlwind of life. Everything one does with money—spending, incurring debt, paying off debt, saving, investing, eating out—has an impact on a net worth score. Tracking net worth is an invaluable tool for making decisions and taking actions. Wealth, in the end, is essentially a number.

"Make it a policy to know your net worth to the penny," advised T. Harv Eker. "Focus on all four of your net worth factors: increasing your income, increasing your savings, increasing your investment returns, and decreasing your cost of living by simplifying your lifestyle."

Keep track of reality.

Keeping score can remind us that when we are not doing anything too exciting, we are doing it right. "If investing is entertaining, if you're having fun," said George Soros, "you're probably not making any money. Good investing is boring." "Investing should be more like watching paint dry or watching grass grow," said Paul Samuelson. "If you want excitement, take $800 and go to Las Vegas." The same boredom should sur-round our personal expenditures.

The thrill is the score—there is joy and wonder in watching little seeds grow.

THE LIFE LESSON: KEEP SCORE

....

I found that not keeping score led to confusion,
But tracking net worth led to consistent right actions.

Inflation: The rising cost of goods and services.

Nature has no mercy at all. Nature says, "I'm going to snow. If you have on a bikini and no snowshoes, that's tough. I am going to snow anyway."

MAYA ANGELOU

"Inflation is a menace that eats money," said the Wealthy Gardener on the seventh day. "It quietly devours our dollars as our savings loses its buying power." He poked the fire and sat on the couch. It was Sunday, and Jimmy thought the Wealthy Gardener looked a bit livelier. Or maybe that was just wishful thinking.

"What do you mean by 'eating money'?" asked Jimmy.

"I mean devaluation of cash. Until now, we've discussed the importance of amassing cash in the bank," said the Wealthy Gardener. "Due to inflation, however, we must find a better use for the cash. It must be moved into investments or it will lose its buying power."

"Okay, so what you're saying now is to move my savings from a bank account and into stocks, bonds, real estate, or maybe even a business?"

"That is the reality of it. Cash in the bank will be eaten by inflation."

Jimmy had no formal investing experience. "Can you elaborate?" he asked.

The Wealthy Gardener considered the simplest way to explain how inflation affects the value of money. "You are surely familiar with the story of Rip Van Winkle, the man who fell asleep and woke up twenty years later, having missed the American Revolution, the death of his wife, the marriage of his daughters, and the birth of his grandson?"

Jimmy nodded without answering.

"What the author didn't mention," the Wealthy Gardener continued, "is that this unfortunate fellow went to sleep with a hundred bucks in his wallet. When he woke up twenty years later, he was glad to find that his one hundred dollars had not been stolen. But then he quickly discovered that the cost of things had doubled during his long nap."

Jimmy smiled. "And so while he didn't physically lose one hundred dollars, he awoke to find that his money could buy only half of what one hundred dollars could buy at the time he went to sleep. Rip woke up poorer due to the effect of rising inflation."

"You must have read this version," huffed the Wealthy Gardener. "And his example is not too different from our own. Given historical inflation rates, the price of things double every twenty years. When you think of your cash in the bank, don't ever forget what happened to poor Rip Van Winkle."

"Got it," Jimmy said. "So we want to get our cash into investments."

"There is really no choice," said the Wealthy Gardener. "We compete with inflation every day. Inflation grows, on average, above two to three percent every year. So tell me, what investment return do you need on your money to not end up like ol' Rip?"

"I need to grow my money at three percent to maintain its buying power."

"That's right. Your money must grow at the rate of inflation—after fees and taxes—to hold its value. This is a crucial point to contemplate—a return that is equal to inflation is a real return of zero. To become wealthy, you must compete fiercely to always beat inflation."

Jimmy nodded with a grin. "What you're talking about is the nominal rate versus the real rate of return. I studied it recently in a finance book."

"You no good rascal!" exclaimed the Wealthy Gardener. "You let me explain this concept until I was blue in the face while all the time you—"

"I wanted to be sure you understood it," Jimmy joked. "Now, the way I comprehend it, we invest money to increase it. We especially want our money to increase more than the rising cost of inflation. Our real return is based on beating the inflation rate. Is that about the sum of it?"

The Wealthy Gardener groaned. "I suppose that about wraps it up."

"Thank you so much," Jimmy said happily. "Keeping up with inflation is important, but it gets you nowhere. It's beating inflation that counts."

INFLATION IS THE RISING COST of goods and services. In 1980 investors could have put their hard-earned cash into a taxable money market at an annual interest rate of 12.68 percent. Those were the good old days, say many unsophisticated investors. These higher interest rates encouraged a trend of saving at the time because a lot of people felt they would be rewarded for their investments.

But what was the *real return* of a money market in 1980?

The question of "real return" is what matters to accumulators who want their savings to grow into substantial wealth.

How do we fare against inflation?

The return of a money market in 1980 was reportedly 12.68 percent, causing an influx of savings from the general population. The rate of inflation reported for that same year, however, was a whopping 13.5 percent.

What then was the real return from a money market account in 1980? To calculate the real return, subtract the percent of inflation from the percent of nominal return:

$$12.68\% - 13.5\% = -0.82\%$$

As you can see, in 1980 the general population actually lost buying power with a return of 12.68 percent. The interest rate that drove so many people to invest ended up being a loser. The irony is that many older folks now speak of the great returns from this bygone era, forgetting the impact inflation had during that time.

Inflation had quietly eaten their money.

Where should they have invested their cash to beat inflation?

This question is one that confronts all who seek to accumulate wealth. The art and skill of investing is knowing what to do when we stare into the future without the benefit of history to serve as a cheat sheet for our brilliance.

The origin of all wealth is initially the ability to stash money in the bank. But engaging those dollars effectively requires a fierce competition with inflation. Beating inflation expands purchasing power and leads to wealth.

There is only one way to keep up with the rising cost of goods and services. We must beat inflation by using cash in the bank to buy appreciating assets.

THE LIFE LESSON: BEAT INFLATION

I thought money grew by its annual rate of return,
But found that it only grows by how much it beats inflation.

LESSON 5-8 · MINIMIZE RISK

Risk: The possibility of loss.

Agriculture will always have changes, always have a set
of risks.

On the eighth day, the Wealthy Gardener said to Jimmy, "The only thing easy about money is losing it. Keep that in mind when you're feeling infallible."

Jimmy paused to consider the statement. "I should avoid risk?"

"I'm not saying to avoid all risk, but I am telling you to pursue risk only in extreme conditions. A healthy respect for loss," said the Wealthy Gardener, "is a sure sign of wisdom. The goal of investing hard-earned cash, before any thought of gains, is always about the avoidance of its departure."

"What about the stock market—it goes up and down, right?"

"During what time frame?"

Jimmy silently grappled with the question.

"The stock market is for those who can endure a twenty to thirty percent drop without panic. If you're in the stock market for decades, you may even see a few forty percent drops. But in the past, the value has always returned for those who wait. So the time frame for stock investing is ten years—at a minimum. Those who stay in the game tend to win. But those who act on their emotions tend to lose."

"What about buying low and selling high?"

"It would be great if it worked, but short-term trading is speculation," said the Wealthy Gardener. "Only buying and holding is real investing."

"Okay, so let's be specific about investing," Jimmy said. "How would I safely move my cash from a bank into the stock market?"

"With a very slow and steady hand," said the Wealthy Gardener.

Jimmy nodded as if he had suspected the approach.

"Risk can be minimized by a technique called dollar-cost averaging. It's a fancy term that means you invest a consistent dollar amount into the stock market every month. The key to this plan is that you absolutely must keep investing during the dips in the market. If you fail to invest when pessimism is rampant, you will fail to gain the benefits of this strategy."

"Buy steadily and consistently," Jimmy said. "What stocks do I buy?"

"The way to minimize risk," the Wealthy Gardener said, "is to never think you're smart enough to pick the winners. The smart move for the average person is to invest in broad index funds. Imagine your money spread among many US stocks, many foreign stocks, and many different bonds. Plow money into broad indexes and you will beat most money managers."

"And that's all there is to it?" Jimmy asked.

"It is ridiculously simple," said the Wealthy Gardener. "The challenge of wealth has very little to do with the complexity of investing. Those who get wealthy focus on their behaviors. They consistently work to earn money and then steadily invest it, even when every genius in the world predicts doom and gloom."

"What about other forms of investing my cash?"

"Real estate investing is more complex," said the Wealthy Gardener, "as you are probably aware from your training—"

"I took classes to be a Realtor," Jimmy interrupted, "not on investing."

"Well, I didn't realize that. Investing in real estate requires a steep learning curve to minimize risk. It also requires a lot more money than investing in stocks. A real estate investor must become familiar with cash flow, cash-on-cash return, estimated repair costs, expense ratios, and real estate appraisal methods. Risk is mitigated by specialized knowledge. Safety in this game requires a disciplined buying criteria."

"It seems that investing is mostly about avoiding stupid mistakes."

"That's true," said the Wealthy Gardener, "but the problem is that stupid mistakes are only seen in the rearview mirror. The challenge for investors is to predict the trouble in advance."

MINIMIZING RISK is reducing the odds of losing money. Peter Bernstein expressed a sentiment that should be written down and hung on every investor's wall: "Maximizing return is a strategy that makes sense only in very specific circumstances. In general, survival is the only road to riches. Let me say that again: Survival is the only road to riches."

Successful investors have a healthy fear of misjudgments and errors.

"Smart people do dumb things," said Charlie Munger. "People are trying to be smart—all I am trying to do is not to be an idiot, but it's harder than most people think." The ability to discern and mitigate financial risks can be a difficult challenge.

"Rule No. 1: Never lose money," said Warren Buffett. "Rule No. 2: Never forget Rule No. 1." If you think you can afford to lose a little, you're going to end up losing a lot. "I hate to be the bearer of bad news but great investing is boring," wrote David Rae. "I mean like really boring."

Slow and steady is wise advice.

In the stock market, maintaining a long-term perspective minimizes risk. "Do not take yearly results too seriously," advised Benjamin Graham. "Instead, focus on four- or five-year averages."

And an index fund is best for average people busily earning excess money to invest. "Most investors, both institutional and individual, will find that the best way to own common stocks is through an index fund that charges minimal fees," advises Buffett.

Index funds outperform most managed funds, so they are an ideal place to put your hard-earned cash. Though unbiased advisers such as CPAs or lawyers will support this common strategy, money managers who cannot profit from index funds will likely deplore it.

Once you've deployed a simple strategy, the risk of investing becomes more about bad behavior. Risk is the result of impulsiveness under the threat of fear or the temptation of greed. Safety requires not selling when the stock market tanks and not getting greedy when others out-perform your steady returns.

If survival is the road to riches, emotional control secures the direction. If you are tempted by an exciting stock or opportunity, regain your senses and choose the dull and boring investment.

THE LIFE LESSON: MINIMIZE RISK

....

I sought to minimize risk with every investment,
And I built consistent momentum with boring strategies.

LESSON 5-9 · MULTIPLY IT

Multiply: To add a number to itself a number of times.

A grain of corn placed in fertile soil shoots up a green
stalk, blossoms and produces an ear of corn containing
hundreds of grains, each capable of doing what the one
grain did.

R. H. JARRETT

"I promise you this," said the Wealthy Gardener on the ninth day,
"great minds are awed by compound interest. It is hard to fathom exactly
how money multiplies over time when all earnings are perpetually reinvested."

Jimmy shook his head. "With all due respect," he said playfully, "I'd
like to challenge my mentor on this one point. What about the rule
of 72?"

"The rule of 72," said the Wealthy Gardener, smiling, "from your recent finance book? It is a useful law, I agree, to determine how long it
takes money to double at a fixed rate of interest. I presume you understand it completely?"

"By simply dividing seventy-two by the interest rate of an investment," Jimmy said, "we find out how long it will take to double our
money. For example, money invested at nine percent would take eight
years to double itself, since seventy-two divided by nine equals eight."

The Wealthy Gardener nodded, closed his eyes, and breathed deeply.
His face was gaunt, and Jimmy sensed that he was holding on to life by a
thread, as if willing himself to stay alive another day.

"Formulas can limit the best possibilities," said the Wealthy Gardener.
"For example, let's say you patiently amass a lifetime savings of $100,000.
You'll then have options—especially if it's saved outside of a normal tax-

deferred retirement account. With $100,000, you can invest in real estate or even in your own small business. Or you can leave the money where it is in the stock market. But know this—with greater savings come greater opportunities."

Jimmy sat in the rocking chair without speaking.

"For example, assume you choose to invest in real estate for positive cash flow," said the Wealthy Gardener. "You study this field, become an expert of the numbers, and then buy a duplex for $100,000. If your positive cash flow after taxes is $12,000, what is your return? And is your money better used in a duplex investment? Or is it better invested in the stock market?"

Jimmy used a calculator. "The duplex example earns a cash-on-cash return of twelve percent," he said. "The duplex seems to make a lot more financial sense."

"It makes financial sense only if you reinvest all the profits," said the Wealthy Gardener. "And it makes practical sense only if you have extra time to manage it. Rental income is not nearly as passive as stock market income."

"Okay, but leverage is a huge advantage in real estate," Jimmy said.

"You're right, and leverage is a strategy for multiplying wealth. What if you bought this duplex with a loan? In this example, you'll invest $20,000 of your own money. But you'll also have a new loan payment of $450 per month. What is your rate of return on the leveraged duplex investment?"

Jimmy did the math. "The annual profit would be reduced to $5,600," he said. "But in this case, the initial cash outlay was only $20,000. And so the cash-on-cash return is . . . twenty-eight percent! Wow—and the duplex is an inflationary asset."

"This return is common in many parts of the country," he said, "but let's do one more example. What if, instead, you started your own small business or purchased a franchise? Say this new business costs $75,000 of your savings, and you get a loan for the rest of the purchase price. Since the business requires time, you decide to quit your day job in favor of the freedom of self-employment."

The Wealthy Gardener paused to let the example sink in with Jimmy. Then he said, "During the next ten years, you live on a salary of $75,000 from this business. What is your return on investment?"

"Do I have profits after my $75,000 salary?"

"As the owner, you can take $75,000—the entire profit of the business."

"Then my investment return is zero," Jimmy said astutely. "I only bought myself a job. I spent $75,000 and gained a working income, which is nothing more than what I already had before the investment. It was a waste of money."

The Wealthy Gardener smiled faintly. "You understand enough. To compound and multiply wealth, you must earn excess and reinvest it."

MULTIPLYING WEALTH is the doubling of money a number of times while adding to it, commonly over a period of decades. Wealth unfolds begrudgingly like the slow growth of an oak tree.

During the first year, an oak grows four feet tall. It then grows just two inches every month, and on its third birthday it's now eight feet tall. After four more years of slow growth, on its seventh birthday, the oak has doubled again to a new height of sixteen feet.

After the initial years, however, the growth of the oak tree is short by days, but huge by decades, much like the multiplying of wealth.

Wealth is the consistent effect of working to earn, followed by urgently saving and investing all excess money over decades.

When we begin saving, our monthly contributions will be the sole source of net worth growth. If we invest $7,000 the first year, then another $7,000 the next year, it's exciting to see $14,000 in the bank. It will take two more years of saving to double our money tree to $28,000. At this level, an interest rate of 10 percent is $2,800.

While this amount is not a lot, we feel an elation to receive money that did not require waking hours or effort. And slowly, money invested wisely begins to add to itself. The seeds of wealth begin to grow.

Steady savings will multiply wealth in unimaginable ways, and we multiply wealth not just by saving, but by planting seeds and leaving them alone.

"The big money is not in the buying and selling. But in the waiting," said Charlie Munger. "Most people are too fretful, they worry too much. Success means being very patient, but aggressive when it's time."

THE LIFE LESSON: MULTIPLY IT

I saw that fretting never makes money grow,
But wealth multiplies best with enduring patience.

LESSON 5-10 · PASSIVE INCOME

Passive income: Continuous cash flow
with little or no effort required.

Better to die fighting for freedom than be a prisoner all
the days of your life.

BOB MARLEY

"The ultimate goal of wealth is security and personal liberty," the Wealthy Gardener said slowly. "When your investments pay you more than you can earn at your day job, you will then drink of a freedom that few ever taste."

It was the tenth day, and Jimmy felt an unshakable melancholy.

"Well, you know I want financial freedom," he said softly. "But last night I was bothered by our conversation. You seemed to imply that putting money into a business was not a very good model for investing."

The Wealthy Gardener exhaled. "A job is trading your hours for money. An investment is trading your money for money. A job is where you work for cash. An investment is where cash works for you. It's a big difference."

Jimmy nodded. "You're referring to active versus passive income?"

"Indeed, I am. Passive income is the aim of those who dream of freedom. It's the profits, cash flow, and earnings from a business or enterprise that do not require direct involvement from an owner. It's the mythical river of gold."

"But can't a business provide passive income?"

"It is the way I myself have achieved freedom," said the Wealthy Gardener, visibly exhausted. "I am a gardener, and my lifestyle is simple. Because my lifestyle is inexpensive, I required little draw from my businesses. This allowed me to use the profits to expand into larger operations. You see, my own businesses made money, and I reinvested my profits. And for twenty long years, these investments have rewarded me with passive income."

"But you have never extricated yourself from business."

"Out of choice," the Wealthy Gardener said, grinning. "For me, the goal of passive income was not idleness or a forced sedentary lifestyle; the goal was to have choices and to increase my options for a richer, fuller life."

"How much money would you need in the stock market to retire?"

"As I look back now, my retirement needs are so few that I can easily live on $30,000 a year. My gardening is free, and reading is free. Exercise, long walks, and meditation are free. I treasure a few key friendships—especially yours," he said. "And I have the weekly classes at the reformatory. But know this: Even my simple lifestyle requires a million dollars in liquid assets."

"A million bucks?" Jimmy shrieked.

"According to a safe retirement rule of thumb," said the Wealthy Gardener, "we can withdraw three percent annually from our amassed savings. And since you're the math whiz kid, you will be quick to see that three percent of a million is $30,000."

"I don't think too many people can do that," Jimmy said.

"Oh, they certainly can, but they won't do it. Freedom requires sacrifice of pleasures and decades of persistence. Saving money must be urgent, and then investments must be given patience without interference or meddling."

"It's a good thing we have Social Security."

"What's even better than Social Security is self-sufficiency," said the Wealthy Gardener. "You can't be secure when you're dependent on others, or even on your government. I gave my early life to gain the freedom I've enjoyed in my later years."

Jimmy looked at his dying friend. "Was the price worth it?"

"I had no choice, really," said the Wealthy Gardener faintly. "And I mean that with every ounce of my being. Some animals are meant to be free, and for them it is wrong to live within fences. Freedom was never a choice for me."

PASSIVE INCOME is cash flow with little or no effort required—it is time freedom. "What is freedom?" asked Archibald MacLeish. "Freedom is the right to choose: the right to create for oneself the alternatives of choice." Passive income is personal liberty.

What exactly is passive income? The profits, cash flow, and earnings from a business that do not require direct involvement from the owner; any type of real estate income; interest income from bank accounts or pensions; royalties paid for inventions, patents, books, or songs; and dividends and interest in the form of cash flow or capital gains from securities and commodities, such as stocks, currencies, gold, silver, ETFs, and bonds.

"You become financially free," said T. Harv Eker, "when your passive income exceeds your expenses." Warren Buffett once warned, "If you don't find a way to make money while you sleep, you will work until you die."

Rental property income tends to be the most common road to passive income for average people with ordinary incomes. When a million dollars is needed for an annual retirement income of $30,000, ambitious middle-class people tend to become creative with limited resources.

I once listened to a real estate investor speak on a podcast. In his late forties, after his kids left the house, his wife demanded a divorce. They had an acrimonious settlement over their assets. Finally, they agreed that she would get his entire life savings and he would keep the rental units, which she never liked anyway—they were just headaches and hassles to her.

When later asked about this deal, which seemed to favor her side, the man chuckled knowingly. "Well, she may have gotten the golden eggs. But I got the geese."

With passive income, we have it all. "Residual income is passive income that comes in every month whether you show up or not," said Steve Fisher. "It's when you no longer get paid on your personal efforts alone . . . It's one of the keys to financial freedom."

Robert Kiyosaki said, "To obtain financial freedom, one must be either a business owner, an investor, or both, generating passive income, particularly on a monthly basis." In the end, wealth is a river of income that flows generously on its own.

THE LIFE LESSON: PASSIVE INCOME

I saw that passive income was the way to freedom,
And my stream of gold was rental property income.

Chapter 6

....

THE 15 VIRTUES
OF WEALTH

The 15 Virtues of Wealth

*Virtue: A characteristic valued as promoting
collective and individual greatness.*

Ponder the fact that God has made you a gardener, to
root out vice and plant virtue.

SAINT CATHERINE OF SIENA

After Jimmy said goodbye, the Wealthy Gardener retreated to his bed. He closed his eyes as tears trickled out. Jimmy was family, like an adopted son, and they would surely never meet again. The Wealthy Gardener's time was nearing its end, and Jimmy's last words to him begged one final question: "Was the price worth it?"

The pursuit of wealth was a spiritual journey that required virtue and nobility. It was the effect of a valued service to mankind, and it was built on a foundation of using the hours of many passing days. It was a life of striving, not settling, to shape his garden by design.

With these thoughts in mind, the Wealthy Gardener eased out of bed and sat at his computer. Thinking of Jimmy, he now contemplated a final lesson to convey in his book. How did he grow in the struggle? What were the virtues learned during the pursuit of his wealth?

Summoning his willpower, he prayed for strength and began typing:

1. SIMPLICITY

If you have a garden and a library, you have everything you need. —CICERO

The pursuit of wealth required simplicity. I meditated each morning to recharge my mental faculties. I was mindful during the days to remain calm and rational under pressure. I focused entirely on the tasks in front of me, and my full concentration seemed to slow time. I planned retreats where I escaped the whirlwind for uninterrupted contemplations. I was free of the burden of distractions. I sought wealth and simple pleasures. Due to the pursuit of financial freedom, I developed the virtue of simplicity.

2. DETACHMENT

The root of suffering is attachment. —BUDDHA

The pursuit of wealth required detachment from material possessions. Due to my ambitions, I forfeited luxuries and indulgences that were basic needs for spenders. I developed restraint and contempt for materialism. I chose a lifestyle less glamorous than I could afford. My aspirations required impulse control, delayed gratification, and vigilance against temptations. Due to the pursuit of wealth, I developed the virtue to resist material consumption.

3. SELF-DISCIPLINE

Through discipline comes freedom. —ARISTOTLE

The pursuit of wealth drove me to self-discipline. It was a daily effort to do the things I knew I had to do, whether I wanted to or not. A strange resistance stood between my goals and me. I disciplined myself to attack the most unwanted tasks of each day first. I let no day pass without reviewing my goals. I let no day pass without exercise to ensure energy and a peak state. I let no day pass without progress. Due to my goal of wealth, I developed the virtue of self-discipline to act, whether I felt like it or not.

4. VITAL ENGAGEMENT

Time is money. —BENJAMIN FRANKLIN

The pursuit of wealth demanded vital engagement. In my free time, I studied, explored curiosities, improved skills, and sought wisdom. I avoided dead time. I forfeited pleasure and entertainment for purpose and meaning. I eliminated time spent with negative minds and, instead, spent many hours alone, thinking, reading, and planning. I worked odd jobs and overtime hours to earn profits that became savings that became investments. Due to a quest for wealth, I learned the virtue of engaging my available hours with purpose.

5. SPIRITUALITY

May the Force be with you. —YODA

The pursuit of wealth led me to spirituality. My wealth required lucky breaks, inspiration, uncanny coincidences, and opportunities. It required good fortune and serendipitous chance. My mental practices of deep concentration seemed to have power, invoke power, or stir the Universal Intelligence. Due to my desire for wealth, I sought to control my opportunities. I cultivated a burning gratitude for wishes fulfilled; I developed absolute faith in my goals; I managed to eliminate all doubts. Due to the pursuit of wealth, I developed an ability to command my inner state of being, and this led to the actualization of coincidence and serendipity.

6. EFFECTIVENESS

It is not enough to be industrious. So are the ants. —HENRY DAVID THOREAU

The pursuit of wealth demanded effectiveness (quality hours and quantity of hours) to most fully use the days. To attain wealth, all work had to contribute to a very clear goal: my net worth. Self-development, goal review, exercise, and planning were all on task. I found my net worth increase most when I tracked impact statistics and money statistics. Sitting alone and thinking, meditating, and imagining were also part of my effectiveness. I cut out most passive indulgences and grew wealthy by avoiding nearly all forms of entertainment. Due to my pursuit of wealth, I lived a fully engaged life and strove to master the virtue of personal effectiveness.

7. PERSISTENCE

Nothing in the world takes the place of persistence. —CALVIN COOLIDGE

The pursuit of wealth forced me to master daily persistence. I learned that all persistence is motivated by a cause, a big why. My purpose for wealth was time freedom, and this dream empowered me through decades of trials and adversities. I also used my discontentment as fuel to endure hard work. At times I even used my greatest fears to drive my persistence until I attained wealth. Due to the pursuit of wealth, I developed the virtue of persistence.

8. PATIENCE

Nature does not hurry, yet everything is accomplished. —LAO TZU

The pursuit of wealth taught me the virtue of patience. I learned the hard way that impatience leads to setbacks. After my money once vanished in risky investments with the promise of high returns, I never again lost money due to impatience. As my patience matured, I gained a reverence for five-year intervals. It was enough time to amass a substantial sum of savings; it was enough time to reap a solid return on investments. Five years was also enough time to transform every unwanted aspect of my life through strategic plans and steady actions. Due to the pursuit of wealth, I learned that all good things take time. I became patient, learning to persist without instant gratification.

9. SACRIFICE

There is no reward without sacrifice. —CARLSON GRACIE

The pursuit of wealth taught me to sacrifice. I accepted that I could not have it all, and so I chose between having money or time. And I opted to sacrifice my time to amass wealth. I also learned to choose between what I wanted now versus what I wanted most. It was a sacrifice to save money while others spent lavishly on possessions, but I was rewarded with the satisfaction of growing security. To obtain wealth, I sacrificed desires to gain savings. Due to the pursuit of wealth, I learned the virtue of personal sacrifice.

10. SELF-MASTERY

Achieve self-mastery over your thoughts. —NAPOLEON HILL

The pursuit of wealth called for the self-mastery of my thoughts. I learned to maintain a vision of wealth in my days. I developed control to focus within. I rebuilt my beliefs about money. I convinced myself that I was worthy of great wealth. Through daily repetition of affirmations, I built beliefs to support my dreams and aspirations. I stopped sabotaging my progress. I noticed opportunities that were previously unseen. With mental control I was compelled to actions that led most directly to wealth. Due to the pursuit of wealth, I grew stronger in character and learned to regulate my thoughts.

11. COURAGE

Fortune befriends the bold. —VIRGIL

The pursuit of wealth required an ongoing battle between fear and courage. When I accepted opportunities with risk, onlookers noted my courage. They didn't know the fear in my steps. My courage was no more than forward motion in times of tremendous uncertainty. Courage for me was making the hard choices that would cause known discomforts. It was the ability to walk into vast uncertainty when it seemed to be the right move. Every time I walked into difficulty, I found that my capabilities rose to match the task. Due to the pursuit of wealth, I learned the virtue of courage.

12. COMMITMENT

Remember it's OK to be yourself. —RICHARD BRANSON

Due to my pursuit of wealth, I learned dedication to strenuous work. As I gained self-knowledge, I chose employment that suited my individuality: my values, inclinations, knacks, ambitions, and inner voice. I chose jobs that interested me, attracted me, and paid me well for my services. To gain a life of prosperity, I committed myself to work that was in harmony with these individual elements. Because I pursued wealth, I learned the virtue of commitment to a labor that I loved and that loved me back with excess income.

13. ACCURATE JUDGMENT

Delay is preferable to error. —THOMAS JEFFERSON

The pursuit of wealth required continual accurate judgments. I faced choices that warranted analytical ability to decipher pros and cons, reasons for and against, and the likelihood of gain versus loss. Correct decisions led to advancements; wrong choices led to crushing setbacks. The net worth scoreboard was a merciless judge of my errors. Detached objectivity and rational thinking proved invaluable in amassing my wealth, but I did not ignore my steadfast intuitions, hunches, or emotional guidance. Due to the pursuit of wealth, I learned to value calm prudence, humility, inner wisdom, and a healthy respect for my own fallibility in critical judgments.

14. CONTRIBUTION

The human contribution is the essential ingredient. —ETHEL PERCY ANDRUS

Due to the pursuit of wealth and freedom, I learned to contribute to the common good. My economic pursuits followed a simple pattern: Money came into my possession according to the need for what I did, how well I did it, how hard it was to replace me, and how many people I served. Money was a tangible measure of the value and magnitude of my personal contribution. Due to the noble pursuit of wealth, I learned the virtue of valuable contribution to the common good.

15. SATISFACTION

Satisfaction lies in the effort. —MAHATMA GANDHI

Due to the pursuit of wealth, I felt empowered, and knew the satisfaction of a great effort in the days. I found unexpected joy in the experience of upward mobility. Financial direction rewarded me in the struggle with a sense of hope and anticipation for the future. But more than anything, I felt the deepest satisfaction knowing that my best effort was offered in a quest to gain complete freedom in this life. My fullest exertions guarded me from regrets on my deathbed due to unmet ambitions. Due to the pursuit of wealth, I learned the virtue of a sacred effort regardless of the ultimate outcome.

THE WEALTHY GARDENER REVIEWED his words on the computer screen and accepted them without revision. He was drained, tired, and spent—it was exactly the state he had always envisioned for his end.

To live fully, one should die wearily, he believed, but also contentedly. It was the reward of a well-used life. He had given his best effort and had lived at the edge of his capacity.

He reviewed the book's table of contents one last time, concerned that his wealth tenets would be castigated. Many jaded people with rational leanings would likely criticize his belief in the Unseen Force. Conversely, those with spiritual leanings would surely criticize his emphasis on amassing money. As he faced death, however, he was glad to have expressed his own truth.

At last he pressed the Submit button on the screen and went to bed. For seven days he clung to life, willing his soul to remain in his body, until a book arrived in his mailbox. When it came, he carried the book to the quiet pond, reviewed it, and scribbled an opening verse in it. And then he trudged home. He wrapped the book in a plastic bag and secretly buried it in the garden. Either Jimmy would find it, or the lessons of his life would be lost to eternity. He offered a prayer to Fate to decide.

And then, content at last, he wearily took to his bed. In his final moments, as his consciousness faded into a most peaceful sleep, he imagined Jimmy finding the book, reading it with an open mind, and *thinking* . . .

PART III

Abundant Harvesting

The only thing that endures over time is the "Law of the Farm." You must prepare the ground, plant the seed, cultivate, and water if you expect to reap the harvest.

STEPHEN R. COVEY

Chapter 7

LEGACY OF THE WEALTHY GARDENER

Legacy of the Wealthy Gardener

Legacy: What one leaves behind.

A society grows great when old men plant trees under
whose shade they know they shall never sit.

GREEK PROVERB

The closed casket lay beside his wife's tombstone overlooking the pond. A steady drizzle had reduced the size of the crowd, and most of the remaining attendees were reformatory students and graduates of the Eagle's Club. Santos and his extended family were there, and they stood beside Connie, who sobbed just as she had at Fred's funeral. Absent was Jared, a fact not missed by Jimmy, who handed bookmarks to mourners as they paid their final respects and left flowers on the casket. On the bookmark was an inscription written days earlier by the Wealthy Gardener.

As people marched past the casket, Jimmy's mind drifted to their past discussions about living an empowered life. The Wealthy Gardener had insisted that there was no "right" or "wrong" design of a garden, but it was wrong not to choose a design at all. And Jimmy recalled a story he'd been told many times, a favorite metaphor comparing life to a plot of land.

A person's time on Earth can be compared to a plot of ground. It exists; it's there. It has within itself an astonishing potential, and it's prepared to react to a person's every action. In fact, it must, he had said. Each of us is given a plot to work, a lifetime, and the work we have chosen. Like a farmer, we can be grateful if we have the vision, imagination, and intelligence to successfully build upon the seemingly unimpressive land of our beginnings. Or we can let it fall into a haphazard condition with no real continuity of purpose behind it, with unpainted, ramshackle buildings, surrounded by weeds and debris. In both cases, the land is the same; it's what we do with it that makes the difference. The potential for a miracle is there, if only we're wise enough to see it and to realize that our fulfillment as people depends upon our reaction to what we've been given. Farmers and gardeners are the shapers of their environments.

The Wealthy Gardener had always sounded so convincing, especially on this topic of living at full capacity. "It seems we each have a potential of unique individuality," he would say, "and just maybe this is what ultimately matters. Maybe it's about choosing our own path in life, standing up for ourselves like we matter, and giving back by engaging our gifts."

If there was any solace in this sad day, Jimmy thought, it was that the Wealthy Gardener had lived a full life. He had lived intentionally, used his time purposefully, given himself to a cause, and lived in harmony with his inner wisdom. He had expressed his own individuality.

The ceremony ended, and so did the day. The sky turned to dusk, the moon started to rise, and Jimmy returned to the silent pond to sit alone on the dark bench under the oak tree. Gazing at the two tombstones on the knoll, Jimmy let his emotions pour out into the desolation of a silent night. The pain of our suffering, he had been told after his tragic accident, is the cure of our suffering.

Finally, his eyes fell to one of the bookmarks he had been handing out during the day. He had chosen this moment of solitude to read the bookmark's message for the first time:

My Dear Gardeners,
    Life is a competition, and your opponent is time. The purpose of life is a life of purpose, and you get to choose the content. There is no destiny. There is only decision. But the clock is ticking. To win the game, you only

need to win the days. To win the day, laugh. To win the day, appreciate. To win the day, use your hours with purpose. Follow your interests, and always be true to your inner wisdom. I beg you to remain filled with love and faith, aware of your freedom to choose your own path. And always know that you—not fate or circumstances—determine the final score against time.

W. G.

THE LEGACY HUNT

A plain envelope arrived in Jimmy's mailbox the day after the funeral. Jimmy, who had taken a week's vacation to mourn the passing of his life mentor, froze upon seeing it. He recognized the Wealthy Gardener's handwriting on the address label. Leaving the rest of the mail behind, he lifted this single envelope and carried it with him inside his townhouse.

He sat on the couch and stared at it in silence. Minutes passed before he gathered his strength, breathed deeply, and slowly opened the envelope. He read the handwritten note:

Jimmy,

I leave you as executor of a trust fund for the reformatory boys and for similar schools for disadvantaged youths. I also leave you a reference manual on prosperity. If you fail to discover the treasure of my lessons, then my final crusade was an old fool's dream. I leave it to Fate to decide. Here are several clues to aid your search: In the garden of life, there are signs if you seek them. There are also lessons in every garden. You must find the signs and then the lessons. The Maker of Gardens doesn't release Her secrets to those who refuse to dig for them. Before all else, discover the inner character of the Wealthiest Gardener—and always look within.

Good luck on your quest,

W. G.

Jimmy studied the enigmatic riddle with complete confusion. And then he recalled the odd statement the Wealthy Gardener had made weeks ago: that if Jimmy was ready to receive it, the book would find him. There was a final lesson to be learned, he was certain, from this suddenly annoying treasure hunt.

Unable to make sense of the clues rationally, he opted to turn the matter over to his subconscious mind, using methods he'd mastered in the past year. He would call upon the help of the Unseen Force, which could always be invoked with concentration and faith. It was fitting, too, that *mental practices* would be required as a final test. We work in concert with a Silent Power, the Wealthy Gardener had preached, that aids our wealth and manifests in mysterious ways.

Jimmy meditated in absolute faith for answers. He knew not to struggle with the problem, but rather to become clear in his mind about what he wanted. Then he'd try to feel, to know, to allow, and to be steady, patient, and assured of a solution. It would require mental control, intuitive awareness, and calm patience. For many hours he sat alone in silence and repeated the words . . . signs . . . lessons . . . And he waited patiently for his own inner voice to emerge.

Nothing happened on the first day.

Jimmy continued his mental practices the next day with faith and grateful expectation. Seeds don't sprout with the first drops of rainfall. In a weak moment, he drove to the Wealthy Gardener's house and ransacked it. He even tried the computer, but it was locked with a password. The password reminder: *The answers we seek are always within.*

This message confirmed that the Wealthy Gardener had created a riddle that required something more than just the physical senses. The solution was beyond reason, and this fact was most likely deliberate. Many of his life lessons on wealth had been about the controlled focus of the mind to engage the aid of Universal Intelligence that operates by immutable laws.

And these laws require our patience.

On the third day, an inspiration flashed into Jimmy's mind as he was taking a morning shower. He recalled a long-forgotten plaque in the garden, a gift from the reform school for the Wealthy Gardener's volunteer work.

And this flash of inspiration—it was so obvious in retrospect—had been the final life lesson, Jimmy thought: When we fix our mental concentration on a desired outcome with intensity and faith, we get ideas and plans to bring it about.

Jimmy returned to the Wealthy Gardener's home. He walked to the rear yard, and came to the iron plaque within the thick ground cover. He knelt and read the Eagle Club's mission statement:

The Wealthiest Gardener

It's the one who shapes life with hours, who is master of attitude regardless of conditions, who feels entitled to nothing except that which is earned, who knows the pride of effort regardless of outcome, and who, instead of settling for less, asks quietly, "Why not me?"

It is the visionary who is impractical, who is even at times ridiculed, but who thinks independently and listens to the still inner voice to avoid the regrets of those who wonder what might have been if only they'd followed the pull of their soul.

It's the one who lives with purpose and intention; who shows up each day and does the hard task; who seeks satisfaction over pleasure; who strives to make a difference, to make the world a better place; but who, when actions fail to produce impact, will know that failure was never due to partial efforts.

It is finally the one who lies spent, exhausted, certain that there's nothing more that could have been offered on the altar of life, who meets the end with a clear conscience of having passed the ultimate test of giving one's best.

This garden plaque described the character of the Wealthiest Gardener, and it was indeed a sign in the garden. Kneeling beside the plaque, Jimmy marveled at the inner wisdom that had led him to it. Isn't a thought, a hunch, or an idea a miracle? Isn't consciousness the greatest marvel? Is it really coincidence when chance favors us? What unfathomable Silent Force is behind serendipity and synchronicity? Who can deny the wonder of Universal Intelligence in every garden?

He recalled the clues that the Wealthy Gardener had given him to arrive at this discovery: *In the garden of life, there are signs if you seek them. There are also lessons in every garden. You must find the signs and then the lessons. The Maker of Gardens doesn't release Her secrets to those who refuse to dig for them.*

Jimmy began digging in the soil under the sign.

Within seconds, he unearthed a plastic bag that had been buried under the plaque. He sat back on the moist ground to investigate its contents; it felt like there was a hardbound book inside. His hands trembled as he opened the treasure.

He saw a note tucked into the pages, but he first examined the book jacket. The title was *Reference Manual for Prosperous Gardeners*, the author unknown. He opened the book and read the dedication page: *Dedicated to troubled gardens and future master gardeners.* He then pulled the handwritten note from the book:

Dear Jimmy,
* I am the Silent Power. I speak to you through thought flashes, hunches, inspirations, ideas, compulsions, inclinations, vibrations, and*

instincts. I am the sixth sense—the repulsion when something isn't quite right, the calmness when it is. I am your inner wisdom, waiting for you to pause and listen. I am the silence of every day seeking to guide you.

I am the Unseen Force. I am the coincidence, the lucky break, the chance occurrence that shows up according to your abiding trust. I am the wonder, the marvel, the awe, the life, and the miracle. I am the cooperative energy, and I aid every aspiration according to your daily clarity, strategy, devotion, attention, and faith. I am the Something More you sense. You honor me most by struggling well in the garden.

—The Anonymous

Jimmy read the note twice, sensing a compulsion to be near the Wealthy Gardener as he opened this book. Following this impulse, he trudged to a solitary bench overlooking the pond with two tombstones on the knoll. He placed the hardcover book on his lap, and scanned a verse that would serve as an introduction to a collection of life lessons:

The moral is clear as I look back
At these lessons, now that I'm of age.
That the book of one's life is determined
By the courage contained in each page.

Material wealth required courage, Jimmy recalled his mentor saying, to know your own mind and live your own life. But the deepest rewards of prosperity were found in the work, the freedom, and the personal growth so necessary to attain wealth. Most unexpectedly, the prosperous life was a spiritual journey. Jimmy turned the page, opened his mind, and began to *think . . .*

LIFE LESSON: SEEK PROSPERITY

I was told that ambition for riches comes from the devil,
But found that the prosperous life was a spiritual adventure.

LIFE LESSON: TIME

I saw that my conditions trail the use of my time,
And I can change what I do or keep what I've got.

LIFE LESSON: IMPACT ACTIVITY

I learned that only a few actions earned tangible rewards,
And so I rearranged my schedule for more effective actions.

Jimmy slowly flipped through the pages, scanning the many lessons about life, success, and wealth the Wealthy Gardener had left behind. As he read, his mind was lifted to the possibilities of his own uncertain future.

Maybe he'd continue to grow his real estate business. Or perhaps he'd focus more on expanding his thriving property management venture. He knew he wanted wealth to gain his freedom. With money, he'd be able to follow his inner voice into the unfamiliar possibilities that awaited him in the years ahead.

Jimmy finished browsing the book and gazed over the pond at the tombstone of his mentor. Two things were sure, he thought.

He would study the Wealthy Gardener's book until he mastered its lessons. And next year, he'd use this manual to instruct the boys at the reformatory.

AFTERWORD: ONE LAST THING

A solitary figure ambled along a bare road, deep in thought, when suddenly he stopped beside a nearby garden. Several moments passed as he observed a gardener vitally engaged in the dull labor at hand, minding his own business. The year was AD 1200, and the gardener was Saint Francis of Assisi.

As the story goes, the stranger on the road stepped forward and asked a peculiar question of the future saint: "If you knew you were going to die tonight, how would you spend this final day of your life?"

Saint Francis paused for a moment, and then he responded profoundly, "I would continue hoeing my garden." And then Saint Francis resumed his work.

The moral is the key to a rich and satisfying way of life.

If you have taken the time to read this book, we've had a long and intimate conversation—and you now know everything that I know. It took me decades to achieve financial freedom, and three years to shape the lessons into an acceptable form. With the advantage of my life lessons, perhaps you can achieve freedom in half that time. Or maybe you just want to achieve a satisfying life without money hassles or worries. It's up to you to know your own mind and live your own life.

I've revealed my private thoughts, beliefs, and mental practices in a public book because I was once whipped and beaten in the arena of financial success. I don't claim to know it all, but I do know what has worked for me. And I can assure you, it wasn't easy to be so open.

If you'd like to keep in touch, visit wealthygardener.com, where you will find all the best ideas from the life lessons. I invite you also to sign up for the email list so that you can receive daily reminders of these principles to keep you focused—and faith-filled—on your own journey to financial success. I want to support your ambitions.

And last, if you have found value in this book, I ask you to leave an online review. I cannot stress enough how valuable reviews are to expose this material to others. Better still . . . if this book helped you, refer it to a friend who is seeking solutions—someone like you with dreams and drive to earn a lifestyle above money concerns.

In parting, I will admit with humility that while I wrote this book for my son, I was hoping it would benefit his own children, and his children's children . . . I wanted them to understand the ways of prosperity.

The means of financial success will surely change with the times, but these principles will remain as changeless as the constellations in the sky. Can you help to share these life lessons with others?

Thank you for your time, your attention, and your support. I hope to meet you in the future. But if we don't meet physically, let me say that our spirits have already met through the pages of this book.

ACKNOWLEDGMENTS

....

Thank you to my editor, Helen Healey, who grasped my vision of a timeless book. You encouraged and supported this ideal beyond my expectations. Thank you to Niki Papadopoulos for helping me join a world-class team at Portfolio. Thank you to my copy editors Zach Gajewski and Ivy McFadden, who offered more insights and corrections than I care to admit. Thank you to Dennis Kleinman, the voice and soul of the audio book. It was a performance for the ages. And last, thank you to my publisher, Adrian Zackheim, whose belief in the book gave it wings. Without you, there would be no thanking all the others.

APPENDIX

Troubleshooting Money Problems

Troubleshoot: To solve serious problems.

Only those who can solve problems are fit to harvest wealth.

This chapter is a reference guide for troubleshooting common money problems in the lives of ambitious people. These twelve everyday problems were used to write this book, and they will point you toward the life lessons that were designed to address them.

Financial challenges indicate problems to solve and lessons to learn. While the solution to your own money problem may not be found in the pages of this book, this troubleshooting section will surely help you find the solution on your own. As you read, stay alert for curious hunches, ideas, inspirations, and creative solutions. Just one sensible thought can alter a currently meager garden.

This printed book was formatted with running headers on pages to make the self-learning process as user-friendly as possible. The ebook version has interactive links of the life lessons for this same purpose.

1. You want wealth and prosperity, but you don't trust that you'll someday have it.
. . . .

2-2. Financial Security 2-5. Mental Practices 3-6. Personal Growth 4-3. Five-Year Crusade 4-6. Peak State 4-7. Self-Trust 4-8. Convictions 4-16. Be Unrealistic 4-19. Decision 4-21. Money Goals 4-25. Certitude 4-26. Intention 4-28. Mindfulness 4-32. Financial Fear 4-33. Straight Edge 4-34. Discomfort Bridges 4-35. Problems 4-36. Think Walks 4-38. Essentialism 4-39. Flexible Plans 4-40. Learning Curves 4-41. Self-Mastery 4-48. Accountability 4-49. Direction 4-51. Impact Statistics 4-55. Success Habits 5-1. Think Wealth 5-9. Multiply It

2. You aim for a balanced life, but you always worry about your money problems.

1-2. Time 2-1. Financial Dignity 2-3. Financial Excess 2-4. Extra Sacrifice 4-1. Purpose 4-3. Five-Year Crusades 4-8. Convictions 4-20. Sacred Effort 4-22. Schedule 4-23. A Big Why 4-31. Discontentment 4-32. Financial Fear 4-36. Think Walks 4-38. Essentialism 4-40. Learning Curves 4-42. Remarkability 4-46. Acquiescence 4-47. Emotional Guidance 4-49. Direction 4-50. Self-Discipline 4-51. Impact Statistics 4-53. Affluence 4-55. Success Habits 5-1. Think Wealth 5-2. Frugality 5-4. Get Out of Debt 5-5. Save Urgently

3. Wealth is difficult for you due to your unique economic disadvantages.

3-1. Challenges 3-2. Crisis 3-6. Personal Growth 4-3. Five-Year Crusades 4-6. Peak State 4-7. Self-Trust 4-8. Convictions 4-15. Courage 4-16. Be Unrealistic 4-17. Fortitude 4-18. Inner Circle 4-20. Sacred Effort 4-22. Schedule 4-23. A Big Why 4-26. Intention 4-34. Discomfort Bridges 4-37. Prudence 4-38. Essentialism 4-39. Flexible Plans 4-40. Learning Curves 4-41. Self-Mastery 4-43. Leverage 4-44. Relationships 4-45. Sour Adversity 4-46. Acquiescence 4-48. Accountability 4-49. Direction 4-54. Self-Forgiveness 4-55. Success Habits 5-1. Think Wealth 5-2. Frugality 5-3. Profitability 5-5. Save Urgently 5-6. Keep Score

4. You are always busy, but you still have little financial direction.

1-3. Impact Activity 1-4. Impact Hours 2-4. Extra Sacrifice 3-5. Wealth Seasons 4-2. Compensation 4-4. Resistance 4-5. Productivity 4-20. Sacred Effort 4-22. Schedule 4-26. Intention 4-28. Mindfulness 4-38. Essentialism 4-41. Self-Mastery 4-42. Remarkability 4-43. Leverage 4-44. Relationships 4-48. Accountability 4-49. Direction 4-51. Impact Statistics 4-52. Asking 4-55. Success Habits 5-1. Think Wealth 5-2. Frugality 5-3. Profitability 5-5. Save Urgently 5-6. Keep Score

5. You struggle financially but are cynical of visualization and the law of attraction.

2-2. Financial Security 2-5. Mental Practices 3-4. Intangible Forces 3-6. Personal Growth 4-8. Convictions 4-14. Inner Voice 4-21. Money Goals 4-24. Gratitude 4-25. Certitude 4-26. Intention 4-28. Mindfulness 4-30. Sixth Sense 4-40. Learning Curves 4-41. Self-Mastery 4-45. Sour Adversity 4-48. Accountability 5-1. Think Wealth

6. Your financial condition seems hopeless due to your current income.

2-5. Mental Practices 3-2. Crisis 3-6. Personal Growth 4-3. Five-Year Crusades 4-6. Peak State 4-7. Self-Trust 4-8. Convictions 4-16. Be Unrealistic 4-19 Decision 4-22. Schedule 4-23. A Big Why 4-24. Gratitude 4-27. Meditation 4-28. Mindfulness 4-33. Straight Edge 4-34. Discomfort Bridges 4-38. Essentialism 4-40. Learning Curves 4-41. Self-Mastery 4-47. Emotional Guidance 4-48. Accountability 4-49. Direction 4-54. Self-Forgiveness 5-1. Think Wealth 5-2. Frugality 5-3. Profitability 5-4. Get Out of Debt 5-5. Save Urgently 5-6. Keep Score 5-9. Multiply It 5-10. Passive Income

7. You have goals, but you don't follow a daily ritual to focus your mind on your desired financial outcomes.

2-2. Financial Security 2-5. Mental Practices 3-1. Challenges 3-4. Intangible Forces 4-1. Purpose 4-3. Five-Year Crusades 4-4. Resistance 4-5. Productivity 4-19. Decision 4-21. Money Goals 4-22. Schedule 4-23. A Big Why 4-24. Gratitude 4-26. Intention 4-27. Meditation 4-28. Mindfulness 4-33. Straight Edge 4-38. Essentialism 4-40. Learning Curves 4-46. Acquiescence 4-48. Accountability 4-50. Self-Discipline 4-55. Success Habits 5-1. Think Wealth 5-6. Keep Score

8. You live in financial anxiety, doubt, worry, and fear of your monthly bills.

1-3. Impact Activity 2-2. Financial Security 2-5. Mental Practices 3-3. Procrastination 3-4. Intangible Forces 4-4. Resistance 4-5. Productivity 4-8. Convictions 4-14. Inner Voice 4-21. Money Goals 4-24. Gratitude 4-25. Certitude 4-26. Intention 4-27. Meditation 4-28. Mindfulness 4-30. Sixth Sense 4-33. Straight Edge 4-36. Think Walks 4-41. Self-Mastery 4-45. Sour Adversity 4-47. Emotional Guidance 4-48. Accountability 4-50. Self-Discipline 5-1. Think Wealth 5-2. Frugality 5-5. Save Urgently

9. You are financially strapped, but you try to be happy and make the best of a life without money.

3-1. Challenges 3-3. Procrastination 3-6. Personal Growth 4-1. Purpose 4-3. Five-Year Crusades 4-6. Peak State 4-7. Self-Trust 4-8. Convictions 4-13. Ambition 4-16. Be Unrealistic 4-17. Fortitude 4-18. Inner Circle 4-21. Money Goals 4-27. Meditation 4-32. Financial Fear 4-33. Straight Edge 4-34. Discomfort Bridges 4-35. Problems 4-36. Think Walks 4-46. Acquiescence 4-47. Emotional Guidance 4-50. Self-Discipline 4-51. Impact Statistics 4-53. Affluence 4-55. Success Habits

10. In your field of work, you are not inclined to be included among the best.

· ·

1-1. Seek Prosperity 1-4. Impact Hours 2-3. Financial Excess 2-6. The Wealthiest Gardener 3-3. Procrastination 4-1. Purpose 4-3. Five-Year Crusades 4-6. Peak State 4-9. Fulfilling Work 4-10. Inner Values 4-11. Inclination 4-12. Knacks 4-13. Ambition 4-14. Inner Voice 4-18. Inner Circle 4-22. Schedule 4-28. Mindfulness 4-29. Retreat 4-31. Discontentment 4-32. Financial Fear 4-33. Straight Edge 4-40. Learning Curves 4-47. Emotional Guidance 4-50. Self-Discipline

11. You've earned various incomes, but you have accumulated little or no cash in the bank.

· ·

2-3. Financial Excess 4-8. Convictions 4-21. Money Goals 4-22. Schedule 4-49. Direction 4-50. Self-Discipline 4-53. Affluence 5-1. Think Wealth 5-2. Frugality 5-3. Profitability 5-5. Save Urgently 5-6. Keep Score 5-10. Passive Income

12. You are hesitant to set a clear goal for uncommon wealth.

· ·

3-3. Procrastination 3-5. Wealth Seasons 3-6. Personal Growth 4-2. Compensation 4-3. Five-Year Crusades 4-13. Ambition 4-14. Inner Voice 4-15. Courage 4-16. Be Unrealistic 4-19. Decision 4-21. Money Goals 4-22. Schedule 4-29. Retreat 4-31. Discontentment 4-33. Straight Edge 4-34. Discomfort Bridges 4-40. Learning Curves 4-41. Self-Mastery 4-45. Sour Adversity 4-47. Emotional Guidance 4-48. Accountability 4-49. Direction 4-51. Impact Statistics 4-52. Asking 4-55. Success Habits 5-9. Multiply It 5-10. Passive Income

As the Gardener Grows, so does the Garden.

—UNKNOWN AUTHOR

LIFE LESSONS INDEX

(summary overview)

GENERAL INDEX

·································

(Life Lessons in bold)

ABOUT THE AUTHOR

I wrote this book about wealth for my son. I felt qualified to speak to him about prosperity due to my own financial freedom. As a father, I was dedicated to offering my best advice without diluting the harshest realities.

Financial success was not easy for me.

I don't have unusual talent, intellect, or special skills. I did not attend a renowned college. I possess no distinctive advantage besides discipline to accumulate wealth. For decades I earned an ordinary living while I also started and ran several small businesses during my working years. These businesses were average, rural, common, and regular operations with steady cash flows.

By age fifty, however, I possessed the one thing that everyone desires at that age: total financial freedom. I had amassed wealth slowly but steadily in the hardworking middle class of America.

Like a soldier who fought in war and emerged victoriously, I felt I had something to say to my son as he was preparing for his own battle. This book contains the life lessons I wanted him to know.